Instrument Pilot

ORAL EXAM GUIDE

JASON BLAIR
Based on original text by Michael D. Hayes

ELEVENTH EDITION

COMPREHENSIVE PREPARATION
FOR THE FAA CHECKRIDE

AVIATION SUPPLIES & ACADEMICS, INC.
NEWCASTLE, WASHINGTON

Instrument Pilot Oral Exam Guide
Eleventh Edition
by Jason Blair
based on original text by Michael D. Hayes

Aviation Supplies & Academics, Inc.
7005 132nd Place SE
Newcastle, Washington 98059
asa@asa2fly.com | 425-235-1500 | asa2fly.com

ASA-OEG-I11
ISBN 978-1-64425-395-3

Additional formats available:
eBook EPUB   ISBN 978-1-64425-396-0
eBook PDF   ISBN 978-1-64425-397-7

Printed in the United States of America
2028   2027   2026   2025   2024   9   8   7   6   5   4   3   2   1

Library of Congress Cataloging-in-Publication Data
Names: Blair, Jason, author. | Hayes, Michael D., author.
Title: Instrument pilot oral exam guide : comprehensive preparation for the FAA
    checkride / Jason Blair, based on original text by Michael D. Hayes.
Other titles: Oral exam guide
Description: Eleventh edition. | Newcastle, Washington : Aviation Supplies & Academics,
    Inc., 2024. | "First edition published 1992."—Title page verso.
Identifiers: LCCN 2024004775 (print) | LCCN 2024004776 (ebook) | ISBN 9781644253953
    (trade paperback) | ISBN 9781644253960 (epub) | ISBN 9781644253977 (pdf)
Subjects: LCSH: United States. Federal Aviation Administration—Examinations—
    Study guides. | Instrument flying—United States—Examinations, questions, etc. |
    Aeronautics—United States—Examinations, questions, etc.
Classification: LCC TL711.B6 B63 2023 (print) | LCC TL711.B6 (ebook) | DDC
    629.132/5214076—dc23/eng/20240205
LC record available at https://lccn.loc.gov/2024004775
LC ebook record available at https://lccn.loc.gov/2024004776

Contents

Contents

About the Author

 Jason Blair is an active single- and multi-engine instructor and an FAA Designated Pilot Examiner (DPE) with over 6,000 hours total time, over 3,500 hours of instruction given, and more than 3,500 hours in aircraft as a DPE. In his role as an Examiner, he has issued more than 2,500 pilot certificates. Blair has worked for and continues to work with multiple aviation associations with his work focusing on pilot training and testing. His experience as a pilot goes back over 30 years, as an instructor spans over 20 years, and includes more than 100 makes and models of aircraft flown. Blair has written and continues to write for multiple aviation publications with a focus on training and safety.

In addition to ASA's Oral Exam Guide series, Blair is also the author of four books in ASA's Aviator's Field Guide series: *Buying an Airplane, Owning an Airplane, Tailwheel Flying,* and *Middle-Altitude Flying.*

Introduction

The *Instrument Pilot Oral Exam Guide* is a comprehensive guide designed for private or commercial pilots who are involved in training for the Instrument Rating. This guide was originally designed for use in a Part 141 flight school but quickly became popular with those training under 14 CFR Part 61 not affiliated with an approved school. This book is also helpful for instrument-rated pilots who wish to refresh their knowledge or are preparing for an instrument proficiency check (IPC).

The *Instrument Rating–Airplane Airman Certification Standards* (FAA-S-ACS-8) specify the areas in which knowledge must be demonstrated by the applicant before a pilot certificate or rating can be issued. This guide has been designed to evaluate a pilot's knowledge of these areas and contains questions and answers organized into four main chapters that represent logical divisions of a typical instrument flight. An FAA evaluator may ask questions from any of the subject areas within these divisions, at any time during the practical test, to determine if the applicant has the required knowledge. For some topics, the evaluator will ask the applicant to describe or explain; for other items, the evaluator will assess the applicant's understanding with a scenario that requires appropriately applying and/or correlating knowledge, experience, and information to the circumstances of the given scenario. Chapter 5 of this guide provides examples of scenario-based questions to help you prepare for typical scenarios that the examiner may present as part of your oral exam. Based on intensive debriefings conducted after instrument checkrides, we have provided you with the questions and topics commonly asked along with the information or the appropriate reference necessary for a knowledgeable response.

At the end of this guide are four appendices. Appendix 1 contains the "Applicant's Practical Test Checklist" to be used when making final preparations for the checkride, and Appendix 2 is the "Flight

Instructor—Instrument Airplane Supplement" that provides additional study material for instrument instructor candidates preparing for the add-on to their existing flight instructor ticket, but it is also of potential interest to pilots preparing for the instrument checkride or an IPC. Appendix 3 contains excerpts from the FAA's "Instrument Proficiency Check Guidance" document and FAA AC 61-98, *Currency Requirements and Guidance for the Flight Review and Instrument Proficiency Check*. These assist an instrument instructor in determining whether a pilot seeking an IPC endorsement has both the knowledge and skills for safe operation in all aspects of instrument flying, and they should also prove very useful to pilots preparing for the instrument checkride or an IPC. Full versions of these FAA documents are available in the reader resources for this book at asa2fly.com/oegi. Appendix 4 contains an instrument proficiency check flight record form.

You may supplement this guide with other comprehensive study materials as noted in parentheses after each question. For example: (FAA-H-8083-15). The abbreviations for these materials and their titles are listed below. Be sure that you use the latest revision of these references when reviewing for the test. Also, check the ASA website at asa2fly.com/oegi for the most recent updates to this book due to changes in FAA procedures and regulations as well as for Reader Resources containing additional relevant information and updates.

14 CFR Part 43	*Maintenance, Preventive Maintenance, Rebuilding, and Alteration*
14 CFR Part 61	*Certification: Pilots, Flight Instructors, and Ground Instructors*
14 CFR Part 91	*General Operating and Flight Rules*
14 CFR Part 93	*Special Air Traffic Rules*
14 CFR Part 95	*IFR Altitudes*
14 CFR Part 97	*Standard Instrument Procedures*
14 CFR Part 142	*Training Centers*
AC 20-113	*Pilot Precautions and Procedures to be Taken in Preventing Aircraft Reciprocating Engine Induction System and Fuel System Icing Problems*
AC 61-65	*Certification: Pilots and Flight and Ground Instructors*

AC 61-67	*Stall and Spin Awareness Training*
AC 61-98	*Currency Requirements and Guidance for the Flight Review and Instrument Proficiency Check*
AC 61-134	*General Aviation Controlled Flight into Terrain Awareness*
AC 61-136	*FAA Approval of Aviation Training Devices and Their Use for Training and Experience*
AC 68-1	*BasicMed*
AC 90-100	*U.S. Terminal and En Route Area Navigation (RNAV) Operations*
AC 90-101	*Approval Guidance for Required Navigation Performance (RNP) Procedures with Authorization Required (AR)*
AC 90-107	*Guidance for Localizer Performance with Vertical Guidance and Localizer Performance without Vertical Guidance Approach Operations in the U.S. National Airspace System*
AC 90-114	*Automatic Dependent Surveillance–Broadcast Operations*
AC 91-73	*Parts 91 and 135 Single Pilot, Flight School Procedures During Taxi Operations*
AC 91-74	*Pilot Guide: Flight in Icing Conditions*
AC 91-78	*Use of Class 1 or Class 2 Electronic Flight Bag (EFB)*
AFM	*Airplane Flight Manual*
AIM	*Aeronautical Information Manual*
AWC	*Aviation Weather Center (aviationweather.gov)*
CS	*Chart Supplement*
FAA Form 7233-4	*AIM Appendix 4: FAA Form 7233-4— International Flight Plan*
faa.gov	*Federal Aviation Administration website*
FAA-H-8083-2	*Risk Management Handbook*
FAA-H-8083-3	*Airplane Flying Handbook*
FAA-H-8083-9	*Aviation Instructor's Handbook*
FAA-H-8083-15	*Instrument Flying Handbook*

(continued)

FAA-H-8083-16	*Instrument Procedures Handbook*
FAA-H-8083-25	*Pilot's Handbook of Aeronautical Knowledge*
FAA-H-8083-28	*Aviation Weather Handbook*
FAA-H-8083-30	*Aviation Maintenance Technician Handbook—General*
FAA-H-8083-31	*Aviation Maintenance Technician Handbook—Airframe*
FAA-H-8083-32	*Aviation Maintenance Technician Handbook—Powerplant*
FAA InFO 15012	*Logging Instrument Approach Procedures (IAP)*
FAA-P-8740-09	*Descent to MDA or DH and Beyond*
FAA-P-8740-30	*How to Obtain a Good Weather Briefing*
FAA-P-8740-36	*Proficiency and the Private Pilot*
FAA-S-8081-9	*Flight Instructor Instrument Practical Test Standards for Airplane Rating and Helicopter Rating*
FAA-S-ACS-8	*Instrument Rating—Airplane Airman Certification Standards*
Order 8260.3	*United States Standard for Terminal Instrument Procedures (TERPs)*
P/CG	*Pilot/Controller Glossary (from AIM)*
POH	*Pilot's Operating Handbook*
TPP	*U.S. Terminal Procedures Publication*
USRGD	*FAA Aeronautical Chart User's Guide*

Most of these documents are available on the FAA's website (faa.gov). Additionally, many of the publications are reprinted by ASA (asa2fly.com) and are available from aviation retailers worldwide.

A review of the information and references presented within this guide should provide the necessary preparation for the oral section of an FAA instrument certification or re-certification check.

Preflight 1

A. Pilot Qualifications

1. What experience requirements must a pilot meet to be eligible for an Instrument Rating in an airplane? (14 CFR 61.65)

A person who applies for an Instrument–Airplane Rating must have logged the following:

a. 50 hours of cross-country flight time as PIC, of which 10 hours must have been in an airplane;

b. 40 hours of actual or simulated instrument time in the Part 61 areas of operation, of which 15 hours must have been received from an authorized instructor who holds an Instrument–Airplane Rating, and the instrument time includes:

- 3 hours of instrument flight training from an authorized instructor in an airplane that is appropriate to the Instrument–Airplane Rating within 2 calendar months before the date of the practical test;

- Instrument flight training on cross country flight procedures, including one cross country flight in an airplane with an authorized instructor, that is performed under IFR, when a flight plan has been filed with an ATC facility, and that involves a flight of 250 NM along airways or ATC-directed routing, an instrument approach at each airport, and 3 different kinds of approaches with the use of navigation systems.

Exam Tip: The evaluator may ask you to demonstrate that you're current and eligible to take the practical test. When preparing for your practical test, verify that you have met all experience requirements, that you have a current flight review (if it has been more than 24 calendar months since you last received a pilot certificate or rating), that you have received the required logged ground training, that you have received the required flight training, and that you have all required endorsements from your recommending instructor(s). It is a good idea to make sure that your logbook pages are totaled and that you can identify in the logbook and training records how you can demonstrate compliance with and completion of all required training and experience.

2. Under what flight operations is a pilot required to be instrument rated? (14 CFR 61.3, 61.133, 91.135, 91.157)

When operations are conducted:

a. Under instrument flight rules (IFR flight plan).

b. In weather conditions less than the minimum for VFR flight.

c. In Class A airspace.

d. Under Special VFR within Class B, Class C, Class D and Class E surface areas between sunset and sunrise.

e. When carrying passengers for hire on cross-country flights in excess of 50 nautical miles or at night.

3. What currency experience requirements must be met for a pilot to act as PIC of a flight under IFR? (14 CFR 61.57)

A pilot acting as PIC under instrument flight rules must meet the following requirements:

a. Meet the requirements of a flight review.

b. To carry passengers, 3 takeoffs and landings within the preceding 90 days in an aircraft of the same category, class, and type, if a type rating is required (landings must be full stop if at night or in a tailwheel).

c. Within the 6 calendar months preceding the month of the flight, performed and logged in actual weather conditions or under simulated conditions using a view-limiting device, at least the following tasks in an airplane:

- [Any] Six instrument approaches.
- Holding procedures and tasks.
- Intercepting and tracking courses through the use of navigational electronic systems.

Note: 14 CFR §61.57(c) allows the use of an aircraft and/or a full flight simulator, flight training device, or aviation training device for maintaining instrument experience, subject to certain limitations.

Study Tip: A common way pilots remember this is to use the pneumonic "**6-6-HIT**." This means a pilot must complete **6** approaches in the previous **6** months including **H**olding, **I**ntercepting, and **T**racking courses. Note that this does not specify any particular approaches to be completed, so a pilot could fly the same approach six times and be "current." This is a good point that an examiner might highlight and then ask you to discuss the difference between "currency" and "proficiency."

4. Explain the difference between being current and being proficient. (FAA-H-8083-2, FAA-P-8740-36)

Being *current* means that a pilot has accomplished the minimum FAA regulatory requirements within a specific time period to exercise the privileges of the certificate. It means that the pilot is legal to make a flight, but it does not necessarily mean that the pilot is proficient or competent to make that flight. A *proficient* pilot is capable of conducting a flight with a high degree of competence; proficiency requires that the pilot have a wide range of knowledge and skills. Being proficient is not only about being legal in terms of the regulations, but it is about being smart and safe in terms of pilot experience and competence.

Checkride tip: Be ready to discuss how you will personally manage your proficiency and how that might affect your personal minimums decisions, risk mitigation, and go/no-go decision-making for flights.

5. May a pilot use a flight simulator to accomplish approaches required to maintain or regain instrument currency? (14 CFR 61.57)

A pilot may "complete the instrument experience in any combination of an aircraft, full flight simulator, flight training device, or aviation training device" (14 CFR 61.57[c][2]). This allows a pilot to utilize a properly certificated full flight simulator, flight training device, or aviation training device for maintaining instrument currency as long as it represents the category of aircraft for the Instrument Rating privileges the pilot needs to maintain and the tasks required for currency are completed in simulated instrument conditions.

Note: Not all simulators are eligible to meet all requirements for instrument proficiency. Many simulators are certified to be used for maintaining or re-establishing currency but may not be able to be used for all requirements of an instrument proficiency check. If you are using a simulator, be sure it is properly qualified to be used for the intended purposes of your currency efforts.

6. You are instrument-rated in both single- and multi-engine airplanes. If you meet the instrument recency of experience requirements in a single-engine airplane, are you also instrument current in a multi-engine airplane? (14 CFR 61.57)

The regulation section that details pilot currency relating to instrument proficiency does not require a pilot to fly the approaches in a particular category or class of aircraft with respect to instrument approaches. A pilot need only fly the approaches in any "airplane, powered-lift, helicopter, or airship for maintaining instrument experience." Any combination of these will keep a pilot current for operations in IFR conditions in any of these aircraft. As such, conducting approaches in a single-engine aircraft would keep a pilot current for instrument flight additionally in a multi-engine aircraft.

7. Must a flight instructor be present if you are planning on using an aviation training device to maintain your IFR currency? (14 CFR 61.51, 61.57)

No. A pilot may accomplish the recency of experience requirements in a full flight simulator, flight training device, or aviation training device, provided the device represents the category of aircraft for the Instrument Rating privileges to be maintained and the pilot performs the tasks and iterations in simulated instrument conditions. A logbook or training record must specify the training device, time, and the content. An instructor is not required to be present.

8. Are you required to have an instructor present when a using time in an FFS, FTD, or ATD to acquire instrument aeronautical experience for a pilot certificate or rating? (14 CFR 61.51)

Yes, an instructor must be present. A person may use time in a full flight simulator, flight training device, or aviation training device for acquiring instrument aeronautical experience for a pilot certificate or rating, provided an authorized instructor is present to observe that time and signs the person's logbook or training record to verify the time and the content of the training session.

9. If a pilot allows his/her instrument currency to expire, what can be done to become current again? (14 CFR 61.57, 91.109)

A pilot is current for the first 6 months following his or her instrument checkride or proficiency check. If the pilot has not accomplished at least 6 approaches (including holding procedures, intercepting/tracking courses through the use of navigation systems) within this first 6 months, he/she is no longer legal to file and fly under IFR. To become legal again, the regulations allow a "grace period" (the second 6-month period), in which a pilot may get current by finding an "appropriately rated" safety pilot, and in simulated IFR conditions only, acquire the 6 approaches, etc. If the second 6-month period also passes without accomplishing the minimum, a pilot may reinstate his/her currency by accomplishing an instrument proficiency check given by an examiner, an authorized instructor, or an FAA-approved person to conduct instrument practical tests.

10. When must a pilot complete an instrument proficiency check to regain instrument currency? (14 CFR 61.57)

A pilot must complete an instrument proficiency check (IPC) when he or she has failed to meet the instrument currency experience requirements for more than six calendar months.

11. If a pilot needs to complete an instrument proficiency check (IPC) to regain currency, who can administer this check? (14 CFR 61.57)

An instrument proficiency check must be given by:

a. An examiner;

b. A person authorized by the U.S. Armed Forces to conduct instrument flight tests, provided the person being tested is a member of the U.S. Armed Forces;

c. A company check pilot who is authorized to conduct instrument flight tests under 14 CFR Part 121, 125, or 135 or Part 91, Subpart K, and provided that both the check pilot and the pilot being tested are employees of that operator or fractional ownership program manager, as applicable;

d. An authorized instructor; or

e. A person approved by the FAA Administrator to conduct instrument practical tests.

12. If a pilot needs to complete an instrument proficiency check (IPC) to regain currency, what must they do on the check? (14 CFR 61.57, FAA-S-ACS-8, AC 61-98)

The *Instrument Rating–Airplane Airman Certification Standards* includes a table in its Appendix 5 that details a selection of items from the Instrument ACS that must be completed to accomplish an instrument proficiency check. Further guidance on the conduct of an IPC is also found in FAA Advisory Circular (AC) 61-98, *Currency Requirements and Guidance for the Flight Review and Instrument Proficiency Check*. Generally, a pilot should know that an IPC will require at least three different approaches to be conducted with one of them being a partial panel simulation, holding, tracking, and navigating procedures. Unlike when maintaining currency, a pilot may not fly the same approaches over and over to regain currency. The sequence of an IPC and required tasks closely resembles what is required on an instrument practical test. It will require a pilot to fly at least one precision or precision-like approach that would include an approach for which a decision altitude is offered, a non-precision approach, and a non-precision approach on which the pilot must fly one procedure with reference to backup or partial panel instrumentation or navigation display, depending on the aircraft's instrument avionics configuration, representing a realistic failure mode(s) for the equipment used. No ground training is required for an IPC.

13. What are the required qualifications for a person to act as a "safety pilot"? (14 CFR 61.3, 61.23, 91.109)

The safety pilot must:

a. Possess at least a Private Pilot Certificate with category and class ratings appropriate to the aircraft being flown.

b. Possess an appropriate medical certificate (the safety pilot is acting as a required crewmember).

c. If the flight is to be conducted on an IFR flight plan, the person acting as PIC of the flight must hold an Instrument Rating and be instrument current.

14. Can a pilot who does not hold a medical certificate but does possess BasicMed authorization act as a safety pilot? (14 CFR 61.23, 61.113, 91.109)

A person may serve as a safety pilot as long as that person holds a Private Pilot or greater certificate for the category and class of aircraft to be operated and is the holder of a Third Class or higher medical certificate, or has alternate means of medical certification through the use of BasicMed as detailed in 14 CFR 61.23(c)(3), as long as the aircraft falls within the aircraft allowed to be operated under such limitations. This is a change from what was originally allowed and became effective in December 2022 through a regulatory change.

15. Can an Instrument-Rated pilot with a Private Pilot Certificate operate an aircraft if that pilot is satisfying medical requirements using BasicMed? (AC 68-1)

Pilots can fly in IFR operations while meeting medical requirements using BasicMed (in covered aircraft) under VFR or IFR. There is no prohibition against flying in IMC, but BasicMed doesn't change the requirement to hold an Instrument Rating and be instrument current to act as PIC under IFR. Further, BasicMed does not relieve an aircraft from the requirement to be approved for IFR operations for flight under IFR.

16. When logging instrument time, what should be included in each logbook entry? (14 CFR 61.51)

Each entry must include the location and type of each instrument approach accomplished and the name of the safety pilot, if required.

17. What is the definition of the term *flight time*? (14 CFR Part 1)

Flight time means pilot time that commences when an aircraft moves under its own power for the purpose of flight and ends when the aircraft comes to rest after landing.

18. What conditions are necessary for a pilot to log instrument time? (14 CFR 61.51)

A person may log instrument time only for that flight time when the person operates the aircraft solely by reference to instruments under actual or simulated instrument flight conditions.

19. What conditions must exist in order to log "actual" instrument flight time? (14 CFR §91.155, AIM 5-3-4)

The FAA has never defined the term "actual" instrument time. 14 CFR Part 61 defines "instrument flight time" as that flight time when a person operates an aircraft solely by reference to instruments under actual or simulated instrument flight conditions. A reasonable guideline for determining when to log "actual instrument time" would be any flight time that is accumulated in IMC conditions with flight being conducted solely by reference to instruments. The definition of IMC is weather conditions in which the pilot would not be able to operate within the prescribed VFR minimums specified for the particular airspace in which the operation takes place. The *Aeronautical Information Manual (AIM)* also indicates that "VFR flight requires visual contact with the ground or water at all times."

A practical way to think about this is that a pilot will be able to log actual instrument time when they are operating on an instrument flight plan whenever operating with less than VFR cloud and/or visibility requirements. The aircraft does not have to be physically in a cloud to be in actual IFR conditions. If you were 100 feet below a cloud in Class E airspace, that would not be operating legally VFR and would require you to be on an IFR flight plan even if you had 10 miles of visibility. The same would hold true if you were flying in Class D airspace with 1 mile visibility 2,000 feet below an overcast layer due to VFR airspace cloud and visibility requirements. If you are unable to legally operate VFR due to weather conditions and are on an IFR flight plan, this would be considered actual IFR conditions.

20. What requirements must be met before a pilot can log an IAP for currency or training? (FAA InFO 15012)

a. When conducted in an aircraft, full flight simulator, flight training device, or aviation training device, the pilot must operate that aircraft or authorized training device solely by reference to instruments. (14 CFR 61.51[g][1])

b. When conducted in an aircraft, full flight simulator, flight training device, or aviation training device, the pilot must be established on each required segment of the IAP to the minimum descent altitude (MDA) or decision altitude/decision height (DA/DH).

c. When conducted in an aircraft simulating instrument flight conditions, a full flight simulator, a flight training device, or an aviation training device, the simulated instrument meteorological conditions (IMC) must continue to MDA or DA/DH.

d. When conducted in an aircraft, the flight must be conducted under actual or simulated instrument flight conditions. (14 CFR 61.51[g][1])

e. When conducted in an aircraft maneuvering in IMC, the aircraft transitions from IMC to visual flight conditions on the final approach segment of the IAP prior to or upon reaching MDA or DA/DH.

21. What are the four methods a pilot may use to conduct and then log IAPs? (FAA InFO 15012)

1. Actual instrument flight conditions flown in an aircraft;

2. Simulated instrument flight conditions, using a view-limiting device, flown in an aircraft with a safety pilot;

3. Simulated instrument flight conditions conducted in any FAA-approved full flight simulator (FFS), flight training device (FTD), or aviation training device (ATD); or

4. A combination of methods 1 through 3 as prescribed by §61.57.

22. Is a pilot required to fly the entire approach procedure in order to log it for currency? (FAA InFO 15012)

Except when being radar vectored to the final approach course, or otherwise directed through an appropriate ATC clearance to a specific IAP, pilots must execute the entire IAP commencing at an IAF or associated feeder route and fly the initial segment, the intermediate segment, and the final segment of an IAP. If the pilot completes these segments, or receives vectors to the final approach course, he or she may log the IAP.

23. When flying an IAP in IMC, does the FAA require the ceiling to be at MDA or DA/DH before the approach may be logged? (FAA InFO 15012)

No; the two possible outcomes are the aircraft will transition from IMC to VMC allowing a landing (in accordance with 14 CFR §91.175), or the aircraft will remain in IMC and execute a missed approach at the MAP or DA/DH. In both cases, the pilot may log the IAP.

B. Preflight Action for Flight

(IFR or Flight Not in the Vicinity of Airport)

1. How can the use of the PAVE checklist during preflight help a pilot to assess and mitigate risk? (FAA-H-8083-9)

Use of the PAVE checklist provides pilots with a simple way to remember each category to examine for risk during flight planning. The pilot divides the risks of flight into four categories:

Pilot—illness, medication, stress, alcohol, fatigue, emotion (I'M SAFE), proficiency, currency.

Aircraft—airworthiness, aircraft equipped for flight, proficiency in aircraft, performance capability.

enVironment—weather hazards, type of terrain, airports/runways to be used, conditions.

External pressures—meetings, people waiting at destination, desire to impress, desire to get there, etc.

2. Explain how the use of a personal minimums checklist can help a pilot control risk. (FAA-H-8083-9)

One of the most important concepts that safe pilots understand is the difference between what is "legal" in terms of the regulations, and what is "smart" or "safe" in terms of pilot experience and proficiency. One way a pilot can control the risks is to set personal minimums for items in each risk category. These are limits

unique to that individual pilot's current level of experience and
proficiency.

Exam Tip: The evaluator will ask you if you have established
your own personal minimums. Prior to the checkride, complete a
personal minimums worksheet if you have not already done so.
Also, at some point during the test, the evaluator will present you
with a scenario to determine if you will actually adhere to your
personal minimums—be prepared. You can download the FAA's
Personal Minimums Worksheet at www.faa.gov.

3. What information must a pilot-in-command be familiar with before a flight? (14 CFR 91.103)

For a flight under IFR or a flight not in the vicinity of an airport,
the PIC must be familiar with all available information, including:

NOTAMs

Weather reports and forecasts

Known ATC traffic delays

Runway lengths at airports of intended use

Alternatives available if the planned flight cannot be completed

Fuel requirements

Takeoff and landing performance data

Remember: NWKRAFT

4. What are the fuel requirements for flight in IFR conditions? (14 CFR 91.167)

The aircraft must carry enough fuel (considering weather reports,
forecasts, and weather conditions) to complete the flight to the first
airport of intended landing, fly from that airport to the alternate
airport, and fly after that for 45 minutes at normal cruising speed.

Note: "Complete the flight," as used in this regulation, means the
aircraft has enough fuel to be flown to, and land at, the first airport
of intended landing. Having fueled the aircraft with only enough
fuel to "attempt an approach" would fall short of the regulatory
requirement (FAA legal interpretation).

5. Before conducting an IFR flight using GPS equipment for navigation, what basic preflight checks should be made? (FAA-H-8083-15)

Preflight preparations should include:

a. Verify that the GPS is properly installed and certified for the planned IFR operation.

b. Verify that the databases (navigation, terrain, obstacle, etc.) have not expired.

c. Review GPS and WAAS NOTAMs.

d. Review GPS RAIM availability for non-WAAS receivers.

e. Review operational status of ground-based NAVAIDs and related aircraft equipment (e.g., 30-day VOR check) appropriate to the route of flight, terminal operations, instrument approaches at the destination, and alternate airports at ETA.

f. Determine that the GPS receiver operation manual or airplane flight manual supplement is on board and available for use.

6. Explain the function of RAIM. (FAA-H-8083-16)

Receiver autonomous integrity monitoring (RAIM) is the self-monitoring function performed by a TSO-129 certified GPS receiver to ensure that adequate GPS signals are being received at all times. The GPS alerts the pilot whenever the integrity monitoring determines that the GPS signals do not meet the criteria for safe navigation use.

7. When is a RAIM check required? (AIM 5-1-16)

TSO-C129 (non-WAAS) equipped aircraft—If TSO-C129 (non-WAAS) equipment is used to solely satisfy the RNAV and RNP requirement, GPS RAIM availability must be confirmed for the intended route of flight (route and time) using current GPS satellite information.

TSO-C145/C146 (WAAS) equipped aircraft—If TSO-C145/C146 (WAAS) equipment is used to satisfy the RNAV and RNP requirement, the pilot/operator need **not** perform the prediction if WAAS coverage is confirmed to be available along the entire route of flight. Outside the U.S. or in areas where WAAS coverage is not available, operators using TSO-C145/C146 receivers are required to check GPS RAIM availability.

(continued)

Note: In the event of a predicted, continuous loss of RAIM of more than five (5) minutes for any part of the intended flight, the flight should be delayed, canceled, or re-routed where RAIM requirements can be met. Pilots should assess their capability to navigate (potentially to an alternate destination) in case of failure of GPS navigation.

8. **What are several methods a pilot can use to satisfy the predictive RAIM requirement (RAIM check)?** (AIM 1-1-17, 5-1-16)

   a. Operators may contact a Flight Service Station to obtain non-precision approach RAIM. Briefers will provide RAIM information for a period of 1 hour before to 1 hour after the ETA, unless a specific time frame is requested by the pilot.

   b. Use the Service Availability Prediction Tool (SAPT) on the FAA enroute and terminal RAIM prediction tool at sapt.faa.gov.

   c. Use a third-party interface, incorporating FAA/Volpe Center RAIM prediction data without altering performance values to predict RAIM outages for the aircraft's predicted flight path and times.

   d. Use the receiver's installed RAIM prediction capability (for TSO-C129a/Class A1/B1/C1 equipment) to provide non-precision approach RAIM.

C. Preflight Action for Aircraft

1. **Who is responsible for determining if an aircraft is in an airworthy condition?** (14 CFR 91.7)

   The pilot-in-command is responsible.

2. **What aircraft instruments/equipment are required for an aircraft to be certificated to operate in IFR operations?** (14 CFR 91.205)

   Those required for VFR day and night flight, plus:

   Generator or alternator of adequate capacity

   Radios (nav. and comm. equipment suitable for the route to be flown)

   Altimeter (sensitive)

   Ball (slip/skid indicator of turn coordinator)

Clock (sweep second hand or digital presentation)

Attitude indicator

Rate of turn (turn coordinator)

Directional gyro

DME or RNAV (for flight at FL240 and above if VOR equipment is required for the route)

3. **What are the required tests and inspections to be performed on an aircraft? Include inspections for IFR.** (14 CFR 91.409, 91.403, 91.417, 91.171, 91.411, 91.413, 91.207)

Annual inspection within the preceding 12 calendar months. (14 CFR 91.409)

Airworthiness directives and life-limited parts complied with, as required. (14 CFR 91.403, 91.417)

VOR equipment check every 30 days (for IFR ops). (14 CFR 91.171)

100-hour inspection, if used for hire or flight instruction in aircraft flight instructor provides. (14 CFR 91.409)

Altimeter, altitude reporting equipment, and static pressure systems tested and inspected (for IFR ops) every 24 calendar months. (14 CFR 91.411)

Transponder tests and inspections, every 24 calendar months. (14 CFR 91.413)

Emergency locator transmitter, operation and battery condition inspected every 12 calendar months. (14 CFR 91.207)

Exam Tip: Be prepared to locate all of the required inspections, ADs, life-limited parts, etc., in the aircraft and engine logbooks and be able to determine when the next inspections are due. Create an aircraft status sheet that indicates the status of all required inspections, ADs, life limited, parts, etc. and/or use post-it notes to tab the specific pages in the aircraft and engine logbooks.

4. **During the preflight inspection in an aircraft, you find a piece of equipment that is inoperative. Describe how you will determine if the aircraft is still airworthy for flight.** (14 CFR 91.213(d), AC 91-67, FAA-H-8083-25)

The pilot must determine if the aircraft can be operated without the piece of equipment for the type of flight operation intended to be completed. The pilot should follow this sequence:

a. Does the aircraft have an approved minimum equipment list (MEL) or kinds of operations equipment list (KOEL) that includes the affected equipment and allows operation with it inoperative?

b. Is the inoperative equipment included in the type certificate data sheet for the aircraft?

c. Is the inoperative equipment required by 14 CFR §91.205, §91.207, or any other rule of 14 CFR Part 91 for the specific kind of flight operation being conducted (for example, VFR, IFR, day, night)?

d. Is the inoperative equipment required to be operational by an AD?

If the equipment is specifically allowed to be inoperative by an approved MEL/KOEL, the pilot may operate the flight with the equipment inoperative. If this is not the case, the pilot will need to have the equipment placarded inoperative, disabled or removed, and the aircraft must be returned to service by a maintenance professional who would also need to complete documentation in the aircraft maintenance logs of the activity.

Note: See Appendix 3 for further explanation of this regulation.

Exam Tip: If an instrument or equipment item is inoperative in your aircraft, be able to explain how you will determine if the aircraft is airworthy and legal for flight and be able to show where proper documentation of the inoperative equipment was completed in the aircraft maintenance logs.

5. **May portable electronic devices be operated on board an aircraft?** (14 CFR 91.21)

No person may operate, nor may any PIC allow the operation of, any portable electronic device:

a. On aircraft operated by an air carrier or commercial operator; or

b. On any other aircraft while it is operated under IFR.

Exceptions are given to this regulation for portable voice recorders, hearing aids, heart pacemakers, electric shavers and most importantly, for "Any other portable electronic device that the operator of the aircraft has determined will not cause interference with the navigation or communication system of the aircraft on which it is to be used."

6. Are electronic chart systems (electronic flight bags) approved for use as a replacement for paper reference material (POH and supplements, charts, etc.) in the flight deck? (AC 91-78)

Yes; electronic flight bags (EFBs) can be used during all phases of flight operations in lieu of paper reference material when the information displayed is the functional equivalent of the paper reference material replaced and is current, up-to-date, and valid. It is recommended that a secondary or back-up source of aeronautical information necessary for the flight be available.

7. What documents are required on board an aircraft prior to flight? (14 CFR 91.9, 91.203)

Supplements (14 CFR §91.9)

Placards (14 CFR §91.9)

Airworthiness Certificate (14 CFR §91.203)

Registration Certificate (14 CFR §91.203)

Radio Station License—if operating outside of U.S.; FCC regulation (47 CFR §87.18)

Operating limitations—AFM/POH and supplements, placards, markings (14 CFR §91.9)

Weight and balance data—current (14 CFR §23.2620)

Compass Deviation Card (14 CFR §23.1547)

External Data Plate/Serial Number (14 CFR §45.11)

Exam Tip: During the practical test, your evaluator may wish to examine the various required aircraft documents (SPARROW) during the preflight inspection, as well as the currency of any aeronautical charts, EFB data, etc., on board the aircraft. Prior to the test, verify that all of the necessary aircraft documentation, onboard databases, charts, etc., are current and available.

8. What additional aircraft documentation should be on board an aircraft equipped with an IFR-approved GPS? (FAA-H-8083-16)

Most systems require an airplane flight manual supplement (AFMS) and cockpit reference guide or quick reference guide to be on board as a limitation of use.

9. How often are GPS databases required to be updated? (FAA-H-8083-15)

The navigation database is updated every 28 days. Obstacle databases may be updated every 56 days, and terrain and airport map databases are updated as needed. Obstacle databases are not necessarily required for IFR navigational operation, unlike the navigation database when using a GPS system for IFR operations.

10. Can a GPS with an expired database be used for navigation under IFR? (AIM 1-1-17, AIM 5-1-16, AC 90-100)

The navigation database contained in the GPS/FMS must be current if the system is to be used for IFR approaches. Some units allow enroute IFR operations with an expired database if the navigation waypoints are manually verified by referencing an official current source, such as a current enroute chart. To determine equipment approvals and limitations, refer to the AFM or AFM supplements.

Note: The FAA-approved airplane flight manual supplement (required to be on board the aircraft) is regulatory and specifies the requirements and operations permitted.

Exam Tip: A most practical approach to GPS databases is to operate only with current GPS database records. While the regulations allow for a pilot to manually identify all used waypoints in an expired database, doing so is not practically applied and would not take into account any deviations in routing that might occur.

11. Can a pilot perform the required database updates, or must this action be accomplished by authorized maintenance personnel? (14 CFR 43.3)

Updates of databases of installed avionics may be performed by pilots provided they can be initiated from the flight deck, performed without disassembly of the avionics unit, and performed without the use of tools and/or special equipment. Updating databases for self-contained, front-panel, or pedestal-mounted GPS units is a non-maintenance task and does not require an entry in the aircraft logbook.

Exam Tip: For practical tests conducted in an aircraft equipped with an installed, instrument flight rules (IFR)-approved RNAV or required navigational performance (RNP) system, or in a flight simulation training device (FSTD) equipped to replicate an installed, IFR-approved RNAV or RNP system, the applicant must demonstrate approach proficiency using that system. The applicant may use a suitable RNAV system on conventional procedures and routes as described in the *Aeronautical Information Manual* (AIM) to accomplish ACS tasks on conventional approach procedures, as appropriate.

12. When utilizing GPS for IFR navigation, are you required to have an alternate means of navigation appropriate for the route of flight? (AIM 1-1-17, FAA-H-8083-16)

Aircraft using GPS TSO-C129 or TSO-C196 (non-WAAS) navigation equipment under IFR must be equipped with an approved and operational alternate means of navigation appropriate to the flight. During preflight, ensure that this equipment is on board and operational, and that all required checks have been performed (e.g., 30-day VOR check). Active monitoring of alternative navigation equipment is not required if the GPS receiver uses RAIM for integrity monitoring. Active monitoring of an alternate means of navigation is required when the RAIM capability of the GPS equipment is lost.

Note: Aircraft equipped with a WAAS receiver may use WAAS as a primary means of navigation. No additional equipment is required.

13. How can a pilot determine what type of operations a GPS receiver is approved for? (FAA-H-8083-16)

The pilot should reference the FAA-approved AFM and AFM supplements to determine the limitations and operating procedures for the particular GPS equipment installed.

14. Can a handheld GPS receiver be used for IFR operations? (AIM 1-1-17)

Visual flight rules (VFR) and hand-held GPS systems are not authorized for IFR navigation, instrument approaches, or as a principal instrument flight reference. During IFR operations they may be considered only as an aid to situational awareness.

Exam Tip: Expect to be tested on the location of the GPS antenna(s) as well as the antenna locations for other installed equipment such as VHF communication radios, transponder/DME, VOR/Localizer/Glideslope receivers, and ELT transmitter.

15. During preflight, you notice several static discharge wicks are missing from your airplane. Explain the function of the static wicks and the problems that could occur in flight if they are missing. (FAA-H-8083-16)

Static dischargers, or wicks, are installed on aircraft to reduce radio receiver interference caused by corona discharge emitted from the aircraft as a result of precipitation static. Precipitation static occurs when an aircraft encounters airborne particles during flight (rain or snow) and develops a negative charge. The problems created by P-static range from serious, such as complete loss of VHF communications and erroneous magnetic compass readings, to the annoyance of high-pitched audio squealing.

Exam Tip: Be aware whether the aircraft POH/AFM or other aircraft documentation indicate a requirement or a minimum number of static wicks that must be in place for the aircraft to be considered airworthy.

D. IFR Flight Plan

1. When must a pilot file an IFR flight plan? (AIM 5-1-6)

Prior to departure from within or prior to entering controlled airspace, a pilot must submit a complete flight plan and receive clearance from ATC if weather conditions are below VFR minimums. The pilot should file the flight plan at least 30 minutes prior to the estimated time of departure to preclude a possible delay in receiving a departure clearance from ATC.

2. The FAA has transitioned to using the ICAO format flight plans for all flights. When is it mandatory to use one? (AIM 5-1-6)

Use of an ICAO flight plan is:

a. Mandatory for assignment of RNAV SIDs and STARs or other PBN routing,

b. Mandatory for all IFR flights that will depart U.S. domestic airspace, and

c. Recommended for domestic IFR flights.

For instrument flight operations in the United States, pilots must file an ICAO flight plan when conducting flights across international borders or when flying in specific controlled airspace designated by the Federal Aviation Administration (FAA). When operating within certain controlled airspace, such as the Class A airspace in the United States or in certain oceanic airspace, pilots are required to file an ICAO flight plan. Additionally, when conducting flights that cross international borders, regardless of the altitude or airspace, filing an ICAO flight plan is mandatory.

3. When will ATC delete from the system a departure flight plan that has not been activated? (AIM 5-1-13)

Most centers have this parameter set so as to delete these flight plans a minimum of 2 hours after the proposed departure time or Expect Departure Clearance Time (EDCT). To ensure that a flight plan remains active, pilots whose actual departure time will be delayed 2 hours or more beyond their filed departure time will need to update their departure time with Flight Service or ATC. Failing to do so may require the pilot to file a new flight plan after it has been deleted.

4. When can you cancel your IFR flight plan? (AIM 5-1-15)

An IFR flight plan may be canceled at any time the flight is operating in VFR conditions outside of Class A airspace. Pilots must be aware that other procedures may be applicable to a flight that cancels an IFR flight plan within an area where a special program, such as a designated TRSA, Class C airspace, or Class B airspace, has been established.

Exam Tip: While many pilots cancel their IFR clearances once they "break out" on an approach and can see the airport environment, technically they must be able to maintain VFR cloud clearances and visibility before canceling the approach.

5. Which altitude for the route of flight does the requested altitude represent—initial, lowest, or highest? (FAA Form 7233-4)

Enter the planned cruising level for the first or the whole portion of the route to be flown, in terms of flight level, expressed as "F" followed by 3 digits (for example, F180; F330), or altitude in hundreds of feet, expressed as "A" followed by 3 digits (for example, A040; A170).

6. On an ICAO flight plan, item 15 requires you to enter your planned cruise speed. Explain what this speed represents. (FAA Form 7233-4)

It represents the true airspeed for the first or the whole cruising portion of the flight, in terms of knots, expressed as N followed by 4 digits (for example, N0485), or Mach number to the nearest hundredth of unit Mach, expressed as M followed by 3 digits (for example, M082).

7. When must a pilot file an alternate airport when flying on an IFR flight plan? (14 CFR 91.169)

1-2-3 Rule—If from 1 hour before to 1 hour after your planned ETA at the destination airport, the weather is forecast to be at least 2,000-foot ceilings and 3-mile visibilities, no alternate is required. If less than 2,000 and 3 miles, an alternate must be filed using the following criteria:

a. If an IAP is published for that airport, the alternate airport minimums specified in that procedure or, if none are specified, the following minimums—

- Precision approach procedure: ceiling 600 feet and visibility 2 statute miles.
- Non-precision approaches: ceiling 800 feet and visibility 2 statute miles.

b. If no IAP has been published for that airport, the ceiling and visibility minimums are those allowing descent from the MEA, approach, and landing under basic VFR.

Exam Tip: After asking the question "when is an alternate required?" an examiner will often follow that with "what factors did you consider when choosing this airport as your alternate?" Be prepared to discuss the various factors that you considered, such as available approaches, distance, non-standard alternate minimums, weather, forecasts, fuel requirements, airport services, etc.

8. **When would an airport not qualify as an alternate airport when filing an IFR flight plan?** (FAA-H-8083-16)

An airport may not be qualified for alternate use if the airport NAVAID is unmonitored, or if it does not have weather reporting capabilities. For an airport to be used as an alternate, the forecast weather at that airport must meet certain qualifications at the ETA. Standard airplane alternate minimums for a precision approach are a 600-foot ceiling and a 2 SM visibility. For a non-precision approach, the minimums are an 800-foot ceiling and a 2 SM visibility. Standard alternate minimums apply unless higher alternate minimums are listed for an airport. For helicopters, alternate weather minimums are a ceiling of 200 feet above the minimum for the approach to be flown, and visibility at least 1 SM but never less than the minimum visibility for the approach to be flown.

Additionally, the presence of a triangle with an "A" on the approach chart indicates the listing of alternate minimums should be consulted. Airports that do not qualify for use as an alternate airport are designated with an A.

9. **What resources may a pilot refer to when determining if an alternate airport is required or if an airport may be used as an alternate when considering weather conditions?** (FAA-H-8083-28)

a. Terminal Area Forecast (TAF); or if the airport is outside the area covered by a TAF,

b. The Graphical Forecasts for Aviation (GFA) tool, on which a pilot may select the "Forecast" and "CIG/VIS" tabs, and then use the Zulu time slider bar to obtain forecast weather at the ETA.

10. When considering potential alternate airports, must an airport have an instrument approach to be legal as an alternate? (14 CFR 91.169)

If no instrument approach procedure has been published in 14 CFR Part 97 and no special instrument approach procedure has been issued by the Administrator to the operator, for the alternate airport, the ceiling and visibility minima are those allowing descent from the MEA, approach, and landing under basic VFR.

11. What size area does a terminal aerodrome forecast (TAF) cover? (FAA-H-8083-28)

A TAF is a concise statement of the expected meteorological conditions significant to aviation for a specified time period within 5 SM of the center of the airport's runway complex (terminal).

12. How far into the future does a TAF forecast weather information? (FAA-H-8083-28)

Terminal aerodrome forecasts (TAFs) are prepared by 123 NWS Weather Forecast Offices (WFOs) for over 700 airports. These forecasts are valid for 24 or 30 hours and are amended as required.

13. During preflight planning, you notice that your destination airport has no published instrument approach procedure. The weather is forecast to be 3,000-foot ceilings with 5 miles of visibility within the 1 hour before to 1 hour after your ETA. Are you required to file an alternate airport? (14 CFR 91.169)

Yes; 14 CFR §91.169 requires that each person filing an IFR flight plan must include in it the following information:

a. Information required under 14 CFR §91.153 (VFR flight plan information), and

b. An alternate airport.

An alternate airport *must* be included in the IFR flight plan *unless* the conditions prescribed in 14 CFR §9l.169(b)(1) and (2) are satisfied:

- *§91.169(b)(1)*—The first airport of intended landing has a Part 97 standard instrument approach procedure (SIAP) or a special instrument approach procedure issued by the Administrator; and

- *§91.169(b)(2)*—Appropriate weather reports or weather forecasts, or a combination of them, indicate the following: For at least 1 hour before and for 1 hour after the ETA, the ceiling will be at least 2,000 feet above the airport elevation and the visibility will be at least 3 statute miles.

In this case, the first airport of intended landing does not have a published SIAP, although it does have the required weather of at least 2,000-foot ceilings and 3 miles of visibility from 1 hour before to 1 hour after ETA. Therefore, the requirements of §91.169(b)(1) and (2) have not been completely satisfied and the pilot is required to include the information specified in §91.169(a) (1) and (2).

14. You have just executed a missed approach at your destination airport due to un-forecast weather, and during the climb, you are unable to contact ATC. You make the decision to proceed to your filed alternate. Does ATC know what your filed alternate is? Can you divert to a different alternate than what is filed? (AIM 5-1-6)

No. Although alternate airport information filed in a flight plan will be accepted by air traffic computer systems, it will not be presented to controllers. If diversion to an alternate airport becomes necessary, pilots are expected to notify ATC and request an amended clearance. There is no requirement for you to proceed to your filed alternate. You may select any airport that you determine is appropriate, considering actual conditions (weather, fuel remaining, etc.) at the time.

Note: In this case, if unable to contact ATC, you would proceed to your alternate or any other airport that you determine is necessary and will result in a safe outcome for your flight. Selecting and filing an alternate is mainly a fuel planning requirement and is done to ensure that you have enough fuel to execute a plan B in the event you cannot land at your destination.

15. What is the definition of the term *ceiling*? (P/CG)

Ceiling is defined as the height above the Earth's surface of the lowest layer of clouds or obscuring phenomena reported as "broken," "overcast," or "obscuration," and not classified as "thin" or "partial."

16. What minimums are to be used on arrival at the alternate? (14 CFR 91.169c)

If an instrument approach procedure has been published for that airport, the minimums specified in that procedure are used.

17. What restrictions apply concerning filing an airport as an alternate when using TSO-C129 and TSO-C196 (non-WAAS) GPS equipment? (AIM 1-1-17)

For the purposes of flight planning, a pilot filing a flight plan to an airport that is served only by GPS approaches is required to file an alternate airport no matter what weather conditions are expected. When filing an alternate airport under these conditions, the alternate airport must have an available instrument approach procedure that does not require the use of GPS (including using the GPS to substitute for DME points if the aircraft does not have a separate DME receiver from the GPS system). This restriction further includes conducting a conventional approach at the alternate airport using a substitute means of navigation that is based upon the use of GPS.

For example, these restrictions would apply when planning to use GPS equipment as a substitute means of navigation for an out-of-service VOR that supports an ILS missed approach procedure at an alternate airport. In this case, some other approach not reliant upon the use of GPS must be available. This restriction does not apply to RNAV systems using TSO-C145/-C146 WAAS capable equipment.

18. What instrument approach procedures may you flight plan to use as the planned approach at the required alternate when using TSO-C145/-C146 (WAAS) equipment? (AIM 1-1-18)

Pilots with TSO-C145/C146 WAAS capable GPS receivers may flight plan to use any instrument approach procedure authorized for use with their WAAS avionics as the planned approach at a required alternate, with certain restrictions. To put this plainly, a pilot with a WAAS-equipped and capable aircraft may use an airport served only with GPS-based approaches as an alternate.

19. **What restrictions apply to flight planning when using WAAS avionics at the alternate airport?** (AIM 1-1-18)

When using WAAS avionics at an alternate airport, flight planning must be based on flying the RNAV (GPS) LNAV or circling minima line, or minima on a GPS approach procedure, or conventional approach procedure with "or GPS" in the title. 14 CFR Part 91 non-precision weather requirements must be used for planning. Upon arrival at an alternate, when the WAAS navigation system indicates that LNAV/VNAV or LPV service is available, then vertical guidance may be used to complete the approach using the displayed level of service.

E. Route Planning

1. **What are preferred routes, and where can they be found?** (P/CG)

Preferred routes are those established between busier airports to increase system efficiency and capacity. Preferred routes are listed in the *Chart Supplement*.

2. **What are enroute low-altitude charts?** (AIM 9-1-4, FAA-H-8083-15)

Enroute low-altitude charts provide aeronautical information for navigation under IFR conditions below 18,000 feet MSL. These charts are revised every 56 days. All courses are magnetic and distances are nautical miles.

3. **What are enroute high-altitude charts?** (AIM 9-1-4)

Enroute high-altitude charts are designed for navigation at or above 18,000 feet MSL. This four-color chart series includes the jet route structure; VHF NAVAIDs with frequency, identification, channel, geographic coordinates; selected airports; and reporting points. These charts are revised every 56 days.

4. **What are area charts?** (AIM 9-1-4)

Area charts show congested terminal areas such as Dallas/ Ft. Worth or Atlanta at a large scale. They are included with subscriptions to any conterminous U.S. set Low (Full set, East or West sets). Revised every 56 days.

5. Where can updated information be obtained about changes to aeronautical charts that occurred between chart publication dates? (AIM 9-1-4)

The *Chart Supplement* provides a means for pilots to update visual charts between edition dates. The *Chart Supplement* is published every 56 days while sectional aeronautical and VFR terminal area charts are generally revised every six months.

6. What other useful information can be found in the *Chart Supplement* that might be helpful in route planning? (Chart Supplement)

a. Special notices—prohibited areas, aerobatic and glider practice areas, noise abatement etc.

b. ARTCCs—low- and high-altitude transmitter site frequencies.

c. FSS frequencies.

d. Routes/waypoints—low- and high-altitude preferred routes; VFR waypoints.

e. GPS Q routes.

f. VOR receiver checkpoints and VOTs.

g. Aeronautical chart bulletins.

7. How does a pilot determine the type and status of an instrument approach light system at the destination airport? (FAA-H-8083-3)

The pilot should check the *Chart Supplement* and any NOTAMs to determine the availability and status of lighting systems, light intensities, and radio-controlled light system frequencies. An FSS briefer will also have access to any recent changes in the status of airport lighting systems.

Exam Tip: Be prepared to determine and explain the type and status of airport lighting, runway lighting, and approach light systems at your departure, destination, and alternate airports.

8. What are NOTAMs? (AIM 5-1-3)

Notice to Air Missions (NOTAM)—Time critical aeronautical information, which is of either a temporary nature or not known sufficiently in advance to permit publication on aeronautical charts or in other operational publications, receives immediate dissemination via the National NOTAM System. It is aeronautical information that could affect a pilot's decision to make a flight. It includes such information as airport or primary runway closures, changes in the status of navigational aids, ILSs, radar service availability, and other information essential to planned en route, terminal, or landing operations.

9. What are the different types of NOTAMs a pilot may encounter? (faa.gov, AIM 5-1-3)

A Notice to Air Missions (NOTAM) is a notice containing information (not known sufficiently in advance to publicize by other means) concerning the establishment, condition, or change in any component (facility, service, or procedure of, or hazard in the National Airspace System) the timely knowledge of which is essential to personnel concerned with flight operations.

Types of NOTAMs include Class I NOTAMs, Class II NOTAMs, International NOTAMs, Domestic NOTAMs, Civil NOTAMs, Military NOTAMs, Published NOTAMs, FDC NOTAMs, Center Area NOTAMs, and NOTAM (D)s including (U) and (O) NOTAMs.

Class I NOTAM (ICAO)—NOTAMs distributed by means of telecommunication.

Class II NOTAM (ICAO) or Published NOTAM—NOTAMs distributed by means other than telecommunications.

International NOTAM—Any NOTAM intended for distribution to more than one country. However, an FSS does not have access to all international NOTAMs. If the definition is limited to international NOTAMs accessible to an FSS, this would include NOTAMs stored in ICAO format in the United States NOTAM System (USNS). The USNS stores international NOTAMs separately from domestic NOTAMs, but only for selected locations both inside and outside the United States. These NOTAMs are not included in a standard weather briefing unless specifically requested.

Domestic NOTAM—A NOTAM that is primarily distributed within the United States, although they may also be available in Canada. Domestic NOTAMs stored in the USNS are coded in a domestic format rather than an ICAO format.

(continued)

Civil NOTAM—Any NOTAM that is part of the civil NOTAM system, which includes any NOTAM that is not part of the military NOTAM system.

Military NOTAM—Any NOTAM that is part of the military NOTAM system, which primarily includes NOTAMs on military airports and military airspace.

FDC NOTAM—Flight Data Center NOTAMs are NOTAMs that are regulatory in nature, such as changes to an instrument approach procedure or airway. Temporary Flight Restrictions (TFRs) are also issued as FDC NOTAMs.

Center Area NOTAM—An FDC NOTAM issued for a condition that is not limited to one airport; therefore, it is filed under the Air Route Traffic Control Center (ARTCC) that controls the airspace involved. TFRs, airway changes, and laser light activity are examples of this type of NOTAM. This is important to know when looking for NOTAMs on your own. For example, you must retrieve ZAN FDC NOTAMs for flights in Alaska because ZAN is the code for Anchorage ARTCC, which is the controlling Center for all of Alaska.

NOTAM (D)—A NOTAM given (in addition to local dissemination) distant dissemination beyond the area of responsibility of the Flight Service Station. This type of NOTAM now includes (U) NOTAMs and (O) NOTAMs. (U) NOTAMs are unverified NOTAMs, which are those that are received from a source other than airport management and have not yet been confirmed by management personnel. This is allowed only at those airports where airport management has authorized it by letter of agreement. (O) NOTAMs are other aeronautical information that does not meet NOTAM criteria but may be beneficial to aircraft operations.

10. All (D) NOTAMs will have keywords contained within the first part of the text. What are several examples of these keywords? (AIM 5-1-3)

RWY, TWY, APRON, AD, OBST, NAV, COM, SVC, AIRSPACE, ODP, SID, STAR, CHART, DATA, IAP, VFP, ROUTE, SPECIAL, SECURITY, (U) or (O).

11. Where can NOTAM information be obtained? (AIM 5-1-1, 5-1-3)

a. Call the Flight Service: 1800WXBRIEF

b. NOTAM search: notams.aim.faa.gov/notamSearch/

c. Flight Service briefing website: 1800wxbrief.com

d. Flight Information Services (FIS-B via ADS-B In)

Note: The NOTAM-D and NOTAM-FDC products broadcast via FIS-B are limited to those issued or effective within the past 30 days. Except for TFRs, NOTAMs older than 30 days are not provided.

12. How can a pilot obtain the latest GPS NOTAMs? (AIM 1-1-17)

A pilot can specifically request GPS aeronautical information from an FSS briefer during preflight briefings. Also, NOTAMs about known GPS service disruptions can be found at notams.aim.faa. gov/notamSearch/.

Exam Tip: Make sure to review all of the NOTAMs along your planned route of flight, at your destination, and at your planned alternate airport for any recent changes that might have occurred after chart publication. Be particularly alert for any changes to the IAPs you might be flying for your checkride.

13. What do the NOTAM terms "UNRELIABLE" and "MAY NOT BE AVAILABLE" indicate when used in conjunction with GPS and WAAS NOTAMs? (AIM 1-1-17, 1-1-18)

The terms "UNRELIABLE" and "MAY NOT BE AVAILABLE" are cautions indicating that the expected level of service might not be available. "UNRELIABLE" does not mean there is a problem with GPS signal integrity. If GPS service is available, pilots may continue operations. If the LNAV or LNAV/VNAV service is available, pilots may use the displayed level of service to fly the approach.

The term MAY NOT BE AVBL is used in conjunction with WAAS NOTAMs and indicates that due to ionospheric conditions, lateral guidance may still be available when vertical guidance is unavailable. Under certain conditions, both lateral and vertical guidance might be unavailable. This NOTAM language is a pilot advisory that the expected level of WAAS service (LNAV/VNAV, LPV, LP) might not be available.

14. When flight planning an RNAV route, where should your route begin and end? (AIM 5-1-8)

Plan the random route portion of the flight plan to begin and end over appropriate arrival and departure transition fixes or appropriate navigation aids for the altitude stratum within which the flight will be conducted. The use of normal preferred departure and arrival routes (DP/STAR), where established, is recommended.

F. Flight Instruments

Pitot/Static System

1. What instruments operate from the pitot/static system? (FAA-H-8083-15)

The pitot/static system operates the altimeter, vertical speed indicator, and airspeed indicator. All three instruments receive static air pressure for operation with only the ASI receiving both pitot and static pressure.

2. How does an altimeter work? (FAA-H-8083-15)

A sensitive altimeter is an aneroid barometer that measures the absolute pressure of the ambient air and displays it in terms of feet or meters above a selected pressure level. The "sensitive element" in a sensitive altimeter is a stack of evacuated, corrugated bronze aneroid capsules. The air pressure acting on these aneroids tries to compress them against their natural springiness, which tries to expand them. The result is that their thickness changes as the air pressure changes. Stacking several aneroids increases the dimension change as the pressure varies over the usable range of the instrument.

3. What type of errors is the altimeter subject to? (FAA-H-8083-15)

a. Mechanical errors—Differences between ambient temperature and/or pressure can cause an erroneous indication on the altimeter.

b. Inherent errors—Non-standard temperature and pressure.

- *Warmer than standard air*—The air is less dense and the pressure levels are farther apart. The pressure level for a given altitude is higher than it would be in air at standard temperature, and the aircraft is higher than it would be if the air were cooler. True altitude is higher than indicated altitude whenever the temperature is warmer than International Standard Atmosphere (ISA).

- *Colder than standard air*—The air is denser and the pressure levels are closer together. The pressure level for a given altitude is lower than it would be in air at standard temperature, and the aircraft is lower than it would be if the air were warmer. True altitude is lower than indicated altitude whenever the temperature is colder than ISA.

- *Extreme cold altimeter errors*—A correctly calibrated pressure altimeter indicates true altitude above mean sea level (MSL) when operating within ISA parameters of pressure and temperature. When operating in extreme cold temperatures (i.e., +10°C to −50°C), pilots may wish to compensate for the reduction in terrain clearance by adding a cold temperature correction.

- *High pressure to low pressure*—If an aircraft is flown from an area of high pressure to an area of lower pressure without adjusting the altimeter, the true altitude of the aircraft will be lower than indicated altitude.

- *Low pressure to high pressure*—If an aircraft is flown from an area of low pressure to an area of higher pressure without adjusting the altimeter, the true altitude of the aircraft will be higher than indicated altitude.

Remember: High to Low or Hot to Cold—look out below!

4. For IFR flight, what is the maximum allowable error for an altimeter? (FAA-H-8083-15, 14 CFR 43 Appendix E)

If the altimeter is off field elevation by more than 75 feet, with the correct pressure set in the Kollsman window, it is considered to be unreliable.

5. Define and state how to determine the following altitudes: indicated altitude, true altitude, absolute altitude, pressure altitude, density altitude.
(FAA-H-8083-25)

Indicated altitude—The altitude read directly from the altimeter (uncorrected) after it is set to the current altimeter setting (QNH) in the Kollsman window.

True altitude—The vertical distance of the aircraft above sea level (MSL). Airport, terrain, and obstacle elevations on aeronautical charts are true altitudes.

Absolute altitude—The vertical distance of the aircraft above the terrain, above ground level (AGL). An altimeter set to the proper pressure reading (QFE setting) indicates zero feet at touchdown. It is referred to as QFE.

Pressure altitude—The indicated altitude with altimeter set to 29.92 inHg. Pressure altitude is used to compute density altitude, true altitude, true airspeed (TAS), and other performance data.

Density altitude—Pressure altitude corrected for variations from standard temperature.

6. Does adjusting the altimeter's Kollsman window have any effect on the altitude that is displayed to an ATC controller? Why? (FAA-H-8083-15)

No, the encoding altimeter measures the pressure referenced to 29.92 inHg (pressure altitude) and delivers this data to the transponder. When a pilot adjusts the barometric scale to the local altimeter setting, the data sent to the transponder is not affected. This is to ensure that all Mode C aircraft are transmitting altitude data referenced to a common pressure level. ATC equipment adjusts the displayed altitudes to compensate for local pressure differences allowing display of targets at correct altitudes.

7. What is the function of the "Kollsman" window on the altimeter? (FAA-H-8083-15)

The Kollsman window on an altimeter provides pilots with a means to adjust the altimeter setting to account for changes in atmospheric pressure during flight, ensuring that altitude readings remain precise and facilitating safe and accurate navigation during flight.

The Kollsman window allows pilots to set the altimeter to the current atmospheric pressure at the aircraft's location. This setting is known as the "altimeter setting" and is usually given in inches of mercury (inHg) or hectopascals (hPa). Pilots obtain the current altimeter setting from air traffic control or automated weather systems.

To make this adjustment, pilots turn the Kollsman window using a knob typically found on the altimeter's outer rim. By setting the altimeter to the correct pressure level, it compensates for variations in atmospheric pressure, providing a more accurate indication of the aircraft's altitude above sea level.

8. How does the airspeed indicator operate?
(FAA-H-8083-15)

The airspeed indicator measures the difference between ram pressure from the pitot head and atmospheric pressure from the static source.

9. What are the limitations the airspeed indicator is subject to? (FAA-H-8083-15)

It must have proper flow of air in the pitot/static system.

10. What are the errors that the airspeed indicator is subject to? (FAA-H-8083-25)

Position error—Caused by the static ports sensing erroneous static pressure; slipstream flow causes disturbances at the static port, preventing actual atmospheric pressure measurement. It varies with airspeed, altitude, and configuration and may be a plus or minus value.

Density error—Changes in altitude and temperature are not compensated for by the instrument.

Compressibility error—Caused by the packing of air into the pitot tube at high airspeeds, resulting in higher-than-normal indications. It usually occurs above 180 KIAS.

11. What are the different types of aircraft speeds?
(FAA-H-8083-15)

Indicated airspeed (IAS)—IAS is the airspeed shown on the dial of the instrument, uncorrected for instrument or system errors.

Calibrated airspeed (CAS)—The speed at which the aircraft is moving through the air, which is found by correcting IAS for instrument and position errors. The POH/AFM has a chart or graph to correct IAS for these errors and provides the correct CAS for the various flap and landing gear configurations.

Equivalent airspeed (EAS)—EAS is CAS corrected for compression of the air inside the pitot tube. EAS is the same as CAS in standard atmosphere at sea level. As the airspeed and pressure altitude increase, the CAS becomes higher than it should be, and a correction for compression must be subtracted from the CAS.

(continued)

True airspeed (TAS)—CAS corrected for nonstandard pressure and temperature. TAS and CAS are the same in standard atmosphere at sea level. Under nonstandard conditions, TAS is found by applying a correction for pressure altitude and temperature to the CAS.

12. What airspeeds are indicated by the various color codes found on the dial of an airspeed indicator?
(FAA-H-8083-25)

Color-coded marking	Indicated limitation
White arc	Flap operating range.
Lower limit of white arc	V_{S0}—stall speed or minimum steady flight speed in landing configuration (gear and flaps down).
Upper limit of the white arc	V_{FE}—maximum speed with the flaps extended. *Note:* Some aircraft allow partial flaps deployment at higher speeds than the maximum speed of the white arc.
Green arc	Normal operating range.
Lower limit of green arc	V_{S1}—stall speed or minimum steady flight speed obtained in a specified or clean configuration.
Upper limit of green arc	V_{NO}—maximum structural cruising speed. Do not exceed this speed except in smooth air.
Yellow arc	Caution range; fly within this range only in smooth air, and then, only with caution.
Red line	V_{NE}—never exceed speed; operating above this speed is prohibited; may result in damage or structural failure.
Red radial line	V_{MC}—a speed established by the manufacturer, published in the AFM/POH, and marked on most airspeed indicators in multi-engine aircraft.
Blue radial line	V_{YSE}—best rate of climb single engine, even if it is negative; marked on most airspeed indicators in multi-engine aircraft.

13. How does the vertical speed indicator work?
(FAA-H-8083-15)

The vertical speed indicator (VSI) is a rate-of-pressure-change instrument that gives an indication of any deviation from a constant pressure level. Inside the VSI instrument case is an aneroid. Both the inside of the aneroid and the inside of the instrument case are vented to the static system. The case is vented through a calibrated orifice that causes the pressure inside the case to change more slowly than the pressure inside the aneroid. Changing pressures inside the case and the aneroid compress and expand the aneroid, moving the pointer upward or downward indicating a climb, a descent, or level flight.

14. What are the limitations of the vertical speed indicator?
(FAA-H-8083-15)

It is not accurate until the aircraft is stabilized. Sudden or abrupt changes in the aircraft attitude will cause erroneous instrument readings as airflow fluctuates over the static port. These changes are not reflected immediately by the VSI due to the calibrated leak. The vertical speed indicator is commonly considered a "trend" instrument.

15. While en route in IMC, ATC clears you to climb to a new altitude. After establishing the appropriate pitch attitude and power setting, your altimeter and VSI correctly indicate a climb, but your airspeed indicator indicates that your airspeed is increasing. What could be the problem? (FAA-H-8083-15, FAA-H-8083-25)

Moisture (including ice), insects, or other foreign matter may have caused a pitot tube blockage. If the pitot tube ram pressure hole and drain hole have become obstructed, the airspeed indicator operates like an altimeter as the aircraft climbs and descends. During a climb, the airspeed increases; during a descent, the airspeed decreases. The danger is that a pilot will not recognize the problem and during a climb, will attempt to reduce airspeed by increasing pitch attitude and/or reducing power, possibly resulting in a stall in IMC.

16. **On takeoff, as you climb away from the runway into IMC, you notice that your vertical speed indicator is indicating zero, your airspeed indicator is still alive but doesn't seem accurate, and the altimeter is frozen. What is the problem?** (FAA-H-8083-25)

    The static system is blocked, and you would observe the following:

    Airspeed indicator—Accurate at the altitude frozen as long as static pressure in the indicator and the system equals outside pressure. If the aircraft descends, the airspeed indicator would read high (outside static pressure would be greater than that trapped). If the aircraft climbs, the airspeed indicator would read low.

    Altimeter—Indicates the altitude at which the system is blocked.

    Vertical speed—Will indicate level flight.

17. **If the air temperature is +6°C at an airport elevation of 1,200 feet and a standard (average) temperature lapse rate exists, what will be the approximate freezing level?**

    4,200 MSL; 6°C at the surface divided by the average temperature lapse rate of 2°C results in a 3,000-foot (AGL) freezing level, converted to sea level by adding the 1,200-foot airport elevation.

18. **What corrective action is needed if the pitot tube freezes?** (FAA-H-8083-15)

    Turn pitot heat on if available. Reference known power settings for level flight until the pitot heat has cleared icing and normal airspeed indications are re-established.

19. **What corrective action is needed if the static port freezes?** (FAA-H-8083-15)

    Turn on static heat if available, use alternate air if available, or break the glass on the VSI. The VSI is not required for instrument flight and breaking the glass provides the altimeter and the ASI a source of static pressure.

20. What instrument indications should you expect to observe should it become necessary to use an alternate source of static pressure vented inside the airplane? (FAA-H-8083-15)

In many unpressurized aircraft equipped with a pitot-static tube, an alternate source of static pressure is provided for emergency use. If the alternate source is vented inside the airplane where static pressure is usually lower than outside, selection of the alternate static source may result in the following indications:

Altimeter—will indicate higher than the actual altitude.

Airspeed—will indicate greater than the actual airspeed.

Vertical speed—will show a momentary climb, then stabilize, if in level flight.

Note: Always consult the AFM/POH to determine the amount of error.

21. In a pressurized aircraft, if the outside pressure source becomes blocked, what will a pilot need to do other than select an alternate static source?

Since alternate static pressure sources are typically inside the aircraft, an alternate static source will only accurately read if the cabin is depressurized. The pilot would need to depressurize the aircraft for the alternate static source to work properly. This could additionally require the pilot to execute a descent to a lower altitude if the aircraft is above the altitude at which oxygen is required.

Gyroscopic System

1. What instruments contain gyroscopes? (FAA-H-8083-15)

The most commonly gyroscopically driven instruments have historically been attitude indicators and heading indicators. Some turn coordinators may also be gyroscopic. Many modern aircraft no longer have vacuum-driven gyroscopic instruments, and a pilot should know which systems are in the aircraft they will be operating.

2. **Name several types of power sources commonly used to power the gyroscopic instruments in an aircraft.** (FAA-H-8083-15)

   Various power sources used are electrical, pneumatic, venturi tube, wet-type vacuum pump, and dry-air pump systems. Aircraft and instrument manufacturers have designed redundancy into the flight instruments so that any single failure will not deprive the pilot of his or her ability to safely conclude the flight. Gyroscopic instruments are crucial for instrument flight; therefore, they are powered by separate electrical or pneumatic sources. Typically, if the heading indicator and attitude indicator are vacuum-driven, the turn coordinator will be electrically driven.

   Note: It is extremely important that pilots consult the POH/AFM to determine the power source of all instruments to know what action to take in the event of an instrument failure.

3. **How does a vacuum system operate?** (FAA-H-8083-25)

   A vacuum or pressure system spins the gyro by drawing a stream of air against the rotor vanes to spin the rotor at high speeds, essentially similar to how a water wheel or turbine operates. The amount of vacuum or pressure required for instrument operation varies by manufacturer and is usually between 4.5 to 5.5 inHg. One source of vacuum for the gyros installed in light aircraft is the vane-type engine-driven pump, mounted on the accessory case of the engine.

4. **What are two important characteristics of gyroscopes?** (FAA-H-8083-15)

   Rigidity—The characteristic of a gyro that prevents its axis of rotation tilting as the Earth rotates; attitude and heading instruments operate on this principle.

   Precession—The characteristic of a gyro that causes an applied force to be felt, not at the point of application, but 90 degrees from that point in the direction of rotation. Rate instruments such as the turn coordinator use this principle.

5. **How does a turn coordinator operate?** (FAA-H-8083-15)

   The turn part of the instrument uses precession to indicate direction and approximate rate of turn. A gyro reacts by trying to move in reaction to the force applied, thus moving the miniature aircraft in proportion to the rate of turn. The inclinometer in the instrument is a black glass ball sealed inside a curved glass tube that is partially filled with a liquid. The ball measures the relative strength of the force of gravity and the force of inertia caused by a turn.

6. What is the definition of a *standard-rate turn*? (FAA-H-8083-15)

A standard-rate turn refers to a turn made by an aircraft at a rate of three degrees per second. This specific rate is standardized to ensure consistency and safety in air navigation. Pilots use this standard rate to execute turns, maintaining a steady and predictable movement through the airspace. In practical terms, a standard-rate turn completes a full 360-degree revolution in two minutes.

7. What information does a turn coordinator provide? (FAA-H-8083-15)

The miniature aircraft in the turn coordinator displays the rate of turn, rate of roll, and direction of turn. The ball in the tube indicates the quality of turn (slip or skid).

Slip—ball on the inside of turn; not enough rate of turn for the amount of bank.

Skid—ball to the outside of turn; too much rate of turn for the amount of bank.

8. What is the source of power for a turn coordinator? (FAA-H-8083-15)

Turn coordinator gyros can be driven by either air or electricity; some are dual-powered. Typically, the turn coordinator is electrically powered, but always refer to the AFM for detailed information about the system in the aircraft you are operating.

9. How does a heading indicator work? (FAA-H-8083-25)

The operation of a heading indicator works on the principle of rigidity in space. The rotor turns in a vertical plane, and fixed to the rotor is a compass card. Since the rotor remains rigid in space, the points on the card hold the same position in space relative to the vertical plane. As the instrument case and the airplane revolve around the vertical axis, the card provides clear and accurate heading information.

10. **What are the limitations of the heading indicator?**
(FAA-H-8083-25)

They vary with the particular design and make of instrument: on some heading indicators in light airplanes, the limits are approximately 55 degrees of pitch and 55 degrees of bank. When either of these attitude limits are exceeded, the instrument "tumbles" or "spills" and no longer gives the correct indication until it is reset with the caging knob. Many modern instruments used are designed in such a manner that they will not tumble.

11. **What type of error is a vacuum-driven gyroscopic heading indicator subject to?** (FAA-H-8083-25)

Because of precession (caused by friction), the heading indicator will creep or drift from the heading it is set to. The amount of drift depends largely upon the condition of the instrument (worn and dirty bearings and/or improperly lubricated bearings). Additionally, the gyro is oriented in space and the earth rotates in space at a rate of 15 degrees in 1 hour; therefore, discounting precession caused by friction, the heading indicator may indicate as much as 15 degrees of error per every hour of operation.

12. **How does a vacuum-driven gyroscopic attitude indicator work?** (FAA-H-8083-25)

The gyro in the attitude indicator is mounted on a horizontal plane and depends upon rigidity in space for its operation. The horizon bar represents the true horizon and is fixed to the gyro; it remains in a horizontal plane as the airplane is pitched or banked about its lateral or longitudinal axis, indicating the attitude of the airplane relative to the true horizon.

13. **What are the limitations of an attitude indicator?**
(FAA-H-8083-25)

Limits depend upon the make and model of the instrument; bank limits are usually from 100° to 110°, and pitch limits are usually from 60° to 70°. If either limit is exceeded, the instrument will tumble or spill and will give incorrect indications until restabilized. Some modern attitude indicators are designed so they will not tumble.

14. Is the attitude indicator subject to errors?
(FAA-H-8083-15)

Attitude indicators are free from most errors, but depending upon the speed with which the erection system functions, there may be a slight nose-up indication during a rapid acceleration and a nose-down indication during a rapid deceleration. There is also a possibility of a small bank angle and pitch error after a 180° turn. On rollout from a 180° turn, the AI will indicate a slight climb and turn in the opposite direction of rollout. These inherent errors are small and correct themselves within a minute or so after returning to straight-and-level flight.

Magnetic Compass

1. How does the magnetic compass work? (FAA-H-8083-15)

Magnets mounted on the compass card align themselves parallel to the Earth's lines of magnetic force.

2. What limitations does the magnetic compass have?
(FAA-H-8083-15)

The jewel-and-pivot type mounting gives the float freedom to rotate and tilt up to approximately 18° angle of bank. At steeper bank angles, the compass indications are erratic and unpredictable.

3. What compass errors must instrument pilots be aware of in their flight operations? (FAA-H-8083-15)

Oscillation error—Erratic movement of the compass card caused by turbulence or rough control technique.

Deviation error—Due to electrical and magnetic disturbances in the aircraft.

Variation error—Angular difference between true and magnetic north; reference isogonic lines of variation.

Dip errors:

a. *Acceleration error*—On east or west headings, while accelerating, the magnetic compass shows a turn to the north, and when decelerating, it shows a turn to the south.
   Remember: ANDS—**A**ccelerate **N**orth, **D**ecelerate **S**outh.

b. *Northerly turning error*—As the airplane turns, the force that results from the magnetic dip causes the float assembly to swing in the opposite direction than the float turns, resulting in a false turn indication opposite from the direction of actual turn. Because of this lag of the compass card, or float assembly, a northerly turn should be continued past arrival at the desired heading by the lag correction value. One rule of thumb to correct for this lag error is to continue the turn 15° plus half of the latitude.

c. *Southerly turning error*—When turning in a southerly direction, the forces are such that the compass float assembly leads rather than lags, resulting in a false excessive turn indication. The compass card, or float assembly, should not be allowed to exceed the rollout point. To correct for this leading error, the aircraft should not be allowed to pass the rollout lead point ahead of the desired compass heading by 15° + half of the latitude.

Remember: UNOS—**U**ndershoot turns in the **N**orth half of the compass, **O**vershoot turns in the **S**outh half of the compass.

Electronic Flight Instrument Displays

1. Describe the function of the following avionics equipment acronyms: PFD, MFD, AHRS, ADC, FMS, FD, TAWS, TIS. (FAA-H-8083-16)

PFD—primary flight display. A PFD provides increased situational awareness to the pilot by replacing the traditional six instruments used for instrument flight with an easy-to-scan display that provides the horizon, airspeed, altitude, vertical speed, trend, trim, and rate of turn, among other key indications.

MFD—multi-function display. A flight deck display capable of presenting information such as navigation data, moving maps, aircraft systems information (engine monitoring), or should the need arise, PFD information.

AHRS—attitude and heading reference system. An integrated flight system composed of three-axis sensors that provide heading, attitude, and yaw information for an aircraft. GPS, solid state magnetometers, solid state accelerometers, and digital air data signals are all combined in an AHRS to compute and output highly reliable information to the flight deck primary flight display (PFD).

ADC—air data computer. An aircraft computer that receives and processes ram air, static air, and temperature information from sensors, and provides information such as altitude, indicated airspeed, vertical speed, and wind direction and velocity to other flight deck systems (PFD, AHRS, transponder).

FMS—flight management system. A computer system containing a database to allow programming of routes, approaches, and departures that can supply navigation data to the flight director/ autopilot from various sources, and can calculate flight data such as fuel consumption, time remaining, possible range, and other values.

FD—flight director. An electronic flight calculator that analyzes the navigation selections, signals, and aircraft parameters. It presents steering instructions on the flight display as command bars or crossbars for the pilot to position the nose of the aircraft over or follow.

TAWS—terrain awareness and warning system. Uses the aircraft's GPS navigation signal and altimetry systems to compare the position and trajectory of the aircraft against a more detailed terrain and obstacle database. This database attempts to detail every obstruction that could pose a threat to an aircraft in flight.

TIS—Traffic Information Service is a ground-based advanced avionics traffic display system which receives transmissions on locations of nearby aircraft from radar-equipped air traffic control facilities and provides alerts and warnings to the pilot.

2. What is the function of a magnetometer? (FAA-H-8083-16)

A magnetometer is a device that measures the strength of the Earth's magnetic field to determine aircraft heading. It provides this information digitally to the AHRS, which relays it to the PFD.

3. Does an aircraft have to remain stationary during AHRS system initialization? (FAA-H-8083-16)

Some AHRSs must be initialized on the ground prior to departure. The initialization procedure allows the system to establish a reference attitude used as a benchmark for all future attitude changes. Other systems are capable of initialization while taxiing as well as in-flight.

4. **If a failure of one of the displays (PFD or MFD) occurs in an aircraft with an electronic flight display, what will happen to the remaining operative display?** (FAA-H-8083-16)

   In the event of a display failure, some systems offer a "reversion" capability to display the primary flight instruments and engine instruments on the remaining operative display. Be sure to know in your particular aircraft how to engage a reversionary mode if available and what systems will or will not be available in the event of a loss of power to a primary or essential electrical bus.

5. **When a display failure occurs, what other system components will be affected?** (AFM/POH)

   In some systems, failure of a display will also result in partial loss of navigation, communication, and GPS capability. Reference your specific AFM/POH and be able to describe to the examiner what systems will or will not be available in the event of failures. An examiner will ask scenario-based questions relating to equipment failure modes.

6. **What display information will be affected when an ADC failure occurs?** (FAA-H-8083-16)

   Inoperative airspeed, altitude, and vertical speed indicators (red Xs) on the PFD indicate the failure of the air data computer.

7. **What display information will be lost when an AHRS failure occurs?** (FAA-H-8083-16)

   An inoperative attitude indicator (red X) on a PFD indicates failure of the AHRS.

8. **How will loss of a magnetometer affect the AHRS operation?** (FAA-H-8083-16)

   Heading information will be lost.

   Exam Tip: If you are flying a technically advanced aircraft (GPS, FMS, autopilot) for the checkride, be capable of describing the failure modes for each piece of equipment and how one component failure could affect another system component (e.g., how an AHRS failure would affect the autopilot). Study the AFM supplements and have thorough knowledge of the normal, abnormal, and emergency operation of each system component.

9. **If you experience an alternator failure and your electrical system is being powered by the main battery, do you immediately lose any equipment functionality? How long will the systems continue to operate before the main battery fails?** (FAA-H-8083-16)

Depending on electrical load and condition of the battery, sufficient power may be available for an hour or more of flight or for only a matter of minutes. The pilot must be familiar with all aircraft systems requiring electricity and which systems will continue to operate without power.

10. **For aircraft with electronic flight instrumentation, what is the function of the standby battery?** (FAA-H-8083-15)

The standby battery is held in reserve and kept charged in case of a failure of the charging system and a subsequent exhaustion of the main battery. The standby battery is brought online when the main battery voltage is depleted to a specific value, approximately 19 volts. Generally, the standby battery switch must be in the ARM position for this to occur, but pilots should refer to the aircraft flight manual (AFM) for specifics on an aircraft's electrical system.

11. **After an alternator failure and depletion of the main battery, what items will still receive power from the standby battery?** (FAA-H-8083-15)

While each aircraft electrical system may be slightly different, the purpose of a standby battery is typically to power an "essential" bus that includes the most critical aircraft equipment intended to allow a pilot to manage a failure of a primary power supply. In most aircraft, the essential bus supply source will power the following critical components:

• AHRS (attitude and heading reference system)
• ADC (air data computer)
• PFD (primary flight display)
• Navigation radio #1
• Communication radio #1
• Standby indicator light

G. Fundamentals of Weather

1. At what rate does atmospheric pressure decrease with an increase in altitude? (FAA-H-8083-28)

Atmospheric pressure decreases approximately 1 inHg per 1,000 feet.

2. What are the standard temperature and pressure values for sea level? (FAA-H-8083-28)

15°C and 29.92 inHg are standard at sea level.

3. State the general characteristics in regard to the flow of air around high-pressure and low-pressure systems in the Northern Hemisphere. (FAA-H-8083-28)

Low pressure—Air flows inward, upward, and counterclockwise.

High pressure—Air flows outward, downward, and clockwise.

4. If your route of flight takes you toward a low-pressure system, what kind of weather in general can you expect? What if you were flying toward a high-pressure system? (FAA-H-8083-28)

A low-pressure system is characterized by rising air, which is conducive to cloudiness, precipitation, and bad weather. A high-pressure system is an area of descending air, which tends to favor dissipation of cloudiness and good weather.

5. Describe the different types of fronts. (FAA-H-8083-28)

Cold front—Occurs when a mass of cold, dense, and stable air advances and replaces a body of warmer air.

Occluded front—A frontal occlusion occurs when a fast-moving cold front catches up with a slow-moving warm front. Two types: cold front occlusion and warm front occlusion.

Warm front—The boundary area formed when a warm air mass contacts and flows over a colder air mass.

Stationary front—When the forces of two air masses are relatively equal, the boundary or front that separates them remains stationary and influences the local weather for days. The weather is typically a mixture of both warm and cold fronts.

6. What are the general characteristics of the weather a pilot would encounter when operating near a cold front? A warm front? (FAA-H-8083-25)

Cold front—As the front passes, expected weather can include towering cumulus or cumulonimbus; heavy rain accompanied by lightning, thunder, and/or hail; tornadoes possible; during passage, poor visibility, winds variable and gusting; temperature/dew point and barometric pressure drop rapidly.

Warm front—As the front passes, expected weather can include stratiform clouds, drizzle, low ceilings, and poor visibility; variable winds; rise in temperature.

Note: The weather associated with a front depends on the amount of moisture available, the degree of stability of the air that is forced upward, the slope of the front, the speed of frontal movement, and the upper wind flow.

7. What is a trough? (FAA-H-8083-28)

A trough (also called a trough line) is an elongated area of relatively low atmospheric pressure. At the surface when air converges into a low, it cannot go outward against the pressure gradient, nor can it go downward into the ground; it must go upward. Therefore, a low or trough is an area of rising air. Rising air is conducive to cloudiness and precipitation; hence the general association of low pressure and bad weather.

8. What is a ridge? (FAA-H-8083-28)

A ridge (also called a ridge line) is an elongated area of relatively high atmospheric pressure. Air moving out of a high or ridge depletes the quantity of air; therefore, these are areas of descending air. Descending air favors dissipation of cloudiness; hence the association of high pressure and good weather.

9. What is a dryline, and why is knowledge of its location important to you? (FAA-H-8083-28)

A dryline is a low-level boundary hundreds of miles long that separates moist and dry air masses. In the United States, it typically lies north-south across the southern and central High Plains during the spring and early summer, where it separates moist air from the Gulf of Mexico to the east and dry desert air from the southwestern states to the west. Severe and sometimes tornadic thunderstorms often develop along a dryline or in the moist air just to the east of it, especially when it begins moving eastward.

10. Why do surface winds generally flow across the isobars at an angle? (FAA-H-8083-28)

Surface friction causes winds to flow across isobars at an angle.

11. When temperature and dew point are close together (within 5°), what type of weather is likely? (AC 00-6)

Visible moisture is likely, in the form of clouds, dew or fog.

12. What factor primarily determines the type and vertical extent of clouds? (FAA-H-8083-28)

The stability of the atmosphere determines the type and vertical extent of clouds.

13. Explain the difference between a stable atmosphere and an unstable atmosphere. Why is the stability of the atmosphere important? (FAA-H-8083-25, FAA-H-8083-28)

The stability of the atmosphere depends on its ability to resist vertical motion. A stable atmosphere makes vertical movement difficult, and small vertical disturbances dampen out and disappear. In an unstable atmosphere, small vertical air movements tend to become larger, resulting in turbulent airflow and convective activity. Instability can lead to significant turbulence, extensive vertical clouds, and severe weather.

14. How do you determine the stability of the atmosphere? (FAA-H-8083-28)

Changes in atmospheric stability are inversely related to temperature (density) changes with height. If temperature lapse rates increase, then stability decreases. Conversely, if temperature lapse rates decrease, then stability increases. Most of these changes occur as a result of the movement of air, but diurnal (day/night) temperature variations can play a significant role. Several stability indexes and other quantities exist that evaluate atmospheric stability and the potential for convective storms. The most common of these are Lifted Index (LI) and Convective Available Potential Energy (CAPE). Observed CAPE values in thunderstorm environments often exceed 1,000 joules per kilogram, and in extreme cases may exceed 5,000 joules per kilogram.

15. List the effects of stable and unstable air on clouds, turbulence, precipitation, and visibility. (FAA-H-8083-28)

	Stable	Unstable
Clouds	Stratiform	Cumuliform
Turbulence	Smooth	Rough
Precipitation	Steady	Showery
Visibility	Fair to Poor	Good

16. What are the two main categories of aircraft icing? (FAA-H-8083-28)

Aircraft icing in flight is usually classified as being either structural icing or induction icing. Structural icing refers to the ice that forms on aircraft surfaces and components, while induction icing refers to ice in the engine's induction system.

17. Name the three types of structural ice that may occur in flight. (FAA-H-8083-28)

Clear icing, or glaze ice, is a glossy, clear, or translucent ice formed by the relatively slow freezing of large, supercooled water droplets. Clear icing conditions exist more often in an environment with warmer temperatures, higher liquid water contents, and larger droplets. It forms when only a small portion of the drop freezes immediately while the remaining unfrozen portion flows or smears over the aircraft surface and gradually freezes.

Rime icing is a rough, milky, and opaque ice formed by the instantaneous freezing of small, supercooled water droplets after they strike the aircraft. Rime icing formation favors colder temperatures (colder than −15°C), lower liquid water content, and small droplets. It grows when droplets rapidly freeze upon striking an aircraft. The rapid freezing traps air and forms a porous, brittle, opaque, and milky-colored ice.

Mixed icing is a mixture of clear ice and rime ice and forms as an airplane collects both rime and clear ice due to small-scale variations in liquid water content, temperature, and droplet sizes. Mixed ice appears as layers of relatively clear and opaque ice when examined from the side. Mixed icing poses a similar hazard to an aircraft as clear ice. It may form horns or other shapes that disrupt airflow and cause handling and performance problems.

(continued)

Note: In general, rime icing tends to occur at temperatures colder than −15°C, clear when the temperature is warmer than −10°C, and mixed ice at temperatures in between. This is only general guidance. The type of icing will vary depending on the liquid water content, droplet size, and aircraft-specific variables.

18. Describe the types of icing found in stratiform clouds, and the types found in cumuliform clouds. (FAA-H-8083-28)

Stratified clouds—Both rime and mixed are found in stratiform clouds. Icing in middle and low-level stratiform clouds is confined, on average, to a layer between 3,000 and 4,000 feet thick. A change in altitude of only a few thousand feet may take the aircraft out of icing conditions, even if it remains in clouds. The main hazard lies in the great horizontal extent of stratiform clouds layers.

Cumuliform clouds—Icing is usually clear or mixed with rime in the upper levels. The icing layer is smaller horizontally but greater vertically than in stratiform clouds. Icing is more variable in cumuliform clouds because the factors conducive to icing depend on the particular cloud's stage of development. Icing intensities may range from a trace in small cumulus to severe in a large towering cumulus or cumulonimbus, especially in the upper portion of the cloud where the updraft is concentrated and supercooled large drops (SLDs) are plentiful.

19. What is necessary for structural icing to occur? (FAA-H-8083-28)

The aircraft must be flying through visible water such as rain or cloud droplets; temperature must be at the point where moisture strikes the aircraft at 0°C or colder.

20. What are the intensity categories of aircraft structural icing? (AIM 7-1-19)

a. *Trace*—Ice becomes noticeable; the rate of accumulation is slightly greater than rate of sublimation; a representative accretion rate for reference purposes is less than ¼ inch (6 mm) per hour on the outer wing. The pilot should consider exiting the icing conditions before they become worse.

b. *Light*—The rate of ice accumulation requires occasional cycling of manual deicing systems to minimize ice accretions on the airframe. A representative accretion rate for reference purposes is ¼ inch to 1 inch (0.6 to 2.5 cm) per hour on the unprotected part of the outer wing. The pilot should consider exiting the icing condition.

c. *Moderate*—The rate of ice accumulation requires frequent cycling of manual deicing systems to minimize ice accretions on the airframe. A representative accretion rate for reference purposes is 1 to 3 inches (2.5 to 7.5 cm) per hour on the unprotected part of the outer wing. The pilot should consider exiting the icing condition as soon as possible.

d. *Severe*—The rate of ice accumulation is such that ice protection systems fail to remove the accumulation of ice and ice accumulates in locations not normally prone to icing. A representative accretion rate for reference purposes is more than 3 inches (7.5 cm) per hour on the unprotected part of the outer wing. By regulation, immediate exit is required.

21. During preflight planning, what type of meteorological information should you be aware of with respect to icing? (AC 91-74)

a. *Location of fronts*—The front's location, type, speed, and direction of movement.

b. *Cloud layers*—The location of cloud bases and tops; this is valuable when determining if you will be able to climb above icing layers or descend beneath those layers into warmer air.

c. *Freezing level(s)*—Important when determining how to avoid icing and how to exit icing conditions if accidentally encountered.

d. *Air temperature and pressure*—Icing tends to be found in low-pressure areas and at temperatures at or around freezing.

e. *Precipitation*—knowing the location and type of precipitation forecast will assist in avoiding areas conducive to severe icing.

Exam Tip: Know what your plan will be if you accidentally encounter in-flight icing. Be able to explain how you will determine the potential for icing during preflight planning. What weather products will you use on the ground and in flight to determine potential areas of icing (GFA, CIP, FIP, prog charts, winds aloft, etc.)?

22. What is the definition of the term *freezing level*, and how can you determine where that level is? (FAA-H-8083-28)

The freezing level is the lowest altitude in the atmosphere over a given location at which the air temperature reaches 0°C. It is possible to have multiple freezing layers when a temperature inversion occurs above the defined freezing level. Potential sources of icing information for determining its location are: GFA, PIREPS, AIRMETs, SIGMETs, convective SIGMETs, low-level significant weather charts, surface analysis (for frontal location and freezing precipitation) and winds and temperatures aloft (for air temperature at altitude). Pilots can use graphical data including freezing level graphics, the current icing product (CIP), and forecast icing product (FIP). These products are available at the NWS Aviation Weather Center website at aviationweather.gov/gfa/#ice.

23. During preflight planning, how can you mitigate the total risk encountered en route when the possibility of operating in or around icing conditions exists? (AC 91-74)

a. When determining routes, consider the climb performance of the airplane and the route's minimum altitude, particularly in mountainous terrain. Airplane climb performance will be degraded if ice is encountered.

b. If the aircraft is loaded near maximum gross weight, climb performance will be degraded, which could increase the time spent in icing conditions.

c. Determine icing exit strategies during preflight. Determine if climbing or descending will be viable options based on the planned route of flight. This includes required altitudes in order to maintain clearance from terrain, airspace, published routes, departure procedures, arrival procedures and approaches.

d. Extra fuel may be necessary because of additional fuel needed to operate icing systems. Additionally, excess drag or weight caused by ice formation may require extra power to maintain altitude or airspeed, increasing fuel consumption.

e. When choosing alternate airports, remember that if structural icing occurs, higher approach speeds and consequently additional runway length may be required for landing.

24. What are the factors necessary for a thunderstorm to form and what are the three stages of thunderstorm development? (FAA-H-8083-28)

For a thunderstorm to form, the air must have sufficient water vapor, an unstable lapse rate, and an initial upward boost (lifting) to start the storm process in motion. During its lifecycle, a thunderstorm cell progresses through three stages:

a. *Cumulus*—Characterized by a strong updraft.

b. *Mature*—Precipitation reaches the surface. The precipitation descends through the cloud and drags the adjacent air downward, creating a strong downdraft alongside the updraft.

c. *Dissipating*—Downdrafts characterize the dissipating stage, and the storm dies rapidly.

25. What are squall line thunderstorms? (FAA-H-8083-28)

A squall line is a non-frontal, narrow band of active thunderstorms. Often it develops ahead of a cold front in moist, unstable air, but it may also develop in unstable air far removed from any front. The line may be too long to easily detour and too wide and severe to penetrate. It often contains severe steady-state thunderstorms and presents the single most intense weather hazard to aircraft. It usually forms rapidly, reaching a maximum intensity during the late afternoon and the first few hours of darkness.

26. How does fog form? (FAA-H-8083-28)

Fog forms when the temperature and dew point of the air become identical (or nearly so). This may occur through cooling of the air to a little beyond its dew point (producing radiation fog, advection fog, or upslope fog), or by adding moisture and thereby elevating the dew point (producing frontal fog or steam fog).

27. Name several types of fog. (FAA-H-8083-28)

a. Radiation fog

b. Advection fog

c. Upslope fog

d. Frontal fog or precipitation-induced fog

e. Steam fog

28. What causes radiation fog to form? (FAA-H-8083-28)

Conditions favorable for radiation fog are a clear sky, little or no wind, and small temperature-dew point spread (high relative humidity). The fog forms almost exclusively at night or near daybreak.

29. What is advection fog, and where is it most likely to form? (FAA-H-8083-28)

Advection fog forms when moist air moves over colder ground or water. It is most common along coastal areas but often develops deep in continental areas. Unlike radiation fog, it may occur with winds, with cloudy skies, over a wide geographic area, and at any time of the day or night. It deepens as wind speed increases up to about 15 knots; wind much stronger than 15 knots lifts the fog into a layer of low stratus or stratocumulus.

30. Define *upslope fog.* (FAA-H-8083-28)

Upslope fog forms as a result of moist, stable air being cooled adiabatically as it moves up sloping terrain. Once the upslope wind ceases, the fog dissipates. Unlike radiation fog, it can form under cloudy skies. It is common along the eastern slopes of the Rockies and somewhat less frequent east of the Appalachians; can often be quite dense and extend to high altitudes.

31. How does steam fog form? (FAA-H-8083-28)

When very cold air moves across relatively warm water, enough moisture may evaporate from the water surface to produce saturation. As the rising water vapor meets the cold air, it immediately re-condenses and rises with the air that is being warmed from below. Because the air is destabilized, fog appears as rising filaments or streamers that resemble steam. This phenomenon is called steam fog. It is commonly observed over lakes and streams on cold autumn mornings, and over the ocean during the winter when cold air masses move off the continents and ice shelves.

32. Explain how frontal (or precipitation-induced) fog forms. (FAA-H-8083-28)

When warm, moist air is lifted over a front, clouds and precipitation may form. If the cold air below is near its dew point, evaporation (or sublimation) from the precipitation may saturate the cold air and form fog. Frontal fog can become quite dense and continue for an extended period of time and may extend over large areas, completely suspending air operations. It is most commonly associated with warm fronts but can occur with other fronts as well.

33. Other than fog, what are several other examples of IFR weather producers? (FAA-H-8083-28)

Other examples of common IFR producers are low clouds (stratus), haze, smoke, blowing obstructions to vision, and precipitation. Fog and low stratus restrict navigation by visual reference more often than all other weather phenomena.

H. Obtaining Weather Information

1. What is a good process that the FAA recommends for obtaining a good weather briefing prior to a flight. (FAA-P-8740-30)

a. First get a "big picture" of weather patterns by watching television (The Weather Channel, etc.) and/or the internet several days prior to a flight.

b. On the day or evening before a flight, obtain an outlook briefing from Flight Service and/or download weather and forecast charts from the internet.

c. As close to departure time as possible, with preliminary flight planning complete (basic route, altitudes, preliminary alternates), call Flight Service or log on to 1800wxbrief.com for a standard briefing. A pilot can also access weather products on the internet or other sources (making sure the products are suitable for aviation use and are current).

d. If a standard briefing is several hours prior to a flight or the weather is questionable, call an FSS for an abbreviated briefing just before takeoff.

2. What are some examples of other sources of weather information? (AIM 7-1-2, 7-1-8, 7-1-9, 7-1-11)

a. The Aviation Weather Center at aviationweather.gov.

b. Leidos Flight Services via the Internet. Pilots can receive preflight weather data and file domestic VFR and IFR flight plans: 1800wxbrief.com or call 1-800-WXBRIEF.

c. Weather and aeronautical information available from numerous private industry sources.

d. Flight Information Services (FIS-B via ADS-B In).

3. What pertinent information should a weather briefing include? (AIM 7-1-5)

a. Adverse conditions

b. VFR flight not recommended

c. Synopsis

d. Current conditions

e. Enroute forecast

f. Destination forecast

g. Winds aloft

h. Notices to Air Missions (NOTAMs)

i. ATC delay

In addition, pilots may obtain the following from FSS briefers upon request: information on special use airspace (SUA) and SUA-related airspace, including alert areas, MOAs, MTRs (IFR, VFR, VR, and SR training routes), warning areas, and ATC assigned airspace (ATCAA); approximate density altitude data; information on air traffic services and rules; customs/immigration procedures; ADIZ rules; search and rescue; GPS RAIM availability for 1 hour before to 1 hour after ETA or a time specified by the pilot; and other assistance as required.

4. While en route, how can a pilot obtain updated weather information? (FAA-H-8083-25)

a. FSS on 122.2 or appropriate frequency; use of remote communication outlet (RCO) frequency, if available.

b. ATIS, Automated Surface Observing System (ASOS), or Automated Weather Observing System (AWOS) broadcasts along your route of flight.

c. Air Route Traffic Control Center (ARTCC) broadcasts—AWW, Convective SIGMET, SIGMET, AIRMET, Urgent PIREP, and CWA alerts are broadcast once on all frequencies, except emergency.

d. Datalink weather—flight deck display of FIS-B information.

e. ATC (workload permitting).

Exam Tip: Be prepared to demonstrate how you would obtain inflight weather advisories and updates and how you would communicate with an FSS while en route.

5. What is Flight Information Service (FIS) and how does it work? (FAA-H-8083-25, AIM 7-1-11)

Flight Information Service–Broadcast (FIS-B) is a ground broadcast service provided through the Automatic Dependent Surveillance–Broadcast (ADS-B) services network over the 978 MHz Universal Access Transceiver (UAT) data link. The FAA FIS-B system provides pilots and flight crews of properly equipped aircraft with a flight deck display of aviation weather and aeronautical information.

I. Aviation Weather Reports and Observations

1. What is a METAR? (AC 00-45)

The aviation routine weather report (METAR) is the weather observer's interpretation of the weather conditions at a given site and time. There are two types of METAR reports: a routine METAR report that is transmitted every hour and an aviation selected special weather report (SPECI). This is a special report that can be given at any time to update the METAR for rapidly changing weather conditions, aircraft mishaps, or other critical information.

2. Describe the basic elements of a METAR.
(FAA-H-8083-28)

A METAR report contains the following elements in the order presented:

a. *Type of report*—The METAR (routine), and SPECI (special observation).

(continued)

b. *Station identifier*—(ICAO) four-letter station identifier; in the conterminous United States, the three-letter identifier is prefixed with K.

c. *Date and time of report*—Six-digit date/time group appended with Z to denote Coordinated Universal Time (UTC). The first two digits are the date followed with two digits for hour and two digits for minutes.

d. *Modifier (as required)*—If used, AUTO identifies a METAR/SPECI report as an automated weather report with no human intervention. If AUTO is shown in the body of the report, AO1 or AO2 will be encoded in the remarks section to indicate the type of precipitation sensor used at the station.

e. *Wind*—Five-digit group (six digits if speed is over 99 knots); first three digits are the wind direction in tens of degrees referenced to true north. Directions less than 100 degrees are preceded with a zero. The next two digits are the average speed in knots, measured or estimated (or if over 99 knots, the next three digits).

f. *Visibility*—Prevailing visibility in statute miles followed by a space; fractions of statute miles, as needed; and the letters SM.

g. *Runway visual range (RVR) (as required)*—Follows the visibility element.

h. *Weather phenomena*—Broken into two categories: qualifiers and weather phenomena.

i. *Sky condition*—Reported in the following format: amount/height/type (as required) or indefinite ceiling/height (vertical visibility). Heights are recorded in feet AGL.

j. *Temperature/dew point group*—Two-digit format in whole degrees Celsius separated by a solidus (/). Temperatures below zero are prefixed with M.

k. *Altimeter*—Four-digit format representing tens, units, tenths, and hundredths of inches of mercury prefixed with A. The decimal point is not reported or stated.

l. *Remarks (RMK) (as required)*—Operationally significant weather phenomena, location of phenomena, beginning and ending times, and/or direction of movement.

Example: METAR KLAX 140651Z AUTO 00000KT 1SM R35L/4500V6000FT -RA BR BKN030 10/10 A2990 RMK AO2

The following is an example of the phraseology used to relay this report to a pilot. Optional words or phrases are shown in parentheses: "Los Angeles (California) (zero six five one observation), wind calm, visibility one, runway three five left RVR, variable between four thousand five hundred and six thousand feet, light rain, mist, broken ceiling 3,000 feet, temperature ten, dew point ten, altimeter two niner niner zero."

3. What are several types of weather observing programs? (AIM 7-1-12)

a. *Manual observations*—Reports made from airport locations staffed by FAA or NWS personnel.

b. *AWOS*—Automated Weather Observing System, which consists of various sensors, a processor, a computer-generated voice sub-system, and a transmitter to broadcast local, minute-by-minute weather data directly to the pilot. Observations include the prefix "AUTO" in the data.

c. *AWOS broadcasts*—Computer-generated voice is used to automate the broadcast of minute-by-minute weather observations.

d. *ASOS/AWSS*—Automated Surface Observing System (ASOS)/ Automated Weather Sensor System (AWSS), the primary U.S. surface weather observing system. AWSS is a follow-on program that provides identical data as ASOS. The system provides continuous minute-by-minute observations generating METARs and other aviation weather information, transmitted over a discrete VHF radio frequency or the voice portion of a local NAVAID.

4. What are PIREPs (UA), and where are they usually found? (FAA-H-8083-28)

A pilot report (PIREP) provides valuable information regarding the conditions as they actually exist in the air, which cannot be gathered from any other source. Pilots can confirm the height of bases and tops of clouds, locations of wind shear and turbulence, and the location of inflight icing. There are two types of PIREPs: routine or "UA," and urgent or "UUA." PIREPs should be given to the ground facility with which communications are established (i.e., FSS, ARTCC, or terminal ATC). Altitudes are MSL, visibilities SM, and distances in NM. PIREPs are available from ATC, FSS, and online at aviationweather.gov/data/pirep/.

5. Where can a pilot find information on the altitudes of cloud-layer tops? (FAA-H-8083-28)

The Cloud Top Heights product is a computer model forecast of the height of the tops of the clouds covering the sky valid for the indicated hour. The heights of cloud tops are depicted using color-shaded contours at specific intervals.

6. What graphical resource may a pilot utilize to determine where across a route freezing levels might occur and incur a risk of icing? (FAA-H-8083-28)

A pilot might utilize the freezing level graphic. Freezing-level graphics are used to assess the lowest freezing-level heights and their values relative to flight paths. Clear, rime, and mixed icing are found in layers with below-freezing (negative) temperatures and supercooled water droplets. Users should be aware that official forecast freezing-level information is specified within the AIRMET Zulu Bulletins (CONUS and Hawaii) and the AIRMET "ICE AND FZLVL" information embedded within the FAs (Alaska only).

J. Aviation Weather Forecasts

1. What is a terminal aerodrome forecast (TAF)? (FAA-H-8083-28)

It is a concise statement of the expected meteorological conditions significant to aviation for a specified time period within a 5 SM radius from the center of an airport's runway complex (terminal). TAFs use the same weather code found in METAR weather reports, in the following format:

a. *Type of reports*—A routine forecast (TAF), an amended forecast (TAF AMD), or a corrected forecast (TAF COR).

b. *ICAO station identifier*—4-letter station identifiers.

c. *Date and time of origin*—The date/time of forecast follows the terminal's location identifier and shows the day of the month in two digits, and the time in which the forecast is completed and ready for transmission in four digits, appended with a Z to denote UTC. Example: 061737Z—the TAF was issued on the 6th day of the month at 1737 UTC.

d. *Valid period date and time*—The first two digits are the day of the month for the start of the TAF, followed by two digits that indicate the starting hour (UTC). The next two digits indicate the day of the month for the end of the TAF, and the last two digits are the ending hour (UTC) of the valid period. Scheduled 24- and 30-hour TAFs are issued four (4) times per day, at 0000, 0600, 1200, and 1800Z. Example: A 00Z TAF issued on the 9th of the month and valid for 24 hours would have a valid period of 0900/0924.

e. *Forecasts*—Wind, visibility, significant and vicinity weather, cloud and vertical obscuration, non-convective low-level wind shear, forecast change indicators (FM, TEMPO and PROB).

2. What is an aviation area forecast? (FAA-H-8083-28)

Area forecasts (FAs) are issued for the Gulf of Mexico, the Caribbean Sea, and Alaska. An FA is an abbreviated plain-language forecast concerning the occurrence or expected occurrence of specified enroute weather phenomena.

The FA (in conjunction with AIRMETs, SIGMETs, convective SIGMETs, CWAs, etc.) is used to determine forecast enroute weather over a specified geographic region. FAs cover an 18- to 24-hour period, depending on the region, and are issued three to four times daily, depending on the region, and are updated as needed.

3. Describe the Graphical Forecast for Aviation (GFA). (AIM 7-1-4)

The Graphical Forecasts for Aviation (GFA) website is intended to provide the necessary aviation weather information to give users a complete picture of the weather that may affect flight in the continental United States (CONUS). The website includes observational data, forecasts, and warnings that can be viewed from 14 hours in the past to 15 hours in the future, including thunderstorms, clouds, flight category, precipitation, icing, turbulence, and wind. Hourly model data and forecasts, including information on clouds, flight category, precipitation, icing, turbulence, wind, and graphical output from the National Weather Service's (NWS) National Digital Forecast Data (NDFD) are available. Wind, icing, and turbulence forecasts are available in 3,000-foot increments from the surface up to 30,000 feet MSL, and in 6,000-foot increments from 30,000 feet MSL to 48,000 feet MSL. Turbulence forecasts are also broken into low (below 18,000 feet MSL) and high (at or above 18,000 feet MSL) graphics. A maximum icing graphic and maximum wind velocity graphic (regardless of altitude) are also available.

The GFA interactive web tool can be viewed at aviationweather .gov/gfa.

4. What type of aviation forecasts are available in the Forecast section of the GFA? (AIM 7-1-4, AWC)

The Forecasts section provides gridded displays of various weather parameters as well as NWS textual weather observations, forecasts, and warnings out to 18 hours. Icing, turbulence, and wind gridded products are three-dimensional. Other gridded products are two-dimensional and may represent a "composite" of a three-dimensional weather phenomenon or a surface weather variable, such as horizontal visibility.

The Forecasts section of the GFA provides the following:

a. Ceiling & visibility (CIG/VIS)

b. Clouds

c. Precipitation/weather (PCPN/WX)

d. Thunderstorm (TS)

e. Temperature

f. Winds

g. Turbulence

h. Icing

5. Describe some of the weather products available on the GFA. (AIM 7-1-4)

Selecting the "Products" tab gives you the option to display weather data for the current time and the previous 18 hours (rounded to the nearest hour) and will provide the following:

a. SIGMET

b. G-AIRMET

c. Center Weather Adv

d. Prog charts

e. TAF map

f. Forecast discussions

g. METAR data

h. TAF data

i. PIREP (pilot reports)

j. Wind/temp data

k. ITWS data

l. WAFS grids

m. TFM convective forecasts

6. What does it mean when a briefing includes the wording "VFR Flight Not Recommended?" (AIM 7-1-5)

When VFR flight is proposed and sky conditions or visibilities are present or forecast, surface or aloft, that in the briefer's judgment would make flight under VFR doubtful, the briefer will describe the conditions, describe the affected locations, and use the phrase "VFR flight not recommended." This recommendation is advisory in nature. The final decision as to whether the flight can be conducted safely rests solely with the pilot. Upon receiving a "VFR flight not recommended" statement, the non-IFR rated pilot will need to make a go or no-go decision. This decision should be based on weighing the current and forecast weather conditions against the pilot's experience and ratings. The aircraft's equipment, capabilities and limitations should also be considered.

7. What are the four types of inflight aviation weather advisories? (AIM 7-1-6)

Inflight aviation weather advisories are forecasts to advise enroute aircraft of the development of potentially hazardous weather in four types: the SIGMET (WS), the convective SIGMET (WST), the AIRMET (WA; text or graphical product), and the Center Weather Advisory (CWA). All heights are referenced MSL, except in the case of ceilings (CIG) which indicate AGL.

8. What is a convective SIGMET? (AIM 7-1-6)

A convective SIGMET (WST) implies severe or greater turbulence, severe icing, and low-level wind shear. It may be issued for any convective situation which the forecaster feels is hazardous to all categories of aircraft. Convective SIGMET bulletins are issued for the Eastern (E), Central (C), and Western

(W) United States (convective SIGMETs are not issued for Alaska or Hawaii). Bulletins are issued hourly at H+55. Special bulletins are issued at any time as required and updated at H+55. The text of the bulletin consists of either an observation and a forecast or just a forecast, which is valid for up to 2 hours. Convective SIGMETs are issued for any of the following:

a. Severe thunderstorm due to:
   - Surface winds greater than or equal to 50 knots.
   - Hail at the surface greater than or equal to ¾ inches in diameter.
   - Tornadoes.

b. Embedded thunderstorms.

c. A line of thunderstorms.

d. Thunderstorms producing precipitation greater than or equal to heavy precipitation that affects 40 percent or more of an area of at least 3,000 square miles.

9. What is a SIGMET? (AIM 7-1-6)

A SIGMET (WS) advises of non-convective weather that is potentially hazardous to all aircraft. SIGMETs are issued for the six areas corresponding to the FA areas. The maximum forecast period is four hours. In the conterminous United States, SIGMETs are issued when the following phenomena occur or are expected to occur:

a. Severe icing not associated with a thunderstorm.

b. Severe or extreme turbulence or clear air turbulence (CAT) not associated with thunderstorms.

c. Widespread dust storms or sandstorms lowering surface visibilities to below 3 miles.

d. Volcanic ash.

10. What is an AIRMET? (AIM 7-1-6)

AIRMETs (WAs) are advisories of significant weather phenomena but describe conditions at intensities lower than those that require the issuance of SIGMETs. AIRMETs are intended for dissemination to all pilots in the preflight and en route phase of flight to enhance safety. AIRMET information is available in two formats: text bulletins (WA) and graphics (G-AIRMET) and are issued on a scheduled basis every 6 hours beginning at 0245 UTC. Unscheduled updates and corrections are issued as necessary. AIRMETs contain details about IFR, extensive mountain obscuration, turbulence, strong surface winds, icing, and freezing levels.

11. What are the different types of AIRMETs? (AIM 7-1-6)

There are three AIRMETs—Sierra, Tango, and Zulu:

a. AIRMET Sierra describes IFR conditions and/or extensive mountain obscurations.

b. AIRMET Tango describes moderate turbulence, sustained surface winds of 30 knots or greater, and/or nonconvective low-level wind shear.

c. AIRMET Zulu describes moderate icing and provides freezing level heights.

12. What is a G-AIRMET? (FAA-H-8083-28)

A G-AIRMET is a graphical advisory of weather that may be hazardous to aircraft, but is less severe than SIGMETs. G-AIRMETs identify hazardous weather in space and time more precisely than text products, enabling pilots to maintain high safety margins while flying more efficient routes. They are issued at 03:00, 09:00, 15:00 and 21:00 UTC (with updates issued as necessary). Hazards depicted in G-AIRMETs include turbulence, low-level wind shear, strong surface winds, icing, freezing level, IFR, and mountain obscurations.

13. What is a winds and temperatures aloft forecast (FB)? (FAA-H-8083-28)

Winds and temperature aloft forecasts are computer-prepared forecasts of wind direction, wind speed, and temperature at specified times, altitudes, and locations. They are produced 4 times daily for specified locations in the continental United States, Hawaii, Alaska and coastal waters, and the western Pacific Ocean. Amendments are not issued to the forecasts. Wind forecasts are not issued for altitudes within 1,500 feet of a location's elevation.

Some of the features of FBs are:

a. Product header includes date and time observations collected, forecast valid date and time, and the time period during which the forecast is to be used.

b. Altitudes up to 15,000 feet referenced to MSL; altitudes at or above 18,000 feet are references to flight levels (FL).

c. Temperature indicated in degrees Celsius (two digits) for the levels from 6,000 through 24,000 feet. Above 24,000 feet, the minus sign is omitted since temperatures are always negative at those altitudes. Temperature forecasts are not issued for altitudes within 2,500 feet of a location's elevation. Forecasts for intermediate levels are determined by interpolation.

d. Wind direction indicated in tens of degrees (two digits) with reference to true north and wind speed is given in knots (two digits). Light and variable wind or wind speeds of less than 5 knots are expressed by 9900. Forecast wind speeds of 100 through 199 knots are indicated by subtracting 100 from the speed and adding 50 to the coded direction. For example, a forecast of 250 degrees, 145 knots, is encoded as 7545. Forecast wind speeds of 200 knots or greater are indicated as a forecast speed of 199 knots. For example, 7799 is decoded as 270 degrees at 199 knots or greater.

14. What valuable information can be determined from a winds and temperatures aloft forecast? (FAA-H-8083-28)

Most favorable altitude—based on winds and direction of flight.

Areas of possible icing—by noting air temperatures of +2°C to −20°C.

Temperature inversions—a temperature increase with altitude can mean a stable layer aloft reducing the chance for convective activity.

Turbulence—by observing abrupt changes in wind direction and speed at different altitudes.

15. What is a Center Weather Advisory (CWA)? (FAA-H-8083-28)

A Center Weather Advisory (CWA) is an aviation warning for use by aircrews to anticipate and avoid adverse weather conditions in the en route and terminal environments. This is not a flight planning product; instead, it reflects current conditions expected at the time of issuance, and/or is a short-range forecast for conditions expected to begin within 2 hours from that time. CWAs are valid for a maximum of 2 hours. If conditions are expected to continue beyond that period, a statement will be included in the CWA.

16. What are several examples of charts, reports, and forecasts that would be useful in determining the potential for and location of thunderstorms along your route? (FAA-H-8083-28)

A pilot might use a convective outlook chart, convective SIGMETs, radar summary charts, or even local TAFs across the route to analyze if convective (thunderstorm) activity is likely to occur across an intended route of flight.

17. Is the wind direction information provided on weather charts and graphics in true or magnetic direction? (FAA-H-8083-28)

The wind direction information provided on weather charts and graphics is typically given in true direction. True direction is the direction of the wind relative to true north, which is the geographic North Pole. This information is essential for flight planning and navigation because it allows pilots to make accurate calculations for headings and crosswind components.

It is important to note that when using wind information from weather charts, pilots must consider the magnetic variation to convert the true direction to magnetic direction. Magnetic variation is the angular difference between true north and magnetic north at a specific location. By accounting for this variation, pilots can align their navigation instruments, such as the magnetic compass, with the true direction of the wind for precise course corrections during flight.

18. Will broadcast ATIS winds be indicated in true or magnetic? (FAA-H-8083-28, AIM 7-1-12)

The winds information provided in the Automatic Terminal Information Service (ATIS) broadcasts is typically given in magnetic direction. ATIS reports include essential information about current weather conditions at an airport, and to ensure compatibility with the aircraft's navigation systems, the wind direction is presented in magnetic degrees.

Pilots can use this magnetic wind direction information directly without the need for conversion since most aviation instruments and charts use magnetic headings. It simplifies the process for pilots in terms of navigation and flight planning, aligning with the standard use of magnetic headings in aviation.

K. Aviation Weather Charts

1. **Give examples of weather charts you will use during the flight planning process.** (FAA-H-8083-28)

   a. Surface analysis chart

   b. Weather depiction chart (being phased out in favor of the CVA, or ceiling and visibility analysis)

   c. Significant weather prognostic chart

   d. Short-range surface prognostic chart

   e. Convective outlook chart

   f. Constant pressure analysis chart (being phased out in favor of upper air constant pressure level forecasts)

   g. Freezing level graphics

2. **What is a surface analysis chart?** (FAA-H-8083-28)

   These are a charted analysis of surface weather observations, depicting the distribution of several items including sea-level pressure; the positions of highs, lows, ridges, and troughs; the location and type of fronts; and the various boundaries such as drylines. Pressure is expressed in mean sea level (MSL); all other elements are presented as they occur at the surface point of observation.

3. **Describe a ceiling and visibility analysis (CVA).** (FAA-H-8083-28)

   A CVA is a real-time analysis (updated every 5 minutes) of current ceiling and visibility conditions across the continental United States. It is intended to aid situational awareness with a quick-glance visualization of current ceiling and visibility conditions across an area or along a route of flight.

   The CVA provides a viewer-selectable representation of ceiling height (AGL), surface visibility in statute miles, and flight category designation. The overview provided by a CVA must be followed by further examination of METARs, TAFs, AIRMETs, the GFA and other weather information.

4. Define the following terms: LIFR, IFR, MVFR, and VFR. (AIM 7-1-7)

LIFR—Low IFR: ceiling less than 500 feet and/or visibility less than 1 mile.

IFR—Ceiling 500 to less than 1,000 feet and/or visibility 1 to less than 3 miles.

MVFR—Marginal VFR: ceiling 1,000 to 3,000 feet and/or visibility 3 to 5 miles inclusive.

VFR—Ceiling greater than 3,000 feet and visibility greater than 5 miles; includes sky clear.

5. What are short-range surface prognostic charts? (FAA-H-8083-28)

Short-range surface prognostic (prog) charts provide a forecast of surface pressure systems, fronts, and precipitation for a two-and-a-half-day period. They cover a forecast area of the 48 contiguous states and coastal waters, and they are prepared by the NWS Weather Prediction Center (and available on the AWC website). Predicted conditions are divided into five forecast periods: 12, 18, 24, 48, and 60 hours. Each chart depicts a snapshot of weather elements expected at the specified valid time. Charts are issued four times a day and can be used to obtain an overview of the progression of surface weather features during the included periods.

6. Describe a U.S. low-level significant weather prog chart. (FAA-H-8083-28)

The low-level significant weather (SIGWX) charts provide a forecast of aviation weather hazards and are primarily intended as guidance products for pre-flight briefings. The forecast domain covers the continental U.S. and the coastal waters for altitudes Flight Level 240 and below. Each depicts a snapshot of weather expected at the specified valid time. The charts depict weather flying categories, turbulence, and freezing levels, and are issued four times per day in two types: a 12-hour and a 24-hour prog.

7. Describe a mid-level significant weather (SIGWX) chart. (FAA-H-8083-28)

This chart provides a forecast and an overview of significant enroute weather phenomena over a range of flight levels from 10,000 feet MSL to FL450, and associated surface weather features. It is a snapshot of weather expected at the specified valid time and depicts numerous weather elements that can be hazardous to aviation. The AWC issues the 24-hour mid-level significant weather chart 4 times daily.

8. What information may be obtained from the U.S. High-Level Significant Weather Prog charts? (FAA-H-8083-28)

High-level significant weather (SIGWX) charts provide a forecast of significant en route weather phenomena over a range of flight levels from FL250 to FL630, and associated surface weather features. Each chart depicts a snapshot of weather expected at the specified valid time. Conditions routinely appearing on the chart are:

a. Thunderstorms and cumulonimbus clouds

b. Moderate or severe turbulence

c. Moderate or severe icing

d. Jet streams

e. Tropopause heights

f. Tropical cyclones

g. Severe squall lines

h. Volcanic eruption sites

i. Widespread sandstorms and dust storms

9. What is a convective outlook chart? (FAA-H-8083-28)

The NWS Storm Prediction Center (SPC) issues narrative and graphical convective outlooks to provide the CONUS NWS WFOs, the public, the media, and emergency managers with the potential for severe (tornado, wind gusts 50 knots or greater, or hail 1 inch in diameter or greater) and non-severe (general) convection, and specific severe weather threats during the following 8 days. The convective outlook defines areas of marginal risk (MRGL), slight risk (SLGT), enhanced risk (ENH), moderate risk (MDT), or high risk (HIGH) of severe weather based on a probability percentage, which varies for time periods from 1 day to 3 days, and then two probability thresholds for days 4 through 8. The day 1, day 2, and day 3 convective outlooks also depict areas of general thunderstorms (TSTMS).

10. What are constant pressure level forecasts? (FAA-H-8083-28)

Constant pressure level forecasts are a computer model depiction of select weather (e.g., wind) at a specified constant pressure level (e.g., 300 MB), along with the altitudes (in meters) of the specified constant pressure level. They are used to provide an overview of weather patterns at specified times and pressure altitudes and are the source for winds and temperatures aloft forecasts. Pressure patterns cause and characterize much of the weather.

Typically, lows and troughs are associated with clouds and precipitation while highs and ridges are associated with fair weather, except in winter when valley fog may occur. The location and strength of the jet stream can be viewed at the 300 MB, 250 MB, and 200 MB levels:

925 mb — 2,500 ft
850 mb — 5,000 ft
700 mb — 10,000 ft
500 mb — 18,000 ft
300 mb — 30,000 ft
250 mb — 34,000 ft
200 mb — 39,000 ft

11. What significance do height contour lines have on a constant pressure chart? (FAA-H-8083-28)

Heights of the specified pressure for each station are analyzed through the use of solid lines called contours to give a height pattern. The contours depict highs, lows, troughs, and ridges aloft in the same manner as isobars on the surface chart. Also, closely spaced contours mean strong winds, as do closely spaced isobars.

12. What significance do isotherms have on a constant pressure chart? (FAA-H-8083-28)

Isotherms (dashed lines) drawn at 5°C intervals show horizontal temperature variations at chart altitude. By inspecting isotherms, you can determine if your flight will be toward colder or warmer air. Subfreezing temperatures and a temperature/dewpoint spread of 5°C or less suggest possible icing.

13. What is the significance of the isotach lines on a constant pressure chart? (FAA-H-8083-28)

Isotachs are lines of constant wind speed analyzed on the 300 and 200 mb charts; they separate higher wind speeds from lower wind speeds and are used to map wind speed variations over a surface. Isotachs are drawn at 20-knot intervals and begin at 10 knots. Isotach gradients identify the magnitude of wind speed variations. Strong gradients are closely spaced isotachs and identify large wind speed variations. Weak gradients are loosely spaced isotachs and identify small wind speed variations. Zones of very strong winds are highlighted by hatches.

14. What information does a freezing level graphics chart provide? (FAA-H-8083-28)

Freezing level graphics are used to assess the lowest freezing level heights and their values relative to flight paths. The chart uses colors to represent the height in hundreds of feet above mean sea level (MSL) of the lowest freezing level(s). The initial analysis and 3-hour forecast graphics are updated hourly. The 6-, 9-, and 12-hour forecast graphics are updated every three hours.

15. Using the Graphical Forecasts for Aviation (GFA) tool, what may a pilot determine about icing probability? (FAA-H-8083-28)

The GFA tool on the Aviation Weather Center (aviationweather.gov /gfa) allows a pilot to select altitudes and times up to 18 hours in the future to analyze icing probability and severity in geographic areas.

Exam Tip: Be prepared to interpret and discuss current and forecast weather along your planned route of flight. The evaluator will want you to demonstrate that you can interpret the various aviation weather reports, forecasts, charts/graphics and make an assessment of how the weather will affect your planned flight. Also, expect the evaluator to place emphasis on your knowledge of weather phenomena that are of particular concern to all instrument-rated pilots such as thunderstorms, turbulence, icing, and visibility.

Departure 2

A. Authority and Limitations of the Pilot

1. Discuss 14 CFR §91.3, "Responsibility and authority of the pilot in command." (14 CFR 91.3)

The pilot-in-command (PIC) of an aircraft is directly responsible for, and is the final authority as to, the operation of that aircraft. Being PIC means you, and only you, are responsible for the operational and safety-related decisions pertaining to your flight. No one else—not the aircraft owner, the FBO, ATC, or anyone else—shares in that responsibility. The decision to begin, cancel, divert, or terminate the flight, determine aircraft airworthiness, or make any other safety or operational decision are yours and yours alone.

2. What are the right-of-way rules pertaining to IFR flights? (14 CFR 91.113)

When weather conditions permit, regardless of whether an operation is under IFR or VFR, vigilance shall be maintained by each person operating an aircraft so as to see and avoid other aircraft. While IFR operations place traffic separation demands on ATC, a pilot is still responsible for seeing and avoiding traffic when able. The responsibility for traffic separation is not solely that of ATC when operating IFR.

3. What are the required reports for equipment malfunction under IFR in controlled airspace? (AIM 5-3-3)

You must report:

a. Any loss in controlled airspace of VOR, TACAN, ADF, or low-frequency navigation receiver capability.

b. GPS anomalies while using installed IFR-certified GPS/GNSS receivers.

c. Complete or partial loss of ILS receiver capability.

d. Impairment of air/ground communication capability.

e. Loss of any other equipment installed in the aircraft which may impair safety and/or the ability to operate under IFR.

B. Departure Clearance

1. How can your IFR clearance be obtained? (AIM 5-2-3)

a. At airports with an ATC tower in operation, clearances may be received from either ground control or a specific clearance delivery frequency when available.

b. For IFR clearances off uncontrolled airports:

- Pilots departing on an IFR flight plan should consult the *Chart Supplement* to determine the frequency or telephone number to use to contact clearance delivery. On initial contact, pilots should advise that the flight is IFR and state the departure and destination airports.

- Air traffic facilities providing clearance delivery services via telephone will have their telephone number published in the *Chart Supplement* of that airport's entry. This same section may also contain a telephone number to use for cancellation of an IFR flight plan after landing. A dedicated clearance number is also available at 888-766-8267 that can be used anywhere in the United States to contact a Flight Services clearance service.

- Except Alaska, pilots of MEDEVAC flights may obtain a clearance by calling 1-877-543-4733.

The procedure may vary due to geographical features, weather conditions, and the complexity of the ATC system. To determine the most effective means of receiving an IFR clearance, pilots should ask an FSS briefer for the most appropriate means of obtaining their IFR clearance.

2. After filing an IFR flight plan, can you depart VFR and pick up your IFR clearance in the air? (FAA-H-8083-16)

A VFR departure can be used as a tool that allows you to get off the ground without having to wait for a time slot in the IFR system; however, departing VFR with the intent of receiving an IFR clearance in the air can also present serious hazards worth considering. A VFR departure dramatically changes the takeoff responsibilities for you and for ATC:

a. Upon receiving clearance for a VFR departure, you are cleared to depart; however, you must maintain separation between yourself and other traffic.

b. You are also responsible for maintaining terrain and obstruction clearance as well as remaining in VFR weather conditions. You cannot fly in IMC without first receiving your IFR clearance.

c. Departing VFR relieves ATC of these duties, and basically requires ATC to only provide you with safety alerts as workload permits.

d. You must maintain VFR until you have obtained your IFR clearance and have ATC approval to proceed on course in accordance with your clearance. If you accept this clearance and are below the minimum IFR altitude for operations in the area, you accept responsibility for terrain/obstruction clearance until you reach that altitude.

3. What does "cleared as filed" mean? (AIM 5-2-6)

ATC will issue an abbreviated IFR clearance based on the route of flight as filed in the IFR flight plan, provided the filed route can be approved with little or no revision.

4. What are pre-taxi clearance procedures? How do you determine if they are available? (AIM 5-2-1)

Certain airports have established pre-taxi clearance programs whereby pilots of departing instrument flight rules (IFR) aircraft may elect to receive their IFR clearances before they start taxiing for takeoff. The following provisions are included in such procedures:

a. Pilot participation is not mandatory.

b. Participating pilots call clearance delivery or ground control not more than 10 minutes before proposed taxi time.

c. IFR clearance (or delay information, if clearance cannot be obtained) is issued at the time of this initial call-up.

d. When the IFR clearance is received on clearance delivery frequency, pilots call ground control when ready to taxi.

e. Normally, pilots need not inform ground control that they have received IFR clearance on clearance delivery frequency. Certain locations may, however, require that the pilot inform ground control of a portion of the routing or that the IFR clearance has been received.

f. If a pilot cannot establish contact on clearance delivery frequency or has not received an IFR clearance before ready to taxi, the pilot should contact ground control and inform the controller accordingly.

Locations where these procedures are in effect are indicated in the *Chart Supplement.*

5. You are cleared to taxi to the active runway for departure. During the taxi, ATC amends the clearance and assigns you an intersection takeoff due to departure delays. Are you required to accept the intersection takeoff? (AIM 4-3-10)

Pilots are expected to assess the suitability of an intersection for use at takeoff during their preflight planning. They must consider the resultant length reduction to the published runway length and to the published declared distances from the intersection intended to be used for takeoff. The minimum runway required for takeoff must fall within the reduced runway length and the reduced declared distances before the intersection can be accepted for takeoff.

6. What responsibilities does a pilot have concerning readback of ATC clearances and instructions?
(AIM 4-4-7)

Pilots of airborne aircraft should read back those parts of ATC clearances and instructions containing altitude assignments, vectors, or runway assignments as a means of mutual verification. The read back of the numbers serves as a double check between pilots and controllers and reduces the kinds of communications errors that occur when a number is either misheard or is incorrect.

a. Include the aircraft identification in all readbacks and acknowledgments. This aids controllers in determining that the correct aircraft received the clearance or instruction. The requirement to include aircraft identification in all readbacks and acknowledgements becomes more important as frequency congestion increases and when aircraft with similar call signs are on the same frequency.
Example: "Climbing to Flight Level three three zero, United Twelve" or "November Five Charlie Tango, roger, cleared to land runway nine left."

b. Read back altitudes, altitude restrictions, and vectors in the same sequence as they are given in the clearance or instruction.

(continued)

c. Altitudes contained in charted procedures, such as DPs, instrument approaches, etc., should not be read back unless they are specifically stated by the controller.

d. Initial read back of a taxi, departure, or landing clearance should include the runway assignment, including left, right, center, etc., if applicable.

7. Which clearance items are given in an abbreviated IFR clearance? (AIM 4-4-3, 5-2-6)

Clearance Limit (destination airport or fix)

Route (initial heading)

Altitude (initial altitude)

Frequency (departure)

Transponder (squawk code)

Note: ATC procedures now require the controller to state the DP name, the current number, and the DP transition name after the phrase "Cleared to (destination) airport" and prior to the phrase, "then as filed," for *all* departure clearances when the DP or DP transition is to be flown.

8. What is the purpose of the term "hold for release" when included in an IFR clearance? (AIM 5-2-7)

ATC may issue "hold for release" instructions in a clearance to delay an aircraft's departure for traffic management reasons (weather, traffic volume, etc.). A pilot may not depart utilizing that IFR clearance until a release time or additional instructions are received from ATC.

9. What does it mean for a pilot when ATC issues a clearance with a "clearance void time?" (AIM 5-2-7)

A pilot may receive a clearance, when operating from an airport without a control tower, which contains a provision for the clearance to be void if not airborne by a specific time. A pilot who does not depart prior to the clearance void time must advise ATC as soon as possible of their intentions. ATC will normally advise the pilot of the time allotted to notify ATC that the aircraft did not depart prior to the clearance void time. This time cannot exceed 30 minutes. Failure of an aircraft to contact ATC within 30 minutes after the clearance void time will result in the aircraft being considered overdue and search and rescue procedures initiated.

10. **ATC may issue a "release time" to an IFR flight. What significance does this have?** (AIM 5-2-7)

    A "release time" is a departure restriction issued to a pilot by ATC, specifying the earliest time an aircraft may depart. ATC will use "release times" in conjunction with traffic management procedures and/or to separate a departing aircraft from other traffic.

C. Departure Procedures

1. **What minimums are necessary for IFR takeoff under 14 CFR Part 91? Under Parts 121, 125, 129, or 135?** (14 CFR 91.175)

    For 14 CFR Part 91, none. For aircraft operated under 14 CFR Parts 121, 125, 129, or 135, if takeoff minimums are not prescribed under Part 97 for a particular airport, the following minimums apply to takeoffs under IFR for aircraft operating under those parts:

    a. For aircraft having two engines or less—1 statute mile visibility.

    b. For aircraft having more than two engines—½ statute mile visibility.

2. **What is considered good operating practice in determining takeoff minimums for IFR flight?**

    If an instrument approach procedure(s) exists for the airport, ensure that the weather is no less than the lowest published minimums for any approach to that airport at departure time. If no approach procedure is available, basic VFR minimums are recommended (1,000 feet and 3 miles).

3. **Explain additional strategies you would use to mitigate risk when considering a takeoff and departure in low IMC.** (AIM 5-2-9)

    a. Use your pre-determined personal minimums.

    b. Determine if obstacles and/or rising terrain exist in the area around the airport.

    c. Determine if your departure airport has published takeoff minimums for your expected departure runway.

    d. Determine if obstacle departure procedures (ODPs) are available.

    (continued)

 e. Use 14 CFR Part 121/135 minimums (1 statute mile, 2 engines or less) as a minimum visibility for your departure.

 f. Consider delaying or cancelling your departure until ceilings/visibilities are equal to or higher than the lowest approach minimums for any approach at your departure airport.

4. What are DPs, and why are they necessary? (AIM 5-2-9)

Departure procedures are preplanned IFR procedures that provide obstruction clearance from the terminal area to the appropriate enroute structure. The primary reason they are established is to provide obstacle clearance protection. Also, at busier airports, they increase efficiency and reduce communication and departure delays. Pilots operating under Part 91 are strongly encouraged to file and fly a DP at night, during marginal VMC, and during IMC, when one is available.

5. What are the two types of DPs? (AIM 5-2-9)

 a. *ODPs (Obstacle Departure Procedures)*—Printed either textually or graphically, ODPs provide obstruction clearance via the least onerous route from the terminal area to the appropriate en route structure. ODPs are recommended for obstruction clearance and may be flown without ATC clearance unless an alternate departure procedure (SID or radar vector) has been specifically assigned by ATC. ODPs are published when obstructions penetrate the 40:1 departure obstacle clearance surface (OCS).

 b. *SIDs (Standard Instrument Departures)*—Always printed graphically, Standard Instrument Departures are air traffic control (ATC) procedures printed for pilot/controller use in graphic form to provide obstruction clearance and a transition from the terminal area to the appropriate en route structure. SIDs are primarily designed for system enhancement and to reduce pilot/controller workload. ATC clearance must be received prior to flying a SID.

6. What are the two types of SIDs? (FAA-H-8083-16)

SIDs are categorized by the type of navigation used to fly the departure, so they are considered either pilot navigation or vector SIDs:

Pilot navigation SIDs—Designed to allow you to provide your own navigation with minimal radio communication. This type of procedure usually contains an initial set of departure instructions followed by one or more transition routes.

Radar vector SIDs—Usually require ATC to provide radar vectors from just after takeoff (ROC is based on a climb to 400 feet above the DER elevation before making the initial turn) until reaching the assigned route or a fix depicted on the SID chart.

7. What criteria are used to provide obstruction clearance during departure? (AIM 5-2-9)

Unless specified otherwise, required obstacle clearance for all departures, including diverse, is based on the pilot crossing the departure end of the runway at least 35 feet above the departure end of runway elevation, climbing to 400 feet above the departure end of runway elevation before making the initial turn, and maintaining a minimum climb gradient of 200 feet per nautical mile (FPNM), unless required to level off by a crossing restriction, until the minimum IFR altitude. A greater climb gradient may be specified in the DP to clear obstacles or to achieve an ATC crossing restriction.

8. What is a diverse vector area (DVA)? (AIM 5-2-9)

DVAs are areas in which ATC may provide random radar vectors during an uninterrupted climb from the departure runway until above the MVA/MIA, established in accordance with the TERPS criteria for diverse departures. The DVA provides obstacle and terrain avoidance in lieu of taking off from the runway under IFR using an ODP or SID.

9. Where are DPs located? (AIM 5-2-9)

DPs will be listed by airport in the IFR Takeoff Minimums and (Obstacle) Departure Procedures section, Section L, of the *Terminal Procedures Publications* (TPPs). SIDs and complex ODPs will be published graphically and given procedure titles.

10. ATC issues you the following clearance: "Cleared to Johnston Airport, Scott One departure, Jonez transition, Q-One Forty-five. Climb via SID." Explain what "Climb via SID" means to you. (AIM 4-4-12)

A clearance for a SID that contains published altitude restrictions may be issued using the phraseology "climb via," which is an abbreviated clearance that requires compliance with the procedure lateral path, associated speed, and altitude restrictions along the cleared route or procedure.

11. How does a pilot determine if takeoff minimums are not standard and/or departure procedures are published for an airport? (FAA-H-8083-16)

If an airport has non-standard takeoff minimums, a "triangle T" (or, "trouble T") symbol—that is, a black triangle with a T inside it—will be placed in the notes sections of the instrument procedure chart.

12. Prior to departing an airport on an IFR flight, a pilot should determine whether they will be able to ensure adequate separation from terrain and obstacles. What information should this include? (AIM 5-2-9)

a. The type of terrain and other obstacles on or in the vicinity of the departure airport.

b. Whether an ODP is available.

c. If obstacle avoidance can be maintained visually or if the ODP should be flown.

d. The effect of degraded climb performance and the actions to take in the event of an engine loss during the departure.

e. Whether a DVA is published and whether the aircraft is capable of meeting the published climb gradient. Advise ATC when requesting the IFR clearance, or as soon as possible, if unable to meet the DVA climb gradient.

f. Check for Takeoff Obstacle Notes published in the TPP for the takeoff runway.

13. If an ODP has been published for the runway you are departing from, are you required to follow it? (FAA-H-8083-16)

No—if a Part 91 pilot is not given a clearance containing an ODP, SID, or radar vectors and an ODP exists, compliance with such a procedure is the pilot's choice.

14. When a DP specifies a climb gradient in excess of 200 feet per nautical mile, what significance should this have to the pilot? (AIM 5-2-9)

If an aircraft may turn in any direction from a runway, and remain clear of obstacles, that runway passes what is called diverse departure criteria and no ODP will be published. A SID may be published if needed for air traffic control purposes. However, if an obstacle penetrates what is called the 40:1 slope obstacle identification surface, then the procedure designer chooses whether to:

a. Establish a steeper than normal climb gradient; or

b. Establish a steeper than normal climb gradient with an alternative that increases takeoff minima to allow the pilot to visually remain clear of the obstacle(s); or

c. Design and publish a specific departure route; or

d. A combination or all of the above.

15. Is the rate-of-climb in feet per nautical mile (ft/NM) found on ODPs based on your aircraft's true airspeed or ground speed? How do you convert that number to feet per minute (fpm)? (TPP)

Rate-of-climb in ft/NM is based on the aircraft's ground speed. To convert ft/NM to fpm, you can use the "Rate of Climb/Descent Table" found in the paper or digital versions of the *Terminal Procedures Publication*. You can also use the following calculation:

$$\frac{Ground\ speed\ (knots,\ or\ NM/hr)}{60\ min./hr} \times Climb\ gradient\ (ft/NM) = Rate\ of\ climb\ (fpm)$$

Therefore:

$$\frac{100\ NM/hr}{60\ min./hr} \times 300\ ft/NM = 500\ fpm$$

16. **ATC has cleared you for a SID that requires a minimum climb gradient of 400 feet per nautical mile to 9,000 feet. You calculate your ground speed in the climb to be 90 knots. What minimum rate-of-climb in feet per minute are you required to maintain during the climb?** (FAA-H-8083-15, TPP)

    By applying the Instrument Takeoff or Approach Procedure Charts Rate of Climb/Descent Table from the digital *Terminal Procedures Publication*, a pilot would find that at 90 knots ground speed, a 400 feet per nautical mile climb gradient would require the pilot to climb at 600 feet per minute with a climb angle of 3.77 degrees along the entire climb. Many general aviation aircraft may not be able to maintain this climb rate to higher altitudes, and this should be a factor in whether or not a pilot would be able to fly a SID that had this requirement.

17. **What is the recommended climb rate procedure when a pilot is issued a climb to an assigned altitude by ATC?** (AIM 4-4-10)

    When ATC has not used the term "at pilot's discretion" or has not imposed any climb or descent restrictions, pilots should initiate climb or descent promptly on acknowledgement of the clearance. Descend or climb at an optimum rate consistent with the operating characteristics of the aircraft to 1,000 feet above or below the assigned altitude, and then attempt to descend or climb at a rate of between 500 and 1,500 fpm until the assigned altitude is reached.

18. **Is an ATC clearance an authorization for a pilot to deviate from any rule, regulation, or minimum altitude?** (AIM 4-4-1)

    A clearance issued by ATC is predicated on known traffic and known physical airport conditions. An ATC clearance means an authorization by ATC, for the purpose of preventing collision between known aircraft, for an aircraft to proceed under specified conditions within controlled airspace. It is not authorization for a pilot to deviate from any rule, regulation, or minimum altitude nor to conduct unsafe operation of the aircraft.

19. **You are airborne, established on the SID, and talking to departure control. You notice that your NEXRAD weather in the flight deck indicates a couple of strong cells up ahead, and you are concerned that your heading and altitude will place you in or too close to that weather. Departure control is busy and has said nothing. Is ATC responsible for providing you vectors around that weather?** (AIM 7-1-12, 5-5-1)

The pilot-in-command of an aircraft is directly responsible for, and is the final authority as to, the safe operation of that aircraft. In an emergency requiring immediate action, the pilot-in-command may deviate from any rule in 14 CFR Part 91, Subpart A (General) and Subpart B (Flight Rules), in accordance with 14 CFR §91.3.

The air traffic controller is responsible to give first priority to the separation of aircraft and to the issuance of radar safety alerts, second priority to other services that are required but do not involve separation of aircraft, and third priority to additional services to the extent possible.

20. **All public performance-based navigation (PBN) SIDs and graphic obstacle departure procedures (ODPs) are normally designed using RNAV 1, RNP 1, or A-RNP NavSpecs. What does this mean?** (AIM 5-2-9, AC 90-100)

RNAV 1 and RNP 1 procedures must maintain a total system error of not more than 1 NM for 95 percent of the total flight time. Minimum values for A-RNP procedures will be charted in the PBN box (for example, 1.00 or 0.30). All pilots are expected to maintain route centerlines, as depicted by onboard lateral deviation indicators and/or flight guidance, during all RNAV operations unless authorized to deviate by ATC or under emergency conditions.

21. **Explain the Visual Climb Over Airport (VCOA) procedure. When would a pilot use this procedure?** (P/CG, AIM 5-2-9)

A VCOA is a departure option for an IFR aircraft, operating in VMC equal to or greater than the specified visibility and ceiling, to visually conduct climbing turns over the airport to the published "climb-to" altitude from which to proceed with the instrument portion of the departure. VCOA procedures are developed to avoid obstacles greater than 3 statute miles from the departure end of the runway as an alternative to complying with climb gradients greater than 200 feet per nautical mile. VCOA textual procedures are published in the "Takeoff Minimums and (Obstacle) Departure Procedures" section of the *Terminal Procedures Publications* and/ or appear as an option on a Graphic ODP.

22. During your departure, while flying an ODP, ATC vectors you off of the ODP for traffic separation. Is the ODP now canceled, and who is responsible for terrain and obstacle clearance? (AIM 5-2-9)

Aircraft may be vectored off of an ODP or issued an altitude lower than a published altitude on an ODP, at which time the ODP is canceled. In these cases, ATC assumes responsibility for terrain and obstacle clearance. In all cases, the minimum 200 feet per nautical mile climb gradient is assumed.

23. If an ODP is published for your airport, are you required to fly it? Can ATC assign an ODP to you? (AIM 5-2-9)

No, if an Obstacle Departure Procedure (ODP) is published for an airport, pilots are not required to fly it. Unlike a Standard Instrument Departure (SID), which is mandatory unless otherwise instructed by air traffic control (ATC), an ODP is a recommended procedure designed to enhance obstacle clearance during the initial phase of departure. Pilots have the discretion to accept or decline an ODP based on their assessment of the situation.

ODPs are particularly useful in situations where terrain or obstacles in the vicinity of the airport could affect the climb gradient required for safe departure. If pilots choose not to follow the published ODP, they are still required to meet the minimum climb gradient specified in the departure procedure or as assigned by ATC.

It is important for pilots to carefully review all available departure procedures, including ODPs, during the pre-flight planning phase. Understanding the potential obstacles and terrain in the departure area and evaluating the benefits of following the ODP contribute to making informed decisions for a safe and efficient departure. ATC may also issue specific departure instructions that supersede the published ODP, and pilots should comply with those instructions.

24. What is meant by ATC when a "climb via" clearance is issued? (P/CG)

When ATC issues a climb via clearance, they will assign a SID and will expect the pilot to comply with all published speed restrictions and comply with all published altitude restrictions in the assigned SID.

25. What is the difference between a VFR over-the-top clearance and a VFR-on-top clearance? (FAA-H-8083-15)

VFR over-the-top must not be confused with VFR-on-top. VFR-on-top is an IFR clearance that allows the pilot to fly VFR altitudes. VFR over-the-top is strictly a VFR operation in which the pilot maintains VFR cloud clearance requirements while operating on top of an undercast layer. This situation might occur when the departure airport and the destination airport are reporting clear conditions, but a low overcast layer is present in between. The pilot could conduct a VFR departure, fly over the top of the undercast in VFR conditions, and then complete a VFR descent and landing at the destination. VFR cloud clearance requirements would be maintained at all times, and an IFR clearance would not be required for any part of the flight.

ATC authorization to "maintain VFR-on-top" is not intended to restrict pilots to operating only above an obscuring meteorological formation (layer). Rather, it permits operation above, below, between layers, or in areas where there is no meteorological obstruction. It is imperative pilots understand, however, that clearance to operate "VFR-on-top/VFR conditions" does not imply cancellation of the IFR flight plan.

D. VOR Accuracy Checks

1. What are the different methods for checking the accuracy of VOR equipment? (14 CFR 91.171)

a. VOR test signal (VOT) check: ±4°; or

b. Radio repair station test signal: ±4°; or

c. VOR ground checkpoint at departure airport: ±4°; or

d. VOR airborne checkpoint: ±6° (if no test signal or ground checkpoint available); or

(continued)

e. Airborne over prominent landmark along centerline of
    established VOR airway (more than 20 NM from VOR): ±6° (if
    no check signal or point is available).

f. Dual VOR system check by checking one system against the
    other; both systems tuned to same VOR and note the indicated
    bearings to station; maximum permissible variation between the
    two indicated bearings is 4°. The dual system check can be used
    in place of all other VOR check procedures specified.

Note: A repair station can use a radiated test signal, but only the
technician performing the test can make an entry in the logbook.

2. What records must be kept concerning VOR checks? (14 CFR 91.171)

Each person making a VOR check shall enter the date, place, and
bearing error, and sign the aircraft log or other reliable record. A
current VOR check is required to be presentable for a flight. There
is no requirement to keep previously expired VOR check records.

3. Where can a pilot find the location of designated airborne checkpoints, ground checkpoints, and VOT testing stations? (AIM 1-1-4)

Locations of airborne checkpoints, ground checkpoints, and VOTs
are published in the *Chart Supplement.*

4. What procedure is used when checking VOR receiver accuracy with a VOT? (FAA-H-8083-15)

Tune in the VOT frequency of 108.0 MHz. With CDI centered, the
OBS should read 0 degrees with TO/FROM indication showing
FROM, or the OBS should read 180 degrees with the TO/FROM
indication showing TO.

Remember: "Cessna 182"—180 TO for VOR accuracy checks
using a VOT.

E. Transponder and ADS-B

1. Where is Mode C transponder and ADS-B Out equipment required? (AIM 4-1-20, 14 CFR 91.215, 91.225, 99.13)

In general, the regulations require aircraft to be equipped with an
operable Mode C transponder and ADS-B Out equipment when
operating:

a. In Class A, Class B, or Class C airspace areas.

b. Above the ceiling and within the lateral boundaries of Class B or Class C airspace up to 10,000 feet MSL.

c. Class E airspace at and above 10,000 feet MSL within the 48 contiguous states and the District of Columbia, excluding the airspace at and below 2,500 feet AGL.

d. Within 30 miles of a Class B airspace primary airport, below 10,000 feet MSL (Mode C veil).

e. For ADS-B Out: Class E airspace at and above 3,000 feet MSL over the Gulf of Mexico from the coastline of the United States out to 12 nautical miles.

f. All aircraft flying into, within, or across the contiguous United States ADIZ.

Note: Civil and military aircraft should operate with the transponder in the altitude reporting mode and ADS-B Out transmissions enabled (if equipped) at all airports, any time the aircraft is positioned on any portion of an airport movement area. This includes all defined taxiways and runways.

2. What are the following transponder codes: 1200, 7700, 7600, and 7500? (AIM 4-1-20, 6-2-2, 6-3-4, 6-4-2)

1200 — VFR
7700 — Emergency
7600 — Communications emergency
7500 — Hijacking in progress

3. Explain transponder and ADS-B operations in the event of a two-way communications failure. (AIM 6-4-2, AC 90-114)

If an aircraft with a coded radar beacon transponder experiences a loss of two-way radio capability, the pilot should adjust the transponder to reply on Mode A/3, Code 7600. The ADS-B message element and transponder code will alert ATC that the aircraft is experiencing emergency conditions and indicate the type of emergency. The pilot should understand that the aircraft may not be in an area of radar coverage.

4. Would an incorrect altimeter setting have an effect on your Mode C/S transponder and ADS-B Out altitude information? (AIM 4-1-20)

While an incorrect altimeter setting has no effect on the transmitted altitude information, it will cause the aircraft to fly at a true altitude different from the assigned altitude. When a controller indicates that an altitude readout is invalid, the pilot should verify that the aircraft altimeter is set correctly.

Note: Altitude encoders are preset at standard atmospheric pressure. Local altimeter correction is applied by the surveillance facility before the altitude information is presented to ATC.

5. For aircraft equipped with ADS-B In, what is TIS-B and FIS-B? (AC 90-114)

TIS-B (Traffic Information Services–Broadcast)—The ground broadcast service provided from an ADS-B ground system network of transponder-based traffic information derived from ATC surveillance systems. It provides ADS-B In-equipped aircraft with a more complete picture of traffic in situations where not all aircraft are equipped with ADS-B Out.

FIS-B (Flight Information Service–Broadcast)—The ground broadcast service provided over the 978 MHz UAT data link that provides ADS-B In-equipped aircraft with a flight deck display of certain aviation weather and aeronautical information for advisory-only use. FIS-B enhances the user's situational awareness.

6. Explain the differences between the Universal Access Transceiver (978 MHz) and 1090ES. What are the advantages and disadvantages of each? (faa.gov)

General aviation users who choose the UAT (978 MHz) link must retain a transponder and can only operate in ADS-B Out required airspace below FL180, unless dual-equipped. 1090ES equipage is required in Class A airspace and users can operate in all ADS-B Out required airspace. 1090ES equipage also ensures compliance with international ADS-B Out requirements.

Users choosing to equip with a UAT ADS-B In device may take advantage of the ADS-B traffic and FIS-B (weather and aeronautical) services that are transmitted on the UAT frequency at no charge. Users equipped with a 1090 MHz ADS-B In device receive ADS-B and TIS-B traffic but cannot receive FIS-B services.

7. What happens to ADS-B functions if there is GPS interference or a GPS outage? (faa.gov, AIM 1-1-13)

The FAA uses back-up systems to provide resiliency and guard against GPS interference, spoofing, or degradation. The FAA also monitors for GPS interference at its ADS-B and WAAS reference sites. In the event of GPS failure, interference, or spoofing, the FAA maintains backup terrestrial radar to provide resiliency for the National Airspace System.

Aircraft contain a number of built-in ADS-B message quality indicators that are constantly checking accuracy and integrity of the position source information.

If operators encounter actual GPS interference during their flight that results in a degradation of ADS-B Out performance, the FAA will not consider these events to constitute noncompliance with 14 CFR §91.227.

8. What is the difference between ADS-B Out and ADS-B In? (FAA-H-8083-25)

ADS-B Out refers to an aircraft broadcasting its position and other information. ADS-B In refers to an aircraft receiving the broadcasts and messages from other aircraft and FAA TIS-B and FIS-B services. ADS-B In is not mandated by the ADS-B Out rule. If an operator chooses to voluntarily equip an aircraft with ADS-B In avionics, a compatible display is also necessary to see the information. Refer to FAA AC 20-165 (*Airworthiness Approval of Automatic Dependent Surveillance–Broadcast Out Systems*) for information on ADS-B Out, and to AC 20-172 (*Airworthiness Approval for ADS-B In Systems and Applications*) for details on ADS-B In installation and certification.

F. Airport Facilities

1. Where can a pilot find information concerning facilities available for a particular airport? (AIM 9-1-4)

The *Chart Supplement* contains data on airports, seaplane bases, heliports, NAVAIDs, communications data, weather data sources, airspace, special notices, and operational procedures. It gives the data that cannot be readily depicted in graphic form and provides a means for pilots to update visual charts between edition dates. It is published every 56 days.

2. What do the following acronyms stand for: ALSF-1, SSALF, MALSR, REIL, MIRL, and PAPI? (P/CG)

ALSF-1—Approach light system with sequenced flashing lights (ILS Cat-I configuration).

SSALF—Simplified short approach light system with sequenced flashing lights.

MALSR—Medium intensity approach light system with runway alignment indicator lights.

REIL—Runway end identifier lights.

MIRL—Medium intensity runway lighting.

PAPI—Precision approach path indicator system.

Exam Tip: Be prepared to locate and explain the type of approach light systems available at your destination and alternate airports. Having the legend for approach lighting systems found in the *Terminal Procedures Publication* (TPP) readily available is highly recommended.

3. What color are runway edge lights? (AIM 2-1-4)

The runway edge lights are white—except on instrument runways, where yellow replaces white on the last 2,000 feet or half the runway length, whichever is less, to form a caution zone for landings.

4. What colors and color combinations of rotating beacons are used to identify airports? (AIM 2-1-9)

a. White and green—lighted land airport.

b. Green alone*—lighted land airport.

c. White and yellow—lighted water airport.

d. Yellow alone*—lighted water airport.

e. Green, yellow, and white—lighted heliport.

f. White (dual peaked) and green—military airport.

* "Green alone" and "yellow alone" beacons are used only in connection with a white-and-green, or white-and-yellow beacon display, respectively.

5. **What does the operation of a rotating beacon at an airport within Class D airspace during daylight hours mean?** (AIM 2-1-9)

In Class B, Class C, Class D, and Class E surface areas, operation of the airport beacon during the hours of daylight often indicates that the ground visibility is less than 3 miles and/or the ceiling is less than 1,000 feet. ATC clearance in accordance with 14 CFR Part 91 is required for landing, takeoff, and flight in the traffic pattern. Pilots should not rely solely on the operation of the airport beacon to indicate if weather conditions are IFR or VFR. There is no regulatory requirement for daylight operation, and it is the pilot's responsibility to comply with proper preflight planning as required by 14 CFR Part 91.

6. **Where would information concerning runway lengths, widths, and weight-bearing capacities be found?**

The *Chart Supplement* has this information.

7. **What are runway touchdown zone markings?** (AIM 2-3-3)

Touchdown zone markings identify the touchdown zone for landing operations and are coded to provide distance information in 500-foot increments. These markings consist of groups of one, two, and three rectangular bars symmetrically arranged in pairs about the runway centerline. Normally, the standard glide slope angle of 3 degrees, if flown to the surface, will ensure touchdown within this zone.

8. **What is the purpose of runway aiming point markings?** (AIM 2-3-3)

The aiming point markings serve as a visual aiming point for a landing aircraft. These two rectangular markings consist of a broad white stripe, located on each side of the runway centerline, and approximately 1,000 feet from the landing threshold. The pilot can estimate a visual glide path that will intersect the marking, ensuring a landing within the 3,000-foot touchdown zone.

9. How far down a runway does the touchdown zone extend? (P/CG)

The touchdown zone is the first 3,000 feet of the runway beginning at the threshold. The area is used for determination of Touchdown Zone Elevation in the development of straight-in landing minimums for instrument approaches.

10. How can you identify an ILS critical area? (AIM 1-1-9, 2-3-5)

Holding position markings for ILS critical areas consist of two yellow solid lines, spaced two feet apart, connected by pairs of solid lines, spaced ten feet apart, extending across the width of the taxiway. When the ILS critical area is being protected, the pilot should stop so no part of the aircraft extends beyond the holding position marking. The area is protected whenever conditions are less than a ceiling of 800 feet and/or visibility less than 2 miles.

11. What does the acronym RWSL stand for? (AIM 2-1-6)

Runway Status Lights system (RWSL) is a fully automated system that provides runway status information to pilots and surface vehicle operators to clearly indicate when it is unsafe to enter, cross, take off from, or land on a runway. The RWSL system processes information from surveillance systems and activates Runway Entrance Lights (REL), Takeoff Hold Lights (THL), Runway Intersection Lights (RIL), and Final Approach Runway Occupancy Signal (FAROS) in accordance with the position and velocity of the detected surface traffic and approach traffic. The status lights have two states—ON: lights are illuminated red; and OFF: lights are not illuminated.

12. Describe runway hold short markings and signs. (AIM 2-3-5)

Runway holding position markings—These indicate where aircraft **must stop** when approaching a runway. They consist of four yellow lines—two solid and two dashed—spaced six or twelve inches apart and extending across the width of the taxiway or runway. The solid lines are always on the side where the aircraft is to hold.

Runway holding position sign—Located at the holding position on taxiways that intersect a runway or on runways that intersect other runways. These signs have a red background with a white inscription and contain the designation of the intersecting runway.

13. Pre-flight planning for taxi operations should be an integral part of the pilot's flight planning process. What information should this include? (AC 91-73)

a. Review and understand airport signage, markings, and lighting.

b. Review the airport diagram, planned taxi route, and identify any hot spots.

c. Review the latest airfield NOTAMs and ATIS (if available) for taxiway/runway closures, construction activity, etc.

d. Conduct a pre-taxi/pre-landing briefing that includes the expected/assigned taxi route, any hold short lines, and restrictions based on ATIS information or previous experience at the airport.

e. Plan for critical times and locations on the taxi route (complex intersections, crossing runways, etc.).

f. Plan to complete as many aircraft checklist items as possible prior to taxi.

14. What is an airport surface *hot spot*? (CS)

A hot spot is a runway safety-related problem area on an airport that presents increased risk during surface operations. Typically, hot spots are complex or confusing taxiway–taxiway or taxiway–runway intersections. The area of increased risk has either a history of or potential for runway incursions or surface incidents due to a variety of causes, such as but not limited to airport layout, traffic flow, airport marking, signage and lighting, situational awareness, and training. Hot spots are depicted on airport diagrams as circles or polygons designated as "HS1," "HS2," etc.

15. When issued taxi instructions to an assigned takeoff runway, are you automatically authorized to cross any runway that intersects your taxi route? (AIM 4-3-18)

No; Aircraft must receive a runway crossing clearance for each runway that their taxi route crosses. When assigned a takeoff runway, ATC will first specify the runway, issue taxi instructions, and state any hold short instructions or runway crossing clearances if the taxi route will cross a runway. When issuing taxi instructions to any point other than an assigned takeoff runway, ATC will specify the point to which to taxi, issue taxi instructions, and state any hold short instructions or runway crossing clearances if the taxi route will cross a runway. ATC is required to obtain from the pilot a readback of all runway hold short instructions.

16. How can a pilot maintain situational awareness during taxi operations? (AC 91-73)

a. Ensure that a current airport diagram is available for immediate reference during taxi.

b. Monitor ATC instructions/clearances issued to other aircraft for the "big picture."

c. Focus attention outside the flight deck while taxiing.

d. Use all available resources (airport diagrams, airport signs, markings, lighting, and ATC) to keep the aircraft on its assigned taxi route.

e. Cross-reference heading indicator to ensure turns are being made in the correct direction and that you're on the assigned taxi route.

f. Prior to crossing any hold short line, visually check for conflicting traffic; verbalize "clear left, clear right."

g. Be alert for other aircraft with similar call signs on the frequency.

h. Understand and follow all ATC instructions and if in doubt—ask!

En Route 3

A. Enroute Limitations

1. Define the following: MEA, MOCA, MCA, MRA, MAA, OROCA, and MTA. (P/CG)

MEA—Minimum enroute altitude; the lowest published altitude between radio fixes that ensures acceptable navigational signal coverage and meets obstacle clearance requirements.

MOCA—Minimum obstruction clearance altitude; the lowest published altitude between radio fixes on VOR airways, off-airway routes, or route segments that meets obstacle clearance requirements, and that ensures acceptable navigational signal coverage only within 25 statute (22 nautical) miles of a VOR.

MCA—Minimum crossing altitude; the lowest altitude at certain fixes at which aircraft must cross when proceeding in the direction of a higher MEA.

MRA—Minimum reception altitude; the lowest altitude at which an intersection can be determined.

MAA—Maximum authorized altitude; the maximum usable altitude or flight level for an airspace structure or a route segment that ensures adequate reception of navigation aid signals.

OROCA—Off-route obstruction clearance altitude; this provides obstruction clearance with a 1,000-foot buffer in non-mountainous terrain areas and a 2,000-foot buffer in designated mountainous areas within the United States. This altitude might not provide signal coverage from ground-based navigational aids, air traffic control radar, or communications coverage.

MTA—Minimum turning altitude (MTA); Due to increased airspeeds at 10,000 feet MSL or above, the published minimum enroute altitude (MEA) may not be sufficient for obstacle clearance when a turn is required over a fix, NAVAID, or waypoint. In these instances, an expanded area in the vicinity of the turn point is examined to determine whether the published MEA is sufficient for obstacle clearance. In some locations (normally mountainous), terrain/obstacles in the expanded search area may necessitate a higher minimum altitude while conducting the turning maneuver. Turning fixes requiring a higher minimum turning altitude (MTA) will be denoted on government charts by the minimum crossing altitude (MCA) icon ("x" flag) and an accompanying note describing the MTA restriction. An MTA restriction will normally consist of the air traffic service (ATS) route leading to the turn point, the ATS route leading from the turn point, and the required altitude; e.g., MTA V330 E TO V520 W 16000. When an MTA is applicable for the intended route of flight, pilots must ensure they are at or above the charted MTA not later than the turn point and maintain at or above the MTA until joining the centerline of the ATS route following the turn point. Once established on the centerline following the turning fix, the MEA/MOCA determines the minimum altitude available for assignment. An MTA may also preclude the use of a specific altitude or a range of altitudes during a turn. For example, the MTA may restrict the use of 10,000 through 11,000 feet MSL. In this case, any altitude greater than 11,000 feet MSL is unrestricted, as are altitudes less than 10,000 feet MSL provided MEA/MOCA requirements are satisfied.

2. If no applicable minimum altitude is prescribed (no MEA or MOCA), what minimum altitudes apply for IFR operations? (14 CFR 91.177, Part 95)

Minimum altitudes are:

a. *Mountainous terrain*—At least 2,000 feet above the highest obstacle within a horizontal distance of 4 NM from the course to be flown. Part 95 designates the location of mountainous terrain.

b. *Other than mountainous terrain*—At least 1,000 feet above the highest obstacle within a horizontal distance of 4 NM from the course to be flown.

3. What cruising altitudes shall be maintained while operating under IFR in controlled airspace (Class A, B, C, D, or E)? In uncontrolled airspace (Class G)? (14 CFR 91.179)

IFR flights within controlled airspace (Class A, B, C, D, or E) shall maintain the altitude or flight level assigned by ATC. In uncontrolled airspace (Class G), altitude is selected based on the magnetic course flown:

Below 18,000 feet MSL:
- 0 to 179°—odd thousand MSL
- 180 to 359°—even thousand MSL

18,000 feet up to but not including 29,000 feet MSL:
- 0 to 179°—odd flight levels
- 180 to 359°—even flight levels

4. What procedures are applicable concerning courses to be flown when operating IFR? (14 CFR 91.181)

Unless otherwise authorized by ATC, no one may operate an aircraft within controlled airspace under IFR except on an air traffic services (ATS) route, along the centerline of that airway, or on any other route along the direct course between the navigational aids or fixes defining that route. However, this does not prohibit maneuvering the aircraft to pass well clear of other air traffic or maneuvering in VFR conditions to clear the intended flight path both before and during climb or descent.

5. On a direct flight not flown on radials or courses of established airways or routes, what points serve as compulsory reporting points? (AIM 5-3-2)

For flights along a direct route, regardless of the altitude or flight level being flown, including flights operating in accordance with an ATC clearance specifying "VFR-on-top," pilots must report over each reporting point used in the flight plan to define the route of flight.

6. What are unpublished RNAV routes? (AIM 5-3-4)

Unpublished RNAV routes are direct routes based on area navigation capability, between waypoints defined in terms of latitude/longitude coordinates, degree-distance fixes, or offsets from established routes/airways at a specified distance and direction. Radar monitoring by ATC is required on all unpublished RNAV routes, except for GNSS-equipped aircraft cleared via filed published waypoints recallable from the aircraft's navigation database.

7. With respect to IFR navigation when using RNAV systems, what is a Magnetic Reference Bearing (MRB)? (AIM 5-3-4)

Magnetic Reference Bearing (MRB) is the published bearing between two waypoints on an RNAV/GPS/GNSS route. The MRB is calculated by applying magnetic variation at the waypoint to the calculated true course between two waypoints. The MRB enhances situational awareness by indicating a reference bearing (no-wind heading) that a pilot should see on the compass/HSI/RMI, etc., when turning prior to/over a waypoint en route to another waypoint. Pilots should use this bearing as a reference only, because their RNAV/GPS/GNSS navigation system will fly the true course between the waypoints.

B. Enroute Procedures

1. What reports should be made to ATC without a specific request (radar and non-radar)? (14 CFR 91.183, 91.187, AIM 5-3-3)

The pilot must report:

Missed approach; request clearance for specific action, such as another approach, alternate airport, etc.

Airspeed change; change in average KTAS at cruising altitude of 5% or 10 knots, whichever is greater.

Reaching a holding fix or point to which cleared; report time and altitude or flight level.

Vacating any previously assigned altitude or flight level.

ETA change when previous estimate is in error in excess of 2 minutes (non-radar).

Leaving assigned holding fix or point.

Outer marker inbound or fix used in lieu of the OM (non-radar).

Unforecast weather.

Safety of flight compromised.

VFR-on-top, when any altitude change is made.

Final approach fix inbound (non-radar).

Radio malfunction—any loss or impairment of navigation/communication receiver capability.

Compulsory reporting points (non-radar).

500 FPM—unable to climb/descend 500 fpm.

Remember: MARVELOUS VFR C500

2. What reporting requirements are required by ATC when not in radar contact? (AIM 5-3-3)

a. When leaving final approach fix inbound on the final (nonprecision) approach, or when leaving the outer marker (or fix used in lieu of the outer marker) inbound on final (precision) approach.

b. A corrected estimate at anytime it becomes apparent that an estimate as previously submitted is in error *in excess of* 2 minutes. For flights in the North Atlantic (NAT), a revised estimate is required if the error is 3 minutes or more.

3. **What items of information should be included in every position report?** (AIM 5-3-2)

   a. Identification

   b. Position

   c. Time

   d. Altitude or flight level

   e. Type of flight plan (not required in IFR position reports made directly to ARTCCs or approach control)

   f. ETA and name of next reporting point

   g. The name only of the next succeeding reporting point along the route of flight, and

   h. Pertinent remarks

4. **When used in conjunction with ATC altitude assignments, what does the term *pilot's discretion* mean?** (P/CG)

   Pilot's discretion means that ATC has offered the pilot the option of starting climb or descent whenever he/she wishes and conducting the climb or descent at any rate he/she wishes. The pilot may temporarily level off at any intermediate altitude. However, after vacating an altitude, the pilot may not return to that altitude.

5. **Explain the terms *maintain* and *cruise* as they pertain to an IFR altitude assignment.** (AIM 4-4-3)

   Maintain—Self-explanatory: maintain last altitude assigned.

   Cruise—Used instead of "maintain" to assign a block of airspace to a pilot, from minimum IFR altitude up to and including the altitude specified in the cruise clearance. The pilot may level off at any intermediate altitude, and climb/descent may be made at the discretion of the pilot. However, once the pilot starts a descent, and *verbally* reports leaving an altitude in the block, the pilot may not return to that altitude without additional ATC clearance.

6. **Can ATC issue you a cruise clearance that authorizes you to proceed to and execute an approach at the destination airport without an operating control tower?** (FAA-H-8083-15, P/CG)

Yes. ATC may issue a cruise clearance that authorizes you to execute an approach upon arrival at the destination airport. When operating in uncontrolled airspace on a cruise clearance, you are responsible for determining the minimum IFR altitude. In addition, descent and landing at an airport in uncontrolled airspace are governed by the applicable visual flight rules and/or operations specifications, i.e. 14 CFR §§91.126, 91.155, 91.175, 91.179, etc.

7. **ATC will issue speed adjustments to pilots of radar-controlled aircraft. Pilots complying with speed adjustments are expected to maintain airspeed within what tolerances?** (AIM 4-4-12)

ATC will express all speed adjustments in terms of knots based on indicated airspeed (IAS) in 5 or 10 knot increments, except that at or above FL 240, speeds may be expressed in terms of Mach numbers in 0.01 increments. The use of Mach numbers is restricted to turbojet aircraft with Mach meters.

8. **Why would a pilot request a VFR-on-top clearance?** (AIM 4-4-8)

A pilot on an IFR flight plan operating in VFR weather conditions may request VFR-on-top in lieu of an assigned altitude. For reasons such as turbulence, more favorable winds aloft, etc., the pilot has the flexibility to select an altitude or flight level of his/her choice (subject to any ATC restrictions). Pilots desiring to climb through a cloud, haze, smoke, or other meteorological formation and then either cancel their IFR flight plan or operate VFR-on-top may request a climb to VFR-on-top.

Note: The ATC authorization must contain either a top report or a statement that no top report is available, and a request to report reaching VFR-on-top. Additionally, the ATC authorization may contain a clearance limit, routing, and an alternative clearance if VFR-on-top is not reached by a specified altitude.

9. **Does an ATC authorization to "maintain VFR-on-top" restrict you to only operating on top or above the cloud layer?** (AIM 4-4-8)

ATC authorization to "maintain VFR-on-top" is not intended to restrict pilots so that they must operate only *above* an obscuring meteorological formation (layer). Instead, it permits operation above, below, between layers, or in areas where there is no meteorological obscuration. It is imperative, however, that pilots understand that clearance to operate "VFR-on-top/VFR conditions" does not imply cancellation of the IFR flight plan.

10. **Which airspace prohibits VFR-on-top clearances?** (AIM 4-4-8)

Class A airspace.

11. **What operational procedures must pilots on IFR flight plans adhere to when operating VFR-on-top?** (AIM 4-4-8)

They must:

a. Fly at the appropriate VFR altitude.

b. Comply with the VFR visibility and distance from cloud criteria.

c. Comply with instrument flight rules that are applicable to this flight; i.e., minimum IFR altitudes, position reporting, radio communications, course to be flown, adherence to ATC clearance, etc.

12. **What is a *clearance limit* and when is it received?** (AIM 4-4-3)

A traffic clearance issued prior to departure will normally authorize flight to the airport of intended landing. Under certain conditions, at some locations, a short-range clearance procedure is used, whereby a clearance is issued to a fix within or just outside of the terminal area, and pilots are advised of the frequency on which they will receive the long-range clearance direct from the center controller.

13. What information will ATC provide when they request a hold at a fix where the holding pattern is not charted? (AIM 5-3-8)

An ATC clearance requiring an aircraft to hold at a fix where the pattern is not charted will include the following information:

a. Direction of holding from the fix, in reference to the eight cardinal compass points (i.e. N, NE, E, SE, etc.).

b. Holding fix (the fix may be omitted if included at the beginning of the transmission as the clearance limit).

c. Radial, course, bearing, airway, or route on which the aircraft is to hold.

d. Leg length in miles if DME or RNAV is to be used (leg length will be specified in minutes on pilot request or if the controller considers it necessary).

e. Direction of turns, if holding pattern is nonstandard (left turns), the pilot requests direction of turns, or the controller considers it necessary to state direction of turns.

f. Time to expect further clearance and any pertinent additional delay information.

14. What are the maximum airspeeds permitted for aircraft while holding? (AIM 5-3-8)

MHA–6,000 feet: 200 KIAS
6,001–14,000 feet: 230 KIAS
14,001 feet and above: 265 KIAS

Note: Holding patterns may be restricted to a maximum speed. Holding patterns from 6,001 to 14,000 feet may be restricted to a maximum airspeed of 210 KIAS. These nonstandard patterns will be depicted by an icon.

15. What is a nonstandard versus a standard holding pattern? (AIM 5-3-8)

In a standard pattern, all turns are to the right. In a nonstandard pattern, all turns are to the left.

16. Describe the procedure for crosswind correction in a holding pattern. (AIM 5-3-8)

Compensate for wind effect primarily by drift correction on the inbound and outbound legs. When outbound, triple the inbound drift correction to avoid major turning adjustments.

17. What action is appropriate when approaching a holding fix at an airspeed in excess of maximum holding speed? (AIM 5-3-8)

Start a speed reduction when 3 minutes or less from the fix. Speed may be reduced earlier, but ATC must be advised of the change.

18. Why is it important for the pilot to receive an EFC time with initial holding instructions? (FAA-H-8083-16)

If you lose two-way radio communication, the EFC allows you to depart the holding fix at a definite time. Plan the last lap of your holding pattern to leave the fix as close as possible to the exact time.

19. Describe the different recommended entry methods for holding. (AIM 5-3-8)

The three types of entry are:

a. Parallel

b. Teardrop

c. Direct

20. What is the leg length for a standard holding pattern? (AIM 5-3-8)

The standard leg length is:

a. 1 minute inbound at or below 14,000 feet MSL, and

b. 1½ minutes inbound above 14,000 feet MSL.

21. If assigned a DME/GPS hold, what procedures should be used? (AIM 5-3-8)

Distance measuring equipment (DME)/GPS along-track distance (ATD) holding is subject to the same entry and holding procedures except that distances (nautical miles) are used in lieu of time values. The outbound course of the DME/GPS holding pattern is called the outbound leg of the pattern. The controller or the instrument approach procedure chart will specify the length of the outbound leg. The end of the outbound leg is determined by the DME or ATD readout.

22. When does the timing for the outbound leg in a holding pattern begin? (AIM 5-3-8)

Outbound leg timing begins over/abeam the fix, whichever occurs later. If the abeam position cannot be determined, start timing when turn to outbound is completed.

23. The distance information indicated by your DME is different from that indicated on the GPS display. Why? (FAA-H-8083-15)

DME signals are line-of-sight; the mileage readout is the straight-line distance from the aircraft antenna to the DME ground facility and is commonly referred to as slant range distance. GPS systems provide distance as the horizontal measurement from the waypoint to the aircraft. Therefore, at 3,000 feet and 0.5 miles, the DME (slant range) would read 0.6 NM while the GPS distance would show the actual horizontal distance of .5 DME. This error is smallest at low altitudes and/or at long ranges.

C. Oxygen Requirements

1. What regulations apply concerning supplemental oxygen? (14 CFR 91.211)

a. At cabin pressure altitudes above 12,500 MSL up to and including 14,000 MSL, the minimum flight crew must use oxygen after 30 minutes.

b. Above 14,000 MSL up to and including 15,000 MSL, the minimum flight crew must continuously use oxygen.

c. Above 15,000 MSL, each passenger must be provided with supplemental oxygen and the minimum flight crew must continuously use oxygen.

D. Emergencies

1. When may the pilot-in-command of an aircraft deviate from an ATC clearance? (14 CFR 91.123)

Except in an emergency, no person may, in an area in which air traffic control is exercised, operate an aircraft contrary to an ATC instruction.

2. If an emergency action requires deviation from 14 CFR Part 91, must a pilot submit a written report, and if so, to whom? (14 CFR 91.123)

Each pilot-in-command who is given priority by ATC in an emergency shall, if requested by ATC, submit a detailed report of that emergency within 48 hours to the manager of that ATC facility.

3. Concerning two-way radio communications failure in VFR and IFR conditions, what is the procedure for altitude, route, leaving holding fix, descent for approach, and approach selection? (14 CFR 91.185)

In VFR conditions—If the failure occurs in VFR, or if VFR is encountered after the failure, each pilot shall continue the flight under VFR and land as soon as practicable.

In IFR conditions—If the failure occurs in IFR conditions, or if VFR conditions are not within range, each pilot shall continue the flight according to the following:

a. Route:

Assigned—By route assigned in last ATC clearance.

Vectored—Go direct from point of radio failure to fix, route, or airway specified in vector clearance.

Expected—By route that ATC has advised may be expected.

Filed—By the route filed in flight plan.

b. Altitude (highest of following altitudes for the route segment being flown):

Minimum—Minimum altitude for IFR operations.

Expected—Altitude/flight level ATC has advised to expect in a further clearance.

Assigned—Altitude/flight level assigned in the last ATC clearance.

c. Leave clearance limit:
  - When the clearance limit is a fix from which the approach begins, commence descent or descent and approach as close as possible to the expect-further-clearance time if one has been received; or if one has not been received, as close as possible to the estimated time of arrival as calculated from the filed or amended (with ATC) estimated time en route.
  - If the clearance limit is not a fix from which the approach begins, leave the clearance limit at the expect-further-clearance time if one has been received; or if none has been received, upon arrival over the clearance limit, and proceed to a fix from which an approach begins and commence descent or decent and approach as close as possible to the estimated time of arrival as calculated from the filed or amended (with ATC) estimated time en route.

Exam Tip: At any given point along your route of flight, be prepared to explain exactly what route to fly, what altitude to fly, and when to continue beyond a clearance limit in the event of a complete communication failure. Knowing the communication failure regulation is a good start, but you must demonstrate that you can apply it in an emergency. Also be able to determine if you were going to arrive ahead of your ETA where you would hold and what kind of hold you would do until your ETA.

4. When may a pilot operate an aircraft below the published MEA? (14 CFR 91.177, AIM 4-5-6)

a. A pilot may operate an aircraft below the MEA down to, but not below, the MOCA, provided the applicable navigation signals are available. For aircraft using VOR for navigation, this applies only when the aircraft is within 22 nautical miles of that VOR (based on the reasonable estimate by the pilot operating the aircraft of that distance); or

b. If no applicable minimum altitude is prescribed in Parts 95 and 97 of this chapter, then—
  - In the case of operations over an area designated as a mountainous area in part 95 of this chapter, an altitude of 2,000 feet above the highest obstacle within a horizontal distance of 4 nautical miles from the course to be flown; or

- In any other case, an altitude of 1,000 feet above the highest obstacle within a horizontal distance of 4 nautical miles from the course to be flown.

An aircraft may also be cleared to operate on jet routes below the MEA (but not below the prescribed minimum altitude for IFR operations) or above the maximum authorized altitude if, in either case, radar service is provided.

5. **Assuming two-way communications failure, discuss the recommended procedure to follow concerning altitudes to be flown for the following trip:**

   The MEA between A and B is 5,000 feet; the MEA between B and C is 5,000 feet; the MEA between C and D is 11,000 feet; and the MEA between D and E is 7,000 feet. You have been cleared via A, B, C, D, to E. While flying between A and B, your assigned altitude was 6,000 feet and you were told to expect a clearance to 8,000 feet at B. Prior to receiving the higher altitude assignment, you experience two-way communication failure. (AIM 6-4-1)

   The correct procedure would be as follows:

   a. Maintain 6,000 feet to B, then climb to 8,000 feet (the altitude you were advised to expect).

   b. Continue to maintain 8,000 feet, then climb to 11,000 feet at C, or prior to C if necessary to comply with an MCA at C.

   c. Upon reaching D, you would descend to 8,000 feet (even though the MEA was 7,000 feet), as 8,000 feet was the highest of the altitude situations stated in the rule.

6. **Assuming two-way communications failure, discuss the recommended procedure to follow concerning altitudes to be flown for the following scenario:**

   A pilot experiencing two-way radio failure while being progressively descended to lower altitudes to begin an approach is assigned 2,700 feet until crossing the VOR and then cleared for the approach. The MOCA along the airway is 2,700 feet and MEA is 4,000 feet. The aircraft is within 22 NM of the VOR. (AIM 6-4-1)

   The pilot should remain at 2,700 feet until crossing the VOR because that altitude is the minimum IFR altitude for the route segment being flown.

7. **In the event of loss of communication with your assigned controller, what other frequencies might you use to try to communicate with ATC before assuming you have fully lost communications?** (AIM 6-4-3)

   The pilot should attempt to reestablish communications by attempting to contact a previously assigned frequency starting with the most recent or attempting to contact Flight Service or remote communications outlet. If communications are thus established, the pilot should advise that radio communications on the assigned frequency had been lost; give the aircraft's position, altitude, and last assigned frequency; and then request further clearance from the controlling facility. The preceding does not preclude the use of 121.5 MHz. There is no priority on which action should be attempted first. If the capability exists, do all at the same time. A pilot might also choose to try to use a sector frequency as depicted on low altitude enroute charts for a center controller or even source local approach plates for a frequency that is designated for use in the nearby area.

8. **While en route, operating in IMC, what procedure would you use if all communication and navigation equipment failed (complete system failure)?** (FAA-H-8083-15)

   In modern aircraft, avionics systems are often more dependent on electrical systems. In the event of a full loss of communication and navigation equipment, typically something that would occur if a generator or alternator had failed and all battery power had been depleted, a pilot would be left with flying toward an area of expected VFR conditions where they might be able to execute an emergency landing. In the absence of other navigation equipment, this would be a last resort option. A pilot might choose to use equipment carried on board such as an EFB or portable GPS device (although these are not IFR-approved equipment) to navigate under such an emergency. This potential is a critical reason pilots even in IFR conditions must know their positioning at all times and should have awareness of where they might proceed to find VFR conditions should it become necessary.

9. If operating on an IFR flight plan but in VFR conditions, what should a pilot do if communications with ATC are lost? (FAA-H-8083-15)

If operating in VFR conditions at the time of the failure, the pilot should continue the flight under VFR and land as soon as practicable.

10. If you become doubtful about your position or adverse weather ahead, should you declare an emergency? (AIM 6-1-2)

An emergency can be either a distress or urgency condition. Pilots do not hesitate to declare an emergency when they are faced with distress conditions such as fire, mechanical failure, or structural damage. However, some are reluctant to report an urgency condition when they encounter situations that may not be immediately perilous but are potentially catastrophic. An aircraft is in at least an urgency condition the moment the pilot becomes doubtful about position, fuel endurance, weather, or any other condition that could adversely affect flight safety. This is the time to ask for help, not after the situation has developed into a distress condition.

11. When would you provide a "minimum fuel" advisory to ATC? (AIM 5-5-15)

A minimum fuel advisory indicates that an aircraft's fuel supply has reached a state where, upon reaching the destination, it can accept little or no delay.

12. **Does ATC consider a "minimum fuel" advisory an emergency, and will they give you priority handling?** (AIM 5-5-15)

No. A minimum fuel advisory by the pilot merely indicates an emergency situation is possible should any undue delay occur and does not imply a need for traffic priority. If the remaining usable fuel supply suggests the need for traffic priority to ensure a safe landing, you should declare an emergency due to low fuel and report fuel remaining in minutes.

E. Single-Pilot Resource Management

1. **Define the term *single-pilot resource management*.** (FAA-H-8083-25)

Single-pilot resource management (SRM) is defined as the art and science of managing all the resources (both on board the aircraft and from outside sources) available to a single pilot (prior to and during flight) to ensure the successful outcome of the flight.

2. **What are the various resources you will use when utilizing your SRM skills?** (FAA-S-8083-9)

SRM available resources can include human resources, hardware, and information. Human resources include all other groups routinely working with the pilot who are involved in decisions required to operate a flight safely. These groups include but are not limited to dispatchers, weather briefers, maintenance personnel, and air traffic controllers. SRM is a set of skill competencies that must be evident in all tasks required by the airman certification standards as applied to single-pilot operation.

3. **What are the six skills you must be competent in for effective SRM?** (FAA-H-8083-25)

Controlled flight into terrain (CFIT) awareness

Aeronautical decision making

Risk management

Automation management

Task management

Situational awareness

4. **A majority of controlled flight into terrain (CFIT) accidents have been attributed to what factors?** (AC 61-134)

   a. Lack of pilot currency

   b. Loss of situational awareness

   c. Pilot distractions and breakdown of SRM

   d. Failure to comply with minimum safe altitudes

   e. Breakdown in effective ADM

   f. Insufficient planning, especially for the descent and arrival segments

5. **Describe several operational techniques that will help you avoid a CFIT accident.** (AC 61-134)

   a. Maintain situational awareness at all times.

   b. Adhere to safe takeoff and departure procedures.

   c. Familiarize yourself with surrounding terrain features and obstacles.

   d. Adhere to published routes and minimum altitudes.

   e. Fly a stabilized approach.

   f. Understand ATC clearances and instructions.

   g. Don't become complacent.

6. **Define the term _aeronautical decision making_.** (FAA-H-8083-9)

   Aeronautical decision making (ADM) is a systematic approach to the mental process used by aircraft pilots to consistently determine the best course of action in response to a given set of circumstances.

7. **The DECIDE model of decision making involves which elements?** (FAA-H-8083-9)

   Detect a change needing attention.

   Estimate the need to counter or react to the change.

   Choose the most desirable outcome for the flight.

   Identify actions to successfully control the change.

   Do something to adapt to the change.

   Evaluate the effect of the action countering the change.

8. What is the definition of *risk*? (FAA-H-8083-2)

Risk is the future impact of a hazard that is not controlled or eliminated.

9. What is the definition of a *hazard*? (FAA-H-8083-2)

A hazard is a present condition, event, object, or circumstance that could lead to or contribute to an unplanned or undesired event such as an accident.

10. Define the term *risk management*. (FAA-H-8083-9)

Risk management is a decision-making process designed to systematically identify hazards, assess the degree of risk, and determine the best course of action. It is a logical process of weighing the potential costs of risks against the possible benefits of allowing those risks to stand uncontrolled.

11. What is one method you can use to control and manage risk? (FAA-H-8083-2)

One way a pilot can limit exposure to risks is to set personal minimums for items in each risk category, using **PAVE**. These are limits unique to that individual pilot's current level of experience and proficiency:

Pilot—experience/recency (takeoffs/landings, hours in make/model), physical/mental condition (IMSAFE).

Aircraft—fuel reserves VFR day/night, aircraft performance (W&B, density altitude, etc.), aircraft equipment (avionics familiarity, charts, survival gear).

EnVironment—airport conditions (runway condition/length), weather (winds, ceilings, visibilities).

External pressures—allowance for delays, diversion, cancelation, alternate plans, personal equipment available for alternate plans (phone numbers, credit cards, medications).

12. Describe the 3P model used in ADM. (FAA-H-8083-2)

The Perceive, Process, Perform (3P) model for ADM offers a simple, practical, and systematic approach that can be used during all phases of flight. To use it, the pilot will:

Perceive the given set of circumstances for a flight; think through circumstances related to the: **Pilot, Aircraft, enVironment,** and

External pressures (**PAVE**). The fundamental question to ask is, "What could hurt me, my passengers, or my aircraft?"

Process by evaluating their impact on flight safety. Think through the Consequences of each hazard, Alternatives available, Reality of the situation, and External pressures (**CARE**) that might influence their analysis.

Perform by implementing the best course of action. Transfer (can the risk decision be transferred to someone else; can you consult someone?); Eliminate (is there a way to eliminate the hazard?); Accept (do the benefits of accepting risk outweigh the costs?); Mitigate (what can you do to reduce the risk?) (**TEAM**)

13. Explain how often a pilot should use the 3P model of ADM throughout a flight. (FAA-H-8083-9)

Once a pilot has completed the 3P decision process and selected a course of action, the process begins again because the circumstances brought about by the course of action require analysis. The decision-making process is a continuous loop of perceiving, processing, and performing.

14. Define the term *situational awareness*. (FAA-H-8083-25)

Situational awareness (SA) is the accurate perception and understanding of all the factors and conditions within the fundamental risk elements (pilot, aircraft, environment, external pressures) that affect safety before, during, and after the flight.

15. What are some of the elements inside and outside the aircraft that a pilot must consider to maintain situational awareness? (FAA-H-8083-9)

Inside the aircraft—the status of aircraft systems, pilot, and passengers.

Outside the aircraft—awareness of where the aircraft is in relation to terrain, traffic, weather, and airspace.

16. What are several factors that reduce situational awareness? (FAA-H-8083-15)

Factors that reduce SA include fatigue, distractions, unusual or unexpected events, complacency, high workload, unfamiliar situations, and inoperative equipment.

17. **What procedures can be used for maintaining situational awareness in technically advanced aircraft?** (FAA-H-8083-25)

   a. Perform verification checks of all programming prior to departure.

   b. Check the flight routing—ensure all routing matches the planned route of flight.

   c. Always verify waypoints.

   d. Make use of all onboard navigation equipment—use VOR to backup GPS, and vice versa.

   e. Match the use of the automated system with pilot proficiency—stay within personal limitations.

   f. Plan a realistic flight route to maintain situational awareness—ATC doesn't always give you direct routing.

   g. Be ready to verify computer data entries—incorrect keystrokes can lead to loss of situational awareness.

F. Adverse Weather

1. **When attempting to circumnavigate thunderstorms, what minimum distance is recommended?** (AIM 7-1-27)

   Thunderstorms identified as severe or displaying an intense radar echo should be avoided by at least 20 miles. This is especially true under the anvil of a large cumulonimbus.

2. **Can onboard datalink weather (FIS-B) be useful in navigating an aircraft safely around an area of thunderstorms?** (FAA-H-8083-28, AIM 7-1-9)

   Weather data linked from a ground weather surveillance radar system is not real-time information; it displays recent rather than current conditions. This data is typically updated every 5 minutes but can be as much as 15 minutes old by the time it displays in the flight deck. Therefore, FIS aviation weather products are not appropriate for tactical avoidance of severe weather such as negotiating a path through a hazardous weather area.

3. **In the event that you inadvertently enter a thunderstorm, what recommended procedures should you follow?** (AIM 7-1-27)

   a. Tighten your safety belt, put on your shoulder harness if you have one, and secure all loose objects.

   b. Keep your eyes on your instruments. Looking outside the flight deck can increase the danger of temporary blindness from lightning.

   c. Plan your course to take you through the storm in a minimum time and hold it. Don't turn back once you are in the thunderstorm. Remember that turning maneuvers increase stresses on the aircraft.

   d. To avoid the most critical icing, establish a penetration altitude below the freezing level or above the level of −15°C.

   e. Turn on pitot heat and carburetor or jet inlet heat. Icing can be rapid at any altitude and cause almost instantaneous power failure or loss of airspeed indication.

   f. Establish power settings for reduced turbulence penetration airspeed recommended in your aircraft manual. Reduced airspeed lessens the structural stresses on the aircraft.

   g. Turn up flight deck lights to highest intensity to lessen danger of temporary blindness from lightning.

   h. If using automatic pilot, disengage altitude hold mode and speed hold mode. The automatic altitude and speed controls will increase maneuvers of the aircraft, thus increasing structural stresses.

   i. Maintain a constant attitude; let the aircraft "ride the waves." Maneuvers to try to maintain constant altitude increase stresses on the aircraft.

4. **Describe the hazardous aircraft icing conditions a pilot may encounter in the following cloud types and conditions: stratus, cumulus, freezing rain, and freezing drizzle.** (AC 91-74)

   Stratus clouds—These form a stratified layer that may cover a wide area; the lifting processes that form them are usually gradual, so they rarely have exceptionally high liquid water content. Icing layers in stratus clouds with a vertical thickness in excess of 3,000 feet are rare, so either climbing or descending may be effective in exiting the icing conditions within the clouds.

Cumuliform clouds—Hazardous icing conditions can occur in cumulus clouds, which sometimes have very high liquid water content. It is not advisable to fly through a series of such clouds or to execute holds within them. However, because these clouds normally do not extend very far horizontally, any icing encountered in such a cloud may be of limited duration and it may be possible to deviate around the cloud.

Freezing rain—Freezing rain forms when rain becomes supercooled by falling through a subfreezing layer of air. It may be possible to exit the freezing rain by climbing into the warm layer.

Freezing drizzle—Because freezing drizzle often forms by the collision-coalescence process, the pilot should not assume that a warm layer of air exists above the aircraft. A pilot encountering freezing drizzle should exit the conditions as quickly as possible either vertically or horizontally. The three possible actions are to ascend to an altitude where the freezing drizzle event is less intense, to descend to an area of warmer air, or to make a level turn to emerge from the area of freezing drizzle.

5. What action is recommended if you inadvertently encounter icing conditions? (FAA-H-8083-15)

You should leave the area of visible moisture. This might mean descending to an altitude below the cloud bases, climbing to an altitude above the cloud tops, or turning to a different course. If this is not possible, then the pilot must move to an altitude where the temperature is above freezing. If you're going to climb, do so quickly; procrastination may leave you with too much ice. If you're going to descend, you must know the temperature of the air and the type of terrain below.

6. If an airplane has anti-icing and/or deicing equipment installed, can it be flown into icing conditions? (FAA-H-8083-3)

The presence of anti-icing and deicing equipment does not necessarily mean that an airplane is approved for flight in icing conditions. The AFM/POH, placards, and manufacturer should be consulted for specific determination of approvals and limitations.

7. **Your aircraft's induction system air filter has become blocked with ice. How will you know this condition has occurred, and does your aircraft have any protection against it?** (AC 20-113, FAA-H-8083-32)

   Induction icing is a type of icing that reduces the amount of air available for combustion. The most commonly found induction icing is carburetor icing. Typically, carburetor-equipped aircraft will have "carb heat" to manage this potential risk. In fuel-injected aircraft, no carburetor is present and therefore the risk is not present.

   In an aircraft equipped with a fixed-pitch propeller, a pilot may notice some loss of engine RPM or engine roughness as an indication that carburetor icing is developing. In an aircraft with a constant-speed propeller, a loss of manifold pressure would be a first indication.

8. **A pilot flying an aircraft certificated for flight in known icing (FIKI) should be aware of a phenomenon known as** *roll upset.* **What is roll upset?** (FAA-H-8083-15)

   Roll upset is an uncommanded and uncontrolled roll phenomenon associated with severe in-flight icing. It can occur without the usual symptoms of ice accumulation or a perceived aerodynamic stall. Pilots flying certificated FIKI aircraft should be aware that severe icing is a condition outside of the aircraft's certification icing envelope. The roll upset that occurs may be caused by airflow separation (aerodynamic stall), which induces self-deflection of the ailerons and loss of or degraded roll handling characteristics. The aileron deflection may be caused by ice accumulating in a sensitive area of the wing aft of the deicing boots.

9. **A pilot building up icing on an aircraft, even in an aircraft equipped with anti-icing or deicing, may experience precipitation static. What possible effects would a pilot expect if this was occurring?** (FAA-H-8083-16)

   Precipitation static, often referred to as P-static, occurs when accumulated static electricity is discharged from the extremities of the aircraft. This discharge has the potential to create problems for the instrument pilot. These problems range from the serious, such as erroneous magnetic compass readings and the complete loss of very high frequency (VHF) communications to the annoyance of high-pitched audio squealing and St. Elmo's fire.

Precipitation static is caused when an aircraft encounters airborne particles during flight (e.g., rain or snow) and develops a negative charge. It can also result from atmospheric electric fields in thunderstorm clouds. When a significant negative voltage level is reached, the aircraft discharges it, which can create electrical disturbances. This electrical discharge builds with time as the aircraft flies in precipitation. It is usually encountered in rain, but snow can cause the same effect. As the static buildup increases, the effectiveness of both communication and navigation systems decreases to the point of potential unusability.

10. What is the recommended recovery procedure for a roll upset? (AC 91-74)

a. Reduce the angle of attack by reducing aircraft pitch. If in a turn, roll wings level.

b. Set appropriate power and monitor the airspeed and angle of attack. A controlled descent is a vastly better alternative than an uncontrolled descent.

c. If flaps are extended, do not retract them unless you can determine that the upper surface of the airfoil is clear of ice, because retracting the flaps will increase the AOA at a given airspeed.

d. Verify that wing ice protection is functioning normally by visual observation of the left and right wing.

11. What is *structural icing*, and when is it likely to occur? (FAA-H-8083-15)

Structural icing refers to the accumulation of ice on the exterior of the aircraft, and it is broken down into three classifications: rime ice, clear ice, and mixed ice. For ice to form, there must be moisture present in the air, and the air must be cooled to a temperature of 0°C (32°F) or less. Aerodynamic cooling can lower the surface temperature of an airfoil and cause ice to form on the airframe even though the ambient temperature is slightly above freezing.

12. **What is the recommended procedure for removing ice from an aircraft equipped with a pneumatic deicing system?** (AFM, AC 91-74)

    The FAA recommends that the deicing system be activated at the first indication of icing. Because some residual ice continues to adhere between pneumatic boot system cycles, the wing is never entirely "clean." The amount of residual ice increases as airspeed or temperature decreases. At airspeeds typical of small airplanes, it may take many boot cycles to effectively shed the ice. It may appear that the boots are not having any effect at all until shedding occurs.

13. **After cruising above an overcast layer en route to your destination, you determine that weather reports and PIREPs at your destination now indicate that your descent will take you through clouds that contain ice. If you cannot divert to your alternate (low fuel), what can you do to prepare for a descent through icing conditions in a non-FIKI (flight in known icing) aircraft?** (FAA-H-8083-15, AFM)

    a. Advise ATC of your situation and declare an emergency.

    b. Apply carburetor heat, windshield heat, and pitot heat.

    c. Set the propeller to max RPM to prevent ice from forming on the propeller blades.

    d. Advise ATC that you would like to remain above the clouds for as long as possible. Ask for a descent at pilot's discretion.

    e. Expedite your descent through the clouds to minimize the aircraft's exposure to icing conditions.

    f. Delay flap and gear extension and maintain a clean configuration for as long as possible.

14. **During your initial climb away from the runway, you hear and see what appears to be small ice pellets hitting the aircraft. Are you in danger? What are ice pellets an indication of?** (AC 91-74)

    Ice pellets by themselves are not a hazard to the airframe with respect to icing, but a ground observation of ice pellets indicates freezing rain or supercooled large drops (SLD) aloft that would be extremely hazardous if encountered.

15. During your descent and while being vectored for an approach, you notice a trace amount of rime ice collecting on the wing's leading edges and struts. The ice is extremely light, and even though you are in a descent, your airspeed is decreasing towards stall speed. What could be the problem? (FAA-H-8083-25)

The pitot tube opening and drain hole are blocked. If the pitot tube ram air input plus the drain hole are blocked, the pressure is trapped in the system and the airspeed indicator will act like an altimeter as the aircraft climbs and descends. If the static port is not blocked, the airspeed indicator will show an increase in a climb and decrease in a descent. During level flight, airspeed indication will not change. Your pitot heat is either off or has failed.

16. If icing is inadvertently encountered, how would configuration for approach and landing be different? (AC 91-74)

a. Extension of landing gear may create excessive drag when coupled with ice. Flaps should be deployed in stages, carefully noting the aircraft's behavior at each stage.

b. If anomalies occur, it is best not to increase the amount of flaps and perhaps even to retract them depending on how much the aircraft is deviating from normal performance.

c. If landing with an accumulation of ice, use a higher approach speed.

d. During the landing flare, carry higher-than-normal power if there is ice on the airplane. Use a longer runway if available.

e. After touchdown, use brakes sparingly to prevent skidding. Be prepared for possible loss of directional control caused by ice buildup on landing gear.

G. Navigation Systems

1. Within what frequency range do VORs operate? (AIM 1-1-3)

VORs operate within the 108.0 to 117.95 MHz VHF band.

2. What restrictions are VORs subject to? (AIM 1-1-3)

VORs are subject to line-of-sight restrictions, and the range varies proportionally to the altitude of the receiving equipment.

3. **What is referred to when describing the VOR Minimum Operational Network (MON) with respect to IFR navigation?** (AIM 1-1-3)

As flight procedures and route structure based on VORs are gradually being replaced with Performance-Based Navigation (PBN) procedures, the FAA is removing selected VORs from service. PBN procedures are primarily enabled by GPS and its augmentation systems, collectively referred to as Global Navigation Satellite System (GNSS). Aircraft that carry DME/DME equipment can also use RNAV which provides a backup to continue flying PBN during a GNSS disruption. For those aircraft that do not carry DME/DME, the FAA is retaining a limited network of VORs, called the VOR Minimum Operational Network (VOR MON), to provide a basic conventional navigation service for operators to use if GNSS becomes unavailable. During a GNSS disruption, the MON will enable aircraft to navigate through the affected area or to a safe landing at a MON airport without reliance on GNSS. Navigation using the MON will not be as efficient as the new PBN route structure, but use of the MON will provide nearly continuous VOR signal coverage at 5,000 feet AGL across the NAS, outside of the Western U.S. Mountainous Area (WUSMA).

4. **What is meant when an airport is described as being a MON serviced airport?** (AIM 1-1-3)

A MON (Minimum Operational Network) serviced airport refers to an airport that is part of the FAA's Minimum Operational Network. The Minimum Operational Network is a concept used by the FAA to designate certain airports that play a crucial role in supporting the overall aviation infrastructure, especially in the event of a GPS (Global Positioning System) outage.

In the context of GPS outages, MON airports are equipped with alternative navigation aids to ensure continued safe and efficient air traffic operations. These airports have specific ground-based navigation equipment that can be utilized by pilots for navigation and instrument approaches when GPS signals are not available or compromised. This would additionally allow a pilot to make an instrument approach to such an airport without GPS or the need to have DME equipment. It does not imply that any particular type of approach will be available at MON airports. In most common instances, it will be a VOR, localizer, or ILS approach available at the airport that would not require use of GPS or DME services to complete the approach. It additionally does not imply that all of the approaches at the MON-designated airport will be usable in such a manner.

5. How can a pilot determine if an airport is a part of the MON network of airports that could be utilized in the event of a GPS outage? (USRGD)

A MON airport is designated on a low altitude enroute chart by having the letters "MON" above the airport information on the chart, as shown in the example below.

MON
SEATTLE
Boeing Fld/King Co Intl
(BFI) D
21 ∟ 100
(A) 127.75

6. What guarantee of coverage can a pilot rely upon for the VOR system in consideration of the Minimum Operational Network (MON)? (AIM 1-1-3)

The VOR MON will ensure that regardless of an aircraft's position in the contiguous United States (CONUS), a MON airport (equipped with legacy ILS or VOR approaches) will be within 100 nautical miles. These airports are referred to as "MON airports" and will have an ILS approach or a VOR approach if an ILS is not available. VORs to support these approaches will be retained in the VOR MON. MON airports are charted on low altitude en route charts and are contained in the *Chart Supplement* and other appropriate publications.

7. What are the normal usable distances for the various classes of VOR stations? (AIM 1-1-8)

A NAVAID will have service volume restrictions if it does not conform to signal strength and course quality standards throughout the published SSV. Service volume restrictions are first published in Notices to Air Missions (NOTAMs) and then with the alphabetical listing of the NAVAIDs in the *Chart Supplement*. Service volume restrictions do not generally apply to published instrument procedures or routes unless published in NOTAMs for the affected instrument procedure or route.

(continued)

VOR Standard Service Volumes

SSV Class Designator	Altitude and Range Boundaries
T Terminal	From 1,000 feet above the transmitter height (ATH) up to and including 12,000 feet ATH at radial distances out to 25 NM.
L Low-altitude	From 1,000 feet ATH up to and including 18,000 feet ATH at radial distances out to 40 NM.
H High-altitude	From 1,000 feet ATH up to and including 14,500 feet ATH at radial distances out to 40 NM. From 14,500 ATH up to and including 60,000 feet at radial distances out to 100 NM. From 18,000 feet ATH up to and including 45,000 feet ATH at radial distances out to 130 NM.
VL VOR Low	From 1,000 feet ATH up to but not including 5,000 feet ATH at radial distances out to 40 NM. From 5,000 feet ATH up to but not including 18,000 feet ATH at radial distances out to 70 NM.
VH VOR High	From 1,000 feet ATH up to but not including 5,000 feet ATH at radial distances out to 40 NM. From 5,000 feet ATH up to but not including 14,500 feet ATH at radial distances out to 70 NM. From 14,500 ATH up to and including 60,000 feet at radial distances out to 100 NM. From 18,000 feet ATH up to and including 45,000 feet ATH at radial distances out to 130 NM.
DL DME Low	For altitudes up to 12,900 feet ATH at a radial distance corresponding to the LOS to the NAVAID. From 12,900 feet ATH up to but not including 18,000 feet ATH at radial distances out to 130 NM.
DH DME High	For altitudes up to 12,900 feet ATH at a radial distance corresponding to the LOS to the NAVAID. From 12,900 ATH up to and including 60,000 feet at radial distances out to 100 NM. From 12,900 feet ATH up to and including 45,000 feet ATH at radial distances out to 130 NM.

8. **What is the meaning of a single coded identification received only once every 30 seconds from a VORTAC station?** (AIM 1-1-7, 1-1-11)

The DME component is operative; the VOR component is inoperative. It is important to recognize which identifier is retained for the operative facility. A single coded identifier with a repeat interval every 30 seconds indicates DME is operative. If no identification is received, the facility has been taken off the air for tune-up or repair, even though intermittent or constant signals are received.

9. **Will all VOR stations have the capability of providing distance information to aircraft equipped with DME?** (AIM 1-1-7)

No, aircraft receiving equipment that provides for automatic DME selection assures reception of azimuth and distance information from a common source, only when designated VOR/DME, VORTAC, ILS/DME, and LOC/DME are selected.

10. **For IFR operations off established airways, the "Route of Flight" portion of an IFR flight plan should list VOR navigational aids that are no further than what distance from each other?** (FAA-H-8083-16)

To facilitate use of VOR, VORTAC, or TACAN aids, consistent with their operational service volume limits, pilot use of such aids for defining a direct route of flight in controlled airspace should not exceed the following:

a. Below 18,000 feet MSL, use aids not more than 80 NM apart.

b. Between 14,500 feet MSL and 17,999 feet MSL in the conterminous U.S., H (high-altitude service volume) facilities not more than 200 NM apart may be used.

11. **What angular deviation from a VOR course is represented by half-scale deflection of the CDI?** (FAA-H-8083-15)

Full scale deflection = 10°; therefore, half-scale deflection = 5°.

12. What are the essential components of all VOR indicator instruments? (FAA-H-8083-15)

   a. Omnibearing selector (OBS)

   b. Course deviation indicator (CDI)

   c. TO/FROM indicator

   d. Flags or other signal strength indicators

13. What is reverse sensing? (FAA-H-8083-15)

Reverse sensing is when the VOR needle indicates the reverse of normal operation. This occurs when the aircraft is headed toward the station with a FROM indication or when the aircraft is headed away from the station with a TO indication. Also, unless the aircraft has reverse sensing capability and it is in use, when flying inbound on the back course or outbound on the front course of an ILS, reverse sensing will occur.

14. What is the procedure for determining an intercept angle when intercepting a VOR radial? (FAA-H-8083-15)

   a. Turn to a heading to parallel the desired course, in the same direction as the course to be flown.

   b. Determine the difference between the radial to be intercepted and the radial on which you are located.

   c. Double the difference to determine the interception angle, which will not be less than 20° nor greater than 90°.

   d. Rotate the OBS to the desired radial or inbound course.

   e. Turn to the interception heading.

   f. Hold this heading constant until the CDI centers, which indicates the aircraft is on course. (With practice in judging the varying rates of closure with the course centerline, you learn to lead the turn to prevent overshooting the course.)

   g. Turn to the MH corresponding to the selected course and follow tracking procedures inbound or outbound.

Note: Steps a. through c. may be omitted if you turn directly to intercept the course without initially turning to parallel the desired course.

15. What degree of accuracy can be expected in VOR navigation? (AIM 1-1-3)

VOR navigation is accurate to ±1°.

16. Explain the function of NDB and ADF equipment. (FAA-H-8083-15)

The non-directional radio beacon (NDB) is a ground-based radio transmitter that transmits radio energy in all directions. NDBs operate within the low-to-medium frequency band, 190 to 535 kHz. The automatic direction finder (ADF) receiver in the airplane determines the bearing from the aircraft to the transmitting station. The ADF needle points to the NDB ground station to determine the relative bearing (RB) to the transmitting station. It is the number of degrees measured clockwise between the aircraft's heading and the direction from which the bearing is taken.

17. When a radio beacon is used in conjunction with an ILS marker beacon, what is it called? (AIM 1-1-2)

It is called a compass locator.

18. There are four types of NDB facilities in use. What are they and what are their effective ranges? (AIM 1-1-8)

HH facilities—2,000 watts; 75 NM
H facilities—50 to 1,999 watts; 50 NM
MH facilities—less than 50 watts; 25 NM
ILS compass locator—less than 25 watts; 15 NM

19. How do you find an ADF magnetic bearing? (FAA-H-8083-15)

A magnetic bearing is the direction of an imaginary line from the aircraft to the station or the station to the aircraft referenced to magnetic north. To determine, use this formula:

$MH + RB = MB$

(Magnetic heading + relative bearing = magnetic bearing)

If the sum is more than 360, subtract 360 to get the magnetic bearing to the station. The reciprocal of this number is the magnetic bearing from the station.

20. What is an HSI? (FAA-H-8083-15)

The horizontal situation indicator (HSI) is a direction indicator that uses the output from a flux valve to drive the compass card. The HSI combines the magnetic compass with navigation signals/ glideslope and gives the pilot an indication of the location of the aircraft with relationship to the chosen course or radial. The aircraft magnetic heading is displayed on the compass card under the lubber line and the course select pointer shows the course selected and its reciprocal. The course deviation bar operates with a VOR/Localizer (VOR/LOC) or GPS navigation receiver to indicate left or right deviations from the course selected with the course select pointer. The desired course is selected by rotating the course select pointer in relation to the compass card by means of the course select knob. The HSI has a fixed aircraft symbol, and the course deviation bar displays the aircraft's position relative to the selected course.

21. If a pilot is flying a back course localizer or ILS approach using an HSI, will reverse sensing be a factor?

An aircraft equipped with an HSI can compensate for reverse sensing by "tuning the needle to the outbound course" and "flying the tail" if they set it up correctly. Most digital HSI indications are capable of compensating for reverse sensing. Understand what is in your aircraft so that if you are flying a back course approach or purposefully reverse sensing on a radial, you turn the correct way for how you have the equipment set up and what it is depicting.

22. What is DME? (AIM 1-1-7)

DME stands for distance measuring equipment. Aircraft equipped with DME are provided with distance and ground speed information when receiving a VORTAC or TACAN facility. In the operation of DME, paired pulses at a specific spacing are sent out from the aircraft and are received at the ground station. The ground station then transmits paired pulses back to the aircraft at the same pulse spacing but on a different frequency. The time required for the round trip of this signal exchange is measured in the airborne DME unit and is translated into distance and ground speed. Reliable signals may be received at distances up to 199 NM at line-of-sight altitude. DME operates on frequencies in the UHF spectrum from 960 MHz to 1215 MHz. Distance information is slant-range distance, not horizontal.

23. When is DME equipment required? (14 CFR 91.205)

If VOR navigational equipment is required for flight at and above FL240, the aircraft must be equipped with approved DME or a suitable RNAV system. If the DME or RNAV system fails at or above FL240, the pilot-in-command shall notify ATC immediately, and then may continue operations to the next airport of intended landing where repairs or equipment replacement can be done.

24. As a rule-of-thumb, to minimize DME slant-range error, how far from the facility should you be to consider the reading accurate? (FAA-H-8083-15)

Slant-range error will be at a minimum if the aircraft is one or more miles from the facility for each 1,000 feet of altitude above the facility.

25. What is RNAV? (P/CG)

Area navigation (RNAV) is a method of navigation that permits aircraft operation on any desired flight path within the coverage of ground- or space-based navigation aids or within the limits of the capability of self-contained aids, or a combination of these.

26. Give a brief description of the Global Positioning System. (AIM 1-1-17)

GPS is a satellite-based radio navigation system that broadcasts a signal used by receivers to determine precise position anywhere in the world. The receiver tracks multiple satellites and determines a pseudo-range measurement that is then used to determine user location.

27. How many satellites does a GPS receiver require to compute its position? (FAA-H-8083-15, AIM 1-1-17)

The GPS constellation of 24 satellites is designed so that a minimum of five satellites are always observable by a user anywhere on earth. The receiver uses data from a minimum of four satellites above the mask angle (the lowest angle above the horizon at which it can use a satellite).

3 satellites—yields a latitude and longitude position only (2D).
4 satellites—yields latitude, longitude, and altitude position (3D).
5 satellites—3D and RAIM.
6 satellites—3D and RAIM isolates corrupt signal and removes
          from navigation solution.

28. **What are the various Technical Standard Orders that apply to GPS navigation equipment?** (AC 90-100)

    - TSO-C129—Airborne Supplemental Navigation Equipment Using the Global Positioning System (GPS) (non-WAAS)
    - TSO-C196—Airborne Supplemental Navigation Sensors for GPS Equipment Using Aircraft-Based Augmentation (non-WAAS)
    - TSO-C145—Airborne Navigation Sensors Using the Global Positioning System Augmented by the Wide Area Augmentation System
    - TSO-C146—Stand-Alone Airborne Navigation Equipment Using the Global Positioning System Augmented by the Wide Area Augmentation System

29. **What is WAAS?** (AIM 1-1-18)

    The Wide Area Augmentation System (WAAS) is a satellite navigation system consisting of the equipment and software that augments the GPS Standard Positioning Service (SPS). The WAAS provides enhanced integrity, accuracy, availability, and continuity over and above GPS SPS. The differential correction function provides improved accuracy required for precision approach.

30. **Briefly describe the operation of WAAS.** (FAA-H-8083-31)

    WAAS ground stations receive GPS signals and forward position errors to two master ground stations. Time and location information is analyzed, and correction instructions are sent to communication satellites in geostationary orbit over the National Airspace System (NAS). The satellites broadcast GPS-like signals that WAAS-enabled GPS receivers use to correct position information received from GPS satellites. A WAAS-enabled GPS receiver (TSO-C145A or TSO-146A) is required to use the wide area augmentation system.

31. **In what ways can RNAV equipment be used as a substitute means of navigation guidance?** (AIM 1-2-3)

    Suitable RNAV Systems (TSO-C129/-C196/-C145/-C146) may be used in the following ways:

    a. To determine aircraft position relative to, or distance from, a VOR, TACAN, NDB, compass locator, DME fix; or a named fix defined by a VOR radial, TACAN course, NDB bearing, or compass locator bearing intersecting a VOR or localizer course.

b. Navigate to or from a VOR, TACAN, NDB, or compass locator.

c. Hold over a VOR, TACAN, NDB, compass locator, or DME fix.

d. Fly an arc based upon DME.

Note: These operations are allowable even when a facility is identified as required on a procedure (for example, "Note ADF required").

32. What are some examples of operations where RNAV equipment cannot be used as a substitute means of navigation? (AIM 1-2-3)

a. Lateral navigation on localizer-based courses (including localizer back-course guidance) without reference to raw localizer data.

b. Procedures that are identified as not authorized ("NA") without exception by a NOTAM.

c. Pilots may not substitute for the NAVAID (for example, a VOR or NDB) providing lateral guidance for the final approach segment. This restriction does not refer to instrument approach procedures with "or GPS" in the title when using GPS or WAAS.

33. When using RNAV equipment for navigation, what is the difference between the terms *Track (TRK)* and *Desired Track (DTK)*? (FAA-H-8083-16, P/CG)

Track—The actual flight path of an aircraft over the surface of the earth. The track, which is the result of aircraft heading and winds, tells you which direction the aircraft is actually flying. Winds make it likely that the track and heading will be different.

Desired Track—The planned or intended track between two waypoints. Desired track is measured in degrees from either magnetic or true north. The instantaneous angle may change from point to point along the great circle track between waypoints. The desired track is the intended course for the active leg in the programmed flight plan.

34. Why is there a difference between the distance information provided by a GPS receiver and the distance information provided by conventional DME equipment? (AIM 1-1-17)

Variations in distances will occur since GPS distance-to-waypoint values are along-track distances (ATD) computed to the next waypoint, and the DME values published on underlying procedures are slant-range distances measured to the station. This difference increases with aircraft altitude and proximity to the NAVAID.

35. When navigating with GPS equipment, explain the CDI scaling changes (sensitivity) that occur for the appropriate route segment and phase of flight. (AIM 1-1-17)

Departures and DPs (Terminal mode)	CDI sensitivity = ±1 NM
More than 30 NM from the destination	CDI sensitivity = ±5 NM (±2 NM WAAS)
Within 30 NM from destination (Terminal mode)	CDI sensitivity = ±1 NM
Within 2 NM from FAWP (Approach mode armed)	CDI sensitivity = ±1 NM to ±0.3 NM at the FAWP
Missed approach segment	CDI sensitivity = ±0.3 NM to ±1 NM

Note: Be familiar with the distance and approach parameters that change the CDI scaling for your aircraft's class of equipment.

36. What is OBS or non-sequencing mode? (FAA-H-8083-16)

OBS or non-sequencing mode is a FMS/RNAV navigation mode that does not automatically sequence between waypoints in the programmed route. The non-sequencing mode maintains the current active waypoint indefinitely and allows the pilot to specify desired track to or from that waypoint.

37. What is the purpose of baro-aiding? (AIM 1-1-17)

Baro-aiding is a method of augmenting the GPS integrity solution by using a non-satellite input source (aircraft static system) to provide a vertical reference. GPS-derived altitude should not be relied upon to determine aircraft altitude since the vertical error can be quite large and no integrity is provided. To ensure that baro-aiding is available, the current altimeter setting must be entered into the receiver. Baro-aiding satisfies the RAIM requirement in lieu of a fifth satellite.

38. Some approaches contain RNP in the approach title, such as "RNAV (RNP) Rwy 17." What does this mean?
(FAA-H-8083-15, AIM 1-2-2)

RNP is RNAV with the added requirement for onboard performance monitoring and alerting (OBPMA). RNP is also a statement of navigation performance necessary for operation within a defined airspace. A critical component of RNP is the ability of the aircraft navigation system to monitor its achieved navigation performance, and to identify for the pilot whether the operational requirement is or is not being met during an operation. The RNP capability of an aircraft will vary depending upon the aircraft equipment and the navigation infrastructure. For example, an aircraft may be equipped and certified for RNP 1.0 but may not be capable of RNP 1.0 operations due to limited NAVAID coverage. RNP levels are actual distances from the centerline of the flightpath, which must be maintained for aircraft and obstacle separation. The U.S. currently supports three standard RNP levels: RNP 0.3—Approach; RNP 1.0—Departure, Terminal; RNP 2.0—En route.

39. What are the two types of ADS-B equipment?
(AC 90-114)

ADS-B Out, or Automatic Dependent Surveillance–Broadcast Out, automatically broadcasts the aircraft's GPS position, altitude, velocity, and other information out to ATC ground-based surveillance stations as well as directly to other aircraft. It is required in all airspace where transponders are required.

ADS-B In, or Automatic Dependent Surveillance–Broadcast In, is the receipt, processing, and display of ADS-B transmissions. ADS-B In capability is necessary to receive ADS-B traffic and broadcast services (e.g., Flight Information Service–Broadcast [FIS-B] and Traffic Information Service–Broadcast [TIS-B]).

H. Airway Route System

1. **The FAA has established three fixed route systems for air navigation purposes. What are these?** (AIM 5-3-4)

   Three fixed route systems are established for air navigation purposes. They are the Federal airway system (consisting of VOR and L/MF routes), the jet route system, and the RNAV route system.

2. **What are the designated altitudes for the airways in the VOR and L/MF Airway System?** (AIM 5-3-4)

   The VOR and L/MF Airway System consists of airways designated from 1,200 feet above the surface (or in some instances higher) up to but not including 18,000 feet MSL. These airways are depicted on enroute low altitude charts.

3. **What are the lateral limits of low altitude federal airways?** (FAA-H-8083-15)

   Each federal airway includes the airspace within parallel boundary lines 4 NM each side of the centerline.

4. **When an airway is denoted in blue and has a MEA with a "-G" after it, what is being depicted?** (AIM 5-3-4)

   Airways that have altitudes so depicted are below the minimum reception altitude (MRA) of the land-based navigation facility defining the route segment, and guarantee standard en route obstacle clearance and two-way communications. They are airways published intended to be used by suitable GPS-based navigation systems.

5. **How are airways and route systems depicted on enroute low altitude charts?** (AIM 5-3-4)

   VHF/UHF data is depicted in black. LF/MF data is depicted in brown.5 RNAV route data is depicted in blue.

   Note: Segments of VOR airways in Alaska are based on L/MF navigation aids and charted in brown instead of black on en route charts.

6. What is the purpose of magnetic reference bearings found on IFR enroute low/high altitude charts? (AIM 5-3-4)

Magnetic Reference Bearing (MRB) is the published bearing between two waypoints on an RNAV/GPS/GNSS route. The MRB is calculated by applying magnetic variation at the waypoint to the calculated true course between two waypoints. The MRB enhances situational awareness by indicating a reference bearing (no-wind heading) that a pilot should see on the compass/HSI/ RMI, etc., when turning prior to/over a waypoint en route to another waypoint. Pilots should use this bearing as a reference only, because their RNAV/GPS/GNSS navigation system will fly the true course between the waypoints.

7. What is a changeover point? (AIM 5-3-6)

It is a point along the route or airway segment between two adjacent navigational facilities or waypoints where changeover in navigational guidance should occur.

8. Why are changeover points established? (AIM 5-3-6)

Changeover points (COPs) are prescribed for Federal airways, jet routes, area navigation routes, or other direct routes for which an MEA is designated under 14 CFR Part 95. The COP is a point along the route or airway segment between two adjacent navigation facilities or waypoints where changeover in navigation guidance should occur. At this point, the pilot should change navigation receiver frequency from the station behind the aircraft to the station ahead.

The COP is normally located midway between the navigation facilities for straight route segments, or at the intersection of radials or courses forming a dogleg in the case of dogleg route segments. When the COP is not located at the midway point, aeronautical charts will depict the COP location and give the mileage to the radio aids.

COPs are established for the purpose of preventing loss of navigation guidance, to prevent frequency interference from other facilities, and to prevent use of different facilities by different aircraft in the same airspace. Pilots are urged to observe COPs to the fullest extent.

9. What is a mileage breakdown point? (FAA-H-8083-15)

Occasionally an "x" will appear at a separated segment of an airway that is not an intersection. The "x" is a mileage breakdown or computer navigation fix and indicates a course change.

10. What is a waypoint? (P/CG)

A waypoint is a predetermined geographical position used for route/instrument approach definition, progress reports, published VFR routes, visual reporting points, or points for transitioning and/or circumnavigating controlled and/or special use airspace. A waypoint is defined relative to a VORTAC station or in terms of latitude/longitude coordinates.

11. What is tower enroute control service? (FAA-H-8083-15)

At many locations, instrument flights can be conducted entirely in terminal airspace. These tower enroute control (TEC) routes are generally for aircraft operating below 10,000 feet, and they can be found in the *Chart Supplement*. Pilots desiring to use TEC should include that designation in the remarks section of the flight plan.

12. Are the courses depicted on an enroute low altitude chart magnetic or true courses? (FAA-H-8083-15)

They are magnetic courses.

13. Describe the climb procedure when approaching a fix beyond which a higher MEA exists. (14 CFR 91.177)

The climb to a higher minimum IFR altitude shall begin immediately after passing the point beyond which that minimum altitude applies, except that when ground obstructions intervene, the point beyond which that higher minimum altitude applies shall be crossed at or above the applicable MCA.

14. Describe the climb procedure when approaching a fix at which a MCA exists. (FAA-H-8083-15)

A pilot should initiate a climb so the MCA is reached by the time the intersection is crossed. An MCA will be charted when a higher MEA route segment is approached. The MCA is usually indicated when you are approaching steeply rising terrain, and obstacle clearance and/or signal reception is compromised.

15. What requirement must be met before ATC will allow an aircraft to operate on an unpublished RNAV route? (AIM 5-3-4)

Unpublished RNAV routes are direct routes, based on area navigation capability between waypoints defined in terms of latitude/longitude coordinates, degree-distance fixes, or offsets from established routes/airways at a specified distance and direction. Radar monitoring by ATC is required on all unpublished RNAV routes, except for GNSS-equipped aircraft cleared via filed published waypoints recallable from the aircraft's navigation database.

16. What are "T," "Q," and "Y" routes? (AIM 5-3-4)

These are published RNAV routes that can be flight-planned for use by aircraft with RNAV capability. They are depicted in blue on aeronautical charts and are identified by the letter Q, T, or Y followed by the airway number (e.g., Q13, T205, and Y280). They provide more direct routing for IFR aircraft and enhance system safety and efficiency.

T-routes—T-routes are available for use by GPS or GPS/WAAS-equipped aircraft from 1,200 feet above the surface (or in some instances higher) up to but not including 18,000 feet MSL. T-routes are depicted on enroute low altitude charts.

Q-routes—Q-routes are available for use by RNAV-equipped aircraft between 18,000 feet MSL and FL450 inclusive. Q-routes are depicted on enroute high altitude charts.

Y-routes—Y-routes generally run in U.S. offshore airspace; however, operators can find some Y-routes over southern Florida. Pilots must use GPS for navigation and meet RNAV 2 performance requirements for all flights on Y-routes.

17. On IFR enroute charts, what does the "MON" designator displayed above the airport name indicate? (USRGD, AIM 1-1-3)

It means that the airport is part of the VOR Minimum Operational Network (MON). The intent of the MON designation is to alert pilots, in the event of a GPS outage, of those airports that have retained ILS and VOR instrument approach procedures for safe recovery during such an outage. The VOR MON includes the minimum number of geographically situated VORs in the contiguous United States (CONUS) necessary to provide coverage at and above 5,000 feet AGL.

18. For the following terms, identify the symbols which correspond to them on enroute low altitude charts. (USRGD)

(These symbols might not all be on your enroute low altitude chart.)

VOR/DME	⬡
TACAN	▽
VOR	⬡
VORTAC	⬟
RNAV waypoint compulsory position point	◆ NAMEE *N00°00.00'* *W00°00.00'*
RNAV waypoint noncompulsory position point	◇ NAMEE *N00°00.00'* *W00°00.00'*
NDB	(Brown)　　(Blue)　　Brown, blue box) ⊚　　⊚　　⊚
Commercial broadcast station	⊙　WKBW 　　1520
Compass locator frequency	***NAME*** **NAM** ⸬⸬ **000** **DME Chan 00**
Localizer facility information box	**NAME** NAM ⸬⸬ 000.0(T) **DME Chan 00** *MN* ⸗ *000*
VORTAC facility information box	LEXINGTON 112.6 HYK 73 ⸬⸬− *N37°57.98' W84°28.35'* ⌐ LOUISVILLE ⌐

Controlling FSS	123.6 122.6 122.1 R **FAYETTEVILLE FYV**	122.1 R WASHINGTON
Remote air/ground communications with ARTCC	NAME Name 134.3 269.5
Airport with a published instrument approach	**AIRPORT DATA** Airports/Seaplane bases shown in BLUE and GREEN have an approved Low Altitude Instrument Approach Procedure published. Those in BLUE have an approved DOD Low Altitude Instrument Approach Procedure and/or DOD RADAR MINIMA published in DOD FLIPS or Alaska Terminal. Airports/Seaplane bases shown in BROWN do not have a published Instrument Approach Procedure.
Airport without a published instrument approach	*(see above)*
Compass rose	0 ... 27 ... 9 ... 18
ATC compulsory reporting point	▲ ▲ **ALANA ATTIC**
ATC noncompulsory reporting point	**ALANA ATTIC** △ △
DME fix distance when not obvious	15 →
DME fix distance when the same as route miles	→
VOR changeover point	42 ⌐ 26
Mileage break at an airway course change, intersection, or breakdown point	⬡ —— 32 —— △/x —— 25 —— ⬡
Mileage between VORs or a VOR and compulsory reporting point	123 123
Mileage breakdown or computer navigation fix	X X
CNF with no ATC function	(RCRCP)

Victor airway	**V10**
ARTCC boundary, controlling ARTCC	NEW YORK ⌇⌇⌇⌇⌇⌇ WASHINGTON
MOCA All altitudes are MSL unless otherwise noted.	LOW ALTITUDE 5500 *3500 **V4** ← MOCA → 5500 *3500 **A0** 7000G *6300 **T266** 112
MEA All altitudes are MSL unless otherwise noted.	LOW ALTITUDE 3500 3000G **V4** RNAV/GPS MEA 3500 **A0** 5500→ ←3500 **V4** Directional MEA 5500→ ←3500 **A0**
Off Route Obstruction Clearance Altitude (OROCA)	LOW ALTITUDE 12^5 Example: 12,500 feet
Change in MEA or MOCA at other than NAVAIDs	⊣ ⊢
Minimum crossing altitude	**MCA V6 4000S** 🅧
Minimum reception altitude	**MRA 9000** 🆁
Maximum authorized altitude	MAA-15500 **V30** MAA-15500 (R5)
Magnetic variation	7°E

Special-use airspace	*(see below)*

AIRSPACE INFORMATION

SPECIAL USE AIRSPACE

Only the airspace effective below 18,000 feet MSL is shown.

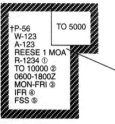

†P-56   TO 5000
W-123
A-123
REESE 1 MOA
R-1234 ①
TO 10000 ②
0600-1800Z
MON-FRI ③
IFR ④
FSS ⑤

A - Alert Area
P - Prohibited Area
R - Restricted Area
W - Warning Area
D - Danger Area (Canada)

Line delimits altitude separation within same Special Use Airspace Area

BROWN MOA
8000 AND ABOVE
INTERMITTENT
BY NOTAM
KANSAS CITY CENTER/FSS

Special Air Traffic Rules

MOA - Military Operations Area

†Indicates complete information in tabulation on front panel

SPECIAL USE AIRSPACE WILL INCLUDE:

① AREA IDENTIFICATION: In Canada area ident is preceded by the letters CY (CANADA) followed by a number (PROVINCE).

② EFFECTIVE ALTITUDE CEILINGS ARE SHOWN UP TO BUT NOT INCLUDING 18,000'. WHEN THE AIRSPACE ENCOMPASSES ALL ALTITUDES IN THE LOW ALTITUDE STRUCTURE, NO ALTITUDE WILL BE SHOWN. THE WORK "TO" (AN ALTITUDE) MEANS "TO AND INCLUDING" (THAT ALTITUDE).

③ OPERATING TIME: When continuous no time is shown.
Days: Sunrise to Sunset.
Nights: Sunset to Sunrise.
Hours: Given in UTC; e.g., 0600-1300Z
Mon-Fri: Indicates area does not exist on Sat. or Sun.

1 Mar.-15 June: Indicates area in use only through dates given. By NOTAM: Area activated by NOTAM. Days are local.

④ Weather Conditions during which the area is in operation. When continuous no weather is shown.
VFR: Used only during VFR conditions. IFR: Used only during IFR conditions.

⑤ Voice Call of Controlling Agency for enroute clearance through area. No A/G unless indicated.

Class B airspace	
Class C airspace	
Class E airspace	**AIRSPACE INFORMATION** **Open area (white) indicates controlled airspace (Class E) unless otherwise indicated.** **All airspace 14,500' and above is controlled (Class E).**

Class G airspace	Shaded area (brown) indicates uncontrolled airspace below 14,500' (Class G).
Mode C area	MODE C 30 NM (a solid blue outline)
ARTCC boundaries	⎍⎍⎍⎍⎍⎍⎍
ARTCC Remoted VHF/ UHF frequency site	NAME Name 000.0 000.0
Air Defense Identification Zone (ADIZ)	....
ASOS/AWOS	**A**
RNAV Q and T routes	**Q00** **T000** (blue)
TWEB (Alaska only)	**T**
ILS localizer course with ATC function	◁▰▰▰▰▰▰▰▰▰▰▱
ATIS	(Airport Name) D 280 L* 43s Automatic Terminal ——→ (A) *109.8 Information Service
Pilot controlled lighting	Ⓛ
Special VFR not authorized	**No SVFR**

Exam Tip: Your ability to interpret the vast amount of information available on IFR enroute, DP and STAR charts, approach charts, and airport diagrams *will* be evaluated. Prior to the checkride, obtain all of the necessary charts, chart supplements, and diagrams and verify that everything is current. Study the chart legends and symbology thoroughly prior to your exam.

I. Airspace

1. What is Class A airspace? (AIM 3-2-2)

Generally, that airspace from 18,000 feet MSL up to and including FL600, including airspace overlying the waters within 12 nautical miles off the coast of the 48 contiguous states and Alaska; and designated international airspace beyond 12 nautical miles off the coast of the 48 contiguous states and Alaska within areas of domestic radio navigational signal or ATC radar coverage, and within which domestic procedures are applied.

2. What is Class B airspace? (AIM 3-2-3)

Generally, that airspace from the surface to 10,000 feet MSL surrounding the nation's busiest airports in terms of IFR operations or passenger enplanements. The configuration of each Class B airspace area is individually tailored and consists of a surface area and two or more layers (some resemble an upside-down wedding cake) and is designated to contain all published instrument procedures once an aircraft enters the airspace. An ATC clearance is required for all aircraft to operate in the area, and all aircraft cleared as such receive separation services within the airspace. The visibility and cloud clearance requirement for VFR operations is 3 statute miles visibility and clear of clouds.

3. What is Class C airspace? (AIM 3-2-4)

Generally, that airspace from the surface to 4,000 feet above the airport elevation (charted in MSL) surrounding airports that have an operational control tower, are serviced by a radar approach control, and that have a certain number of IFR operations or passenger enplanements. Although the configuration of each Class C airspace area is individually tailored, the airspace usually consists of a 5 NM radius core surface area that extends from the surface up to 4,000 feet above the airport elevation, and a 10 NM radius shelf area that extends from 1,200 feet to 4,000 feet above the airport elevation.

4. What is Class D airspace? (AIM 3-2-5)

Generally, that airspace from the surface to 2,500 feet above the airport elevation (charted in MSL) surrounding airports that have an operational control tower. The configuration of each Class D airspace area is individually tailored, and when instrument procedures are published, the airspace will usually be designed to contain those procedures.

5. **When a control tower located at an airport within Class D airspace ceases operation for the day, what happens to the lower limit of the controlled airspace?** (AIM 3-2-5)

   During the hours the tower is not in operation, Class E surface area rules, or a combination of Class E rules to 700 feet AGL and Class G rules to the surface, will become applicable. Check the *Chart Supplement* for specifics.

6. **What is the definition of Class E (controlled) airspace?** (P/CG)

   Controlled airspace is airspace of defined dimensions within which air traffic control service is provided to IFR flights and to VFR flights in accordance with the airspace classification. Controlled airspace is a generic term that covers Class A, Class B, Class C, Class D, and Class E airspace.

7. **What is the floor of Class E airspace when designated in conjunction with an airport with an approved IAP?** (14 CFR 71.71)

   700 feet AGL.

8. **What is the floor of Class E airspace when designated in conjunction with a federal airway?** (14 CFR 71.71)

   1,200 feet AGL.

9. **How can a pilot identify where Class E airspace begins at the surface?** (14 CFR 71.71)

   At some airports, Class E airspace begins at the surface. This will be depicted by a dashed magenta circle on a VFR sectional chart.

10. **Explain the purpose of Class E transition areas.** (AIM 3-2-6)

    Class E transition areas extend upward from either 700 feet AGL (magenta vignette) or 1,200 feet AGL (blue vignette) and are designated for airports with an approved instrument procedure. Class E transition areas exist to help separate (via cloud clearance) arriving and departing IFR traffic from VFR aircraft operating in the vicinity.

    Note: Do not confuse the 700-foot and 1,200-foot Class E transition areas with surface areas or surface area extensions.

11. What is Class G airspace? (AIM 3-3-1)

Class G airspace (uncontrolled) is that portion of airspace that has not been designated as Class A, Class B, Class C, Class D, or Class E airspace.

12. What are the vertical limits of Class G airspace? (FAA-H-8083-25)

Class G airspace begins at the surface and continues up to but not including the overlying controlled airspace, or 14,500 MSL, or where Class E airspace begins, whichever occurs first.

Exam Tip: Be prepared to explain the type of airspace your planned route of flight will take you through from departure to arrival at your destination. Even though you are flying under IFR, you should know the required visibility, cloud clearance, and communication and equipment requirements at any point and altitude along your route of flight. Also, expect the "what if you're here" questions concerning VFR-on-top clearances, visual and contact approach clearances, etc.

J. Special Use Airspace

1. Define the following types of airspace: Prohibited Area, Restricted Area, Military Operations Area, Warning Area, Alert Area, Controlled Firing Area, National Security Areas, Temporary Flight Restrictions, and Special Flight Rules Area. (AIM 3-4-2 through 3-4-8, 3-5-3, 3-5-7)

Prohibited Area—For security or other reasons, aircraft flight is prohibited.

Restricted Area—Contains unusual, often invisible hazards to aircraft, flights must have permission from the controlling agency, if VFR. IFR flights will be cleared through or vectored around it.

Military Operations Area—MOAs consist of airspace of defined vertical and lateral limits established for the purpose of separating certain military training activities from IFR traffic. Permission is not required for VFR flights, but extreme caution should be exercised. IFR flights will be cleared through or vectored around it.

Warning Area—Airspace of defined dimensions extending from 3 nautical miles outward from the coast of the U.S. containing activity that may be hazardous to nonparticipating aircraft. A warning area may be located over domestic or international waters or both. Permission is not required but a flight plan is advised.

Alert Area—Depicted on aeronautical charts to inform nonparticipating pilots of areas that may contain a high volume of pilot training or an unusual type of aerial activity. No permission is required, but VFR flights should exercise extreme caution. IFR flights will be cleared through or vectored around it.

Controlled Firing Areas—CFAs contain activities which, if not conducted in a controlled environment, could be hazardous to nonparticipating aircraft. These activities are suspended immediately when spotter aircraft, radar, or ground lookout positions indicate an aircraft might be approaching the area. CFAs are not charted.

National Security Areas—Airspace of defined vertical and lateral dimensions established at locations where there is a requirement for increased security and safety of ground facilities. Pilots are requested to voluntarily avoid flying through the depicted NSA. When it is necessary to provide a greater level of security and safety, flight in NSAs may be temporarily prohibited by regulation under the provisions of 14 CFR §99.7.

Temporary Flight Restrictions—A TFR is a regulatory action issued via the U.S. NOTAM system to restrict certain aircraft from operating within a defined area, on a temporary basis, to protect persons or property in the air or on the ground. They may be issued due to a hazardous condition, a special event, or as a general warning for the entire FAA airspace. TFR information can be obtained from a FSS or on the internet at www.faa.gov.

Special Flight Rules Area—Airspace of defined dimensions, above land areas or territorial waters, within which the flight of aircraft is subject to the rules set forth in 14 CFR Part 93, unless otherwise authorized by ATC. Not all areas listed in 14 CFR Part 93 are designated SFRA, but special air traffic rules (SATR) apply to all areas described in 14 CFR Part 93.

2. Where can information on special use airspace be found? (AIM 3-4-1)

Special use airspace (SUA) areas are depicted on aeronautical charts, except for CFAs, temporary MOAs, and TFRs. A permanent SUA is charted on sectional aeronautical, VFR terminal area, and applicable enroute charts, and includes the hours of operation, altitudes, and the controlling agency. Current and scheduled status information on SUAs can be found on the FAA's SUA website at sua.faa.gov.

Arrival 4

A. Approach Control

1. What is a STAR? (AIM 5-4-1)

A Standard Terminal Arrival Route (STAR) is an ATC-coded IFR arrival route established for use by arriving IFR aircraft destined for certain airports. Its purpose is to simplify clearance delivery procedures and facilitate transition between enroute and instrument approach procedures. Reference the *Terminal Procedures Publication* (TPP) for the availability of STARs.

2. If ATC issues your flight a STAR, must you accept it? (AIM 5-4-1)

You are not required to accept a STAR, but if you do, you must be in possession of at least the approved chart. RNAV STARs must be retrievable by the procedure name from the aircraft database and conform to the charted procedure. Pilots should notify ATC if they do not wish to use a STAR by placing "NO STAR" in the remarks section of the flight plan, or by the less desirable method of verbally stating the same to ATC.

3. What is an RNAV STAR? (FAA-H-8083-16)

STARs designated RNAV serve the same purpose as conventional STARs but are only used by aircraft equipped with FMS or GPS. An RNAV STAR or STAR transition typically includes fly-by waypoints, with fly-over waypoints used only when operationally required. These waypoints may be assigned crossing altitudes and speeds to optimize the descent and deceleration profiles.

4. What does the notation "RNAV1" on an RNAV STAR indicate? (AIM 5-4-1, AC 90-100)

RNAV 1 terminal procedures require that the aircraft's track keeping accuracy remain bound by +1 nautical mile (NM) for 95 percent of the total flight time. All pilots are expected to maintain route centerlines, as depicted by onboard lateral deviation indicators and/or flight guidance during all RNAV operations unless authorized to deviate by ATC or under emergency conditions. Public PBN STARs are normally designed using RNAV 1, RNP 1, or A-RNP NavSpecs.

5. What does the clearance "descend via" authorize you to do when navigating on a STAR or RNAV STAR procedure? (AIM 5-4-1)

Clearance to "descend via" authorizes pilots to:

a. Descend at pilot's discretion to meet published restrictions and laterally navigate on a STAR.

b. When cleared to a waypoint depicted on a STAR, to descend from a previously assigned altitude at pilot's discretion to the altitude depicted at that waypoint.

c. Once established on the depicted arrival, to descend and to meet all published or assigned altitude and/or speed restrictions.

6. What is a terminal arrival area (TAA)? (FAA-H-8083-16)

A terminal arrival area (TAA) is a published or assigned track by which aircraft are transitioned from the en route structure to the terminal area. A terminal arrival area consists of a designated volume of airspace designed to allow aircraft to enter a protected area with obstacle clearance and signal reception guaranteed where the initial approach course is intercepted.

7. If you are cleared direct to an IAF or IF/IAF within a TAA, but not cleared for the approach by ATC, are you automatically cleared to descend to a TAA altitude? (AIM 5-4-5)

An ATC clearance direct to an IAF or to the IF/IAF without an approach clearance does not authorize a pilot to descend to a lower TAA altitude. If a pilot desires a lower altitude without an approach clearance, the pilot should request the lower TAA altitude from ATC. Pilots entering the TAA with two-way radio communications failure must maintain the highest altitude prescribed by 14 CFR §91.185 until arriving at the appropriate IAF.

8. Will all RNAV (GPS) approaches have a TAA? (FAA-H-8083-16)

No; The TAA will not be found on all RNAV procedures, particularly in areas of heavy concentration of air traffic. When the TAA is published, it replaces the MSA for that approach procedure.

9. **How are fly-over and fly-by waypoints used in a GPS approach procedure?** (AIM 1-1-17, 1-2-1)

Fly-by waypoints are used when an aircraft should begin a turn to the next course prior to reaching the waypoint separating the two route segments. This is known as turn anticipation and is compensated for in the airspace and terrain clearances. Approach waypoints, except for the MAWP and the missed approach holding waypoint (MAHWP), are normally fly-by waypoints.

Fly-over waypoints are used when the aircraft must fly over the point prior to starting a turn. New approach charts depict fly-over waypoints as a circled waypoint symbol. Overlay approach charts and some early stand-alone GPS approach charts may not reflect this convention.

10. **When being radar-vectored for an approach, at what point may you start a descent from your last assigned altitude to a lower altitude if "cleared for the approach"?** (AIM 5-5-4)

Upon receipt of an approach clearance while on an unpublished route or being radar vectored, a pilot will comply with the minimum altitude for IFR and maintain the last assigned altitude until established on a segment of a published route or IAP, at which time published altitudes apply.

11. **Define the terms *initial approach segment*, *intermediate approach segment*, *final approach segment*, and *missed approach segment*.** (P/CG)

An instrument approach procedure may have as many as four separate segments depending upon how the approach procedure is structured.

The *initial approach segment* is that segment between the initial approach fix and the intermediate fix, or the point where the aircraft is established on the intermediate course or final approach course.

The *intermediate approach segment* is between the intermediate fix or point and the final approach fix.

The *final approach segment* is between the final approach fix or point and the runway, airport, or missed approach point.

The *missed approach segment* is between the missed approach point or the point of arrival at decision height, and the missed approach fix at the prescribed altitude.

12. What are standard IFR separation minimums?
(AIM 4-4-11)

When radar is employed in the separation of aircraft at the same altitude, a minimum of 3 miles separation is provided between aircraft operating within 40 miles of the radar antenna site, and 5 miles between aircraft operating beyond 40 miles from the antenna site. These minima may be increased or decreased in certain specific situations.

13. What is a minimum vectoring altitude (MVA)? (P/CG, AIM 5-4-5)

MVA is the lowest MSL altitude at which an IFR aircraft will be vectored by a radar controller, except as otherwise authorized for radar approaches, departures, and missed approaches. The altitude meets IFR obstacle clearance criteria. It may be lower than the published MEA along an airway or J-route segment. It may be used for radar vectoring only upon the controller's determination that an adequate radar return is being received from the aircraft being controlled. Charts depicting minimum vectoring altitudes are normally available only to the controllers and not to the pilots.

14. Your approach chart indicates a MSA circle in the plan view. What is an MSA, and when would you use it? (FAA-H-8083-16, P/CG)

A minimum safe altitude (MSA) circle depicts altitudes on approach charts that provide at least 1,000 feet of obstacle clearance within a 25-mile radius of the navigation facility, waypoint, or airport reference point upon which the MSA is predicated. MSAs are for emergency use only and do not necessarily assure acceptable navigational signal coverage. For RNAV approaches, the MSA is based on either the runway waypoint (RWY WP), the MAWP for straight-in approaches, or the airport waypoint (APT WP) for circling only approaches.

15. What are feeder routes? (FAA-H-8083-16)

A feeder route is a route depicted on IAP charts to designate courses for aircraft to proceed from the enroute structure to the IAF. When a feeder route is designated, the chart provides the course or bearing to be flown, the distance, and the minimum altitude. Enroute airway obstacle clearance criteria apply to feeder routes, providing 1,000 feet of obstacle clearance (2,000 feet in mountainous areas).

16. Is the ATC clearance "cleared for the visual" a VFR clearance or an IFR clearance? What requirements must be met in order to accept such a clearance? (AIM 5-4-23)

A visual approach is conducted on an IFR flight plan and authorizes a pilot to proceed visually and clear of clouds to the airport. The pilot must have either the airport or the preceding identified aircraft in sight. This approach must be authorized and controlled by the appropriate air traffic control facility. Reported weather at the airport must have a ceiling at or above 1,000 feet and visibility 3 miles or greater.

Visual approaches are an IFR procedure conducted under IFR in visual meteorological conditions. Cloud clearance requirements of 14 CFR §91.155 are not applicable.

17. Describe the term *contact approach*. (P/CG)

A contact approach is an approach in which an aircraft on an IFR flight plan, having an air traffic control authorization, operating clear of clouds with at least 1 mile flight visibility and a reasonable expectation of continuing to the destination airport in those conditions, may deviate from the instrument approach procedure and proceed to the destination airport by visual reference to the surface. This approach will only be authorized when requested by the pilot and the reported ground visibility at the destination airport is at least 1 statute mile.

18. When is a procedure turn not required? (AIM 5-4-9, 14 CFR 91.175)

A procedure turn is not required when:

Straight in approach—ATC specifies in approach clearance "Cleared straight-in (type) Approach."

Holding pattern replaces the procedure turn, the holding pattern must be followed.

Arc—when flying a DME arc.

Radar vectored to final approach course.

Procedure turn barb is absent in the plan view or the "NoPT" symbol is depicted on the initial segment being used.

Timed approach—when conducting a timed approach from a holding fix.

Teardrop procedure turn is depicted and a course reversal is required, this type turn must be executed.

Note: If a pilot is uncertain whether the ATC clearance intends for a procedure turn to be conducted or to allow for a straight-in approach, the pilot must immediately request clarification from ATC (14 CFR §91.123).

19. What are standard procedure turn limitations? (AIM 5-4-9)

a. Turn on the depicted (protected) side.

b. Adhere to depicted minimum altitudes.

c. Complete the maneuver within the distance specified in the profile view.

d. Maneuver at a maximum speed not greater than 200 knots (IAS).

20. What procedure is followed when a holding pattern is specified in lieu of a procedure turn? (AIM 5-4-9)

A holding pattern, in lieu of a procedure turn, may be specified for course reversal in some procedures: the holding pattern is established over an intermediate fix or final approach fix. The holding pattern distance or time specified in the profile view must be observed. Maximum holding airspeed limitations apply, as set forth for all holding patterns. The holding pattern maneuver is completed when the aircraft is established on the inbound course after executing the appropriate entry. If cleared for the approach prior to returning to the holding fix, and the aircraft is at the prescribed altitude, additional circuits of the holding pattern are not necessary nor expected by ATC. If pilots elect to make additional circuits to lose altitude or to become better established on course, it is their responsibility to so advise ATC upon receipt of their approach clearance.

B. Precision Approaches

1. What is a precision approach (PA)? (AIM 5-4-5)

A precision approach (PA) is an instrument approach that is based on a navigation system that provides course and glidepath deviation information meeting the precision standards of ICAO Annex 10. For example, PAR, ILS, and GLS are precision approaches.

2. What are the basic components of a standard ILS? (AIM 1-1-9)

Guidance information—localizer, glide slope

Range information—marker beacons, DME

Visual information—approach lights, touchdown and centerline lights, runway lights

3. Describe both visual and aural indications that a pilot would receive when crossing the outer, middle, and inner markers of a standard ILS. (AIM 1-1-9)

Outer Marker	Middle Marker	Inner Marker
blue light	amber light	white light
dull tone	medium tone	high tone
slow speed	medium speed	high speed
– – – – –	– . – . – .	. . . . . .

Note: An MM is no longer operationally required. There are some MMs still in use, but there are no MMs being installed at new ILS sites by the FAA.

4. What are the distances from the landing threshold of the outer, middle, and inner markers? (AIM 1-1-9)

Outer marker—4 to 7 miles from threshold.

Middle marker—3,500 feet from threshold.

Inner marker—between middle marker and threshold.

5. When is the inner marker used? (P/CG)

The inner marker beacon is used with an ILS Category II precision approach and is located between the middle marker and the end of the ILS runway. It indicates the point at which an aircraft is at decision height on the glide path of a CAT II approach. It also marks progress during a CAT III approach.

6. While flying a 3° glide slope, which conditions should the pilot expect concerning airspeed, pitch attitude, and altitude when encountering a wind shear situation where a tailwind shears to a calm or headwind? (FAA-H-8083-28)

Pitch attitude—Increase.

Required thrust—Reduced, then increased.

Vertical speed—Decreases, then increases.

Airspeed—Increases, then decreases.

Reaction—Reduce power initially, then increase.

7. While flying a 3° glide slope, which conditions should the pilot expect concerning airspeed, pitch attitude, and altitude when encountering a wind shear situation where a headwind shears to a calm or tailwind? (FAA-H-8083-28)

Pitch attitude—Decrease.

Required thrust—Increased, then reduced.

Vertical speed—Increases.

Airspeed—Decreases, then increases.

Reaction—Increased power, then a decrease in power.

8. Localizers operate within what frequency range? (AIM 1-1-9)

Localizers operate on odd tenths within the 108.10 to 111.95 MHz band.

9. Where is the localizer/transmitter antenna installation located in relation to the runway? (AIM 1-1-9)

The antenna is located at the far end of the approach runway.

10. Where is the glide slope antenna located, and what is its normal usable range? (AIM 1-1-9)

The glide slope transmitter is located between 750 feet and 1,250 feet from the approach end of the runway (down the runway) and offset 250 feet to 650 feet from it. The glide slope is normally usable to a distance of 10 NM.

11. What range does a standard localizer have? (AIM 1-1-9)

The localizer signal provides course guidance throughout the descent path to the runway threshold from a distance of 18 NM from the antenna site.

12. What is the angular width of a localizer signal? (AIM 1-1-9)

The localizer signal is adjusted to provide an angular width of between 3° to 6°, as necessary to provide a linear width of 700 feet at the runway approach threshold.

13. What is the normal glide slope angle for a standard ILS? (AIM 1-1-9)

The glide path projection angle is normally 3 degrees above horizontal so that it intersects the MM at about 200 feet and the OM at about 1,400 feet above the runway elevation.

14. What is the sensitivity of a CDI tuned to a localizer signal compared with a CDI tuned to a VOR? (FAA-H-8083-15)

Full left or full right deflection occurs at approximately 2.5° from the centerline of a localizer course, which is 4 times greater than when tuned to a VOR, where full-scale deflection equals 10° from the centerline.

15. Define the term *decision altitude* (DA). (P/CG)

A specified altitude (MSL) on an instrument approach procedure (ILS, GLS, vertically guided RNAV) at which the pilot must decide whether to continue the approach or initiate an immediate missed approach if the pilot does not see the required visual references.

16. When flying an instrument approach procedure, when can the pilot descend below MDA or DA/DH? (14 CFR 91.175)

No pilot may operate an aircraft below the authorized MDA or continue an approach below the authorized DA/DH unless:

a. The aircraft is continuously in a position from which a descent to a landing on the intended runway can be made at a normal rate of descent using normal maneuvers.

b. The flight visibility is not less than the visibility prescribed in the standard instrument approach procedure being used.

c. When at least one of the following visual references for the intended runway is distinctly visible and identifiable to the pilot:

- The approach light system (except that the pilot may not descend below 100 feet above the touchdown zone elevation using the ALS as a reference unless the red terminating bars or the red side row bars are also distinctly visible and identifiable)
- The threshold
- The threshold markings
- The threshold lights
- REIL
- Visual glideslope indicator
- The touchdown zone or touchdown zone markings
- The touchdown zone lights
- The runway or runway markings
- The runway lights

17. What are the legal substitutions for an inoperative outer marker? (14 CFR 91.175)

Compass locator; precision approach radar (PAR), or airport surveillance radar (ASR); DME, VOR, or NDB fixes authorized in the standard instrument approach procedure; or a suitable RNAV system in conjunction with a fix identified in the standard instrument approach procedure.

18. What are PAR and ASR approaches? (AIM 5-4-11)

A precision approach radar (PAR) approach is a type of radar approach in which a controller provides highly accurate navigational guidance in azimuth and elevation to the pilot (precision approach). An airport surveillance radar (ASR) approach is a type of radar approach in which a controller provides navigational guidance in azimuth only (nonprecision approach).

19. What is a no-gyro approach? (P/CG, AIM 5-4-11)

A no-gyro approach is a radar approach/vector provided in case of a malfunctioning gyro-compass or directional gyro. Instead of providing the pilot with headings to be flown, the controller observes the radar track and issues control instructions "Turn right/left," or "Stop turn," as appropriate.

20. What rate of turn is recommended during execution of a no-gyro approach procedure? (AIM 5-4-11)

On a no-gyro approach, all turns should be standard rate until on final; then one-half standard rate on final approach.

21. Are the minimums for an ASR approach expressed as DA or MDA? (AIM 5-4-11)

MDA; Guidance in elevation is not possible, but the pilot will be advised when to commence descent to the minimum descent altitude or, if appropriate, to an intermediate step-down fix minimum crossing altitude and subsequently to the prescribed MDA.

22. What is the definition of TDZE? (P/CG)

Touchdown zone elevation (TDZE) is the highest elevation in the first 3,000 feet of the landing surface. TDZE is indicated on the instrument approach procedure chart when straight-in landing minimums are authorized.

23. After completing an ILS approach, you touch down and begin decelerating down the runway. You notice the white runway centerline lights begin to alternate with red centerline lights. What does this indicate to you about distance remaining on the runway? (AIM 2-1-5)

Runway centerline lights are installed on some precision approach runways to facilitate landing under adverse visibility conditions.

When viewed from the landing threshold, the runway centerline lights are white until the last 3,000 feet of the runway. The white lights begin to alternate with red for the next 2,000 feet, and for the last 1,000 feet of the runway, all centerline lights are red.

C. Nonprecision Approaches

1. What is the definition of the term *nonprecision approach*? (AIM 5-4-5)

A nonprecision approach (NPA) is an instrument approach based on a navigation system that provides course deviation information, but no glidepath deviation information such as VOR, NDB and LNAV.

2. Name the types of nonprecision approach procedures available. (P/CG)

The types of nonprecision approaches available are LNAV, VOR, TACAN, NDB, LOC, ASR, LDA, and SDF.

3. Define MDA. (P/CG)

The minimum descent altitude (MDA) is the lowest altitude, expressed in feet above MSL, to which descent is authorized on final approach or during circle-to-land maneuvering, in execution of a standard instrument approach procedure where no electronic glide slope is provided.

4. What is the definition of a *stabilized approach*? (AC 61-98)

The airplane must be stabilized by 1,000 feet above airport elevation in IMC and by 500 feet above airport elevation during straight-in approaches in VMC. The FAA considers an approach to touchdown stabilized when the airplane meets all of the following criteria, with only minor deviations:

a. *Glide path*—On the correct flight path, normally 3 degrees to the runway TDZ, obstructions permitting.

b. *Heading*—Tracking extended centerline to runway with only minor heading/pitch changes to correct for wind, turbulence, and maintain alignment. Bank angle should not exceed 15 degrees on final.

(continued)

c. *Airspeed*—Maintains a constant airspeed within +10/−5 KIAS of the recommended landing speed.

d. *Configuration*—In the correct landing configuration (flaps as required, landing gear extended, and airplane is in trim).

e. *Rate of descent*—Constant and no greater than 500 fpm; if a descent greater than 500 fpm is required due to approach considerations, it must be reduced prior to 300 feet AGL and well before the landing flare and touchdown phase.

f. *Power setting*—Appropriate for the airplane configuration and not below the minimum power for approach.

g. *Checklists/briefings*—All briefings and checklists (except the landing checklist) completed prior to initiating the approach.

5. Define VDP. (P/CG, AIM 5-4-5)

A visual descent point (VDP) is a defined point on the final approach course of a nonprecision straight-in approach procedure from which normal descent from the MDA to the runway touchdown point may be commenced, provided the approach threshold of that runway, or approach lights or other markings identifiable with the approach end of that runway, are clearly visible to the pilot. Pilots not equipped to receive the VDP should fly the approach procedure as though no VDP had been provided. On an approach chart, a VDP is identified in the profile view by a "V."

6. While flying the final segment of a non-precision approach with a VDP, a pilot breaks out of the clouds prior to the VDP and has the required visibility and necessary visual references available to begin the descent. Does the pilot have to wait until the VDP is reached before descending below the MDA? (AIM 5-4-5, 8-1-5)

The pilot should not descend below the MDA prior to reaching the VDP and acquiring the necessary visual references.

Note: By delaying your descent until crossing the VDP, you mitigate the risk of hitting an unseen obstacle or experiencing an optical illusion during your descent from MDA (rain on windscreen, at night/featureless terrain illusion, etc.).

7. If no VDP is provided on an IAP, how can you compute your own VDP? (FAA-H-8083-16)

Height above touchdown (HAT) in ft ÷ 300 ft/NM = VDP (in NM from threshold); or

10% of HAT = seconds to subtract from the time to MAP

8. What is a VDA? (FAA-H-8083-15)

The vertical descent angle (VDA) found on non-precision approach charts provides the pilot with information required to establish a stabilized approach descent from the FAF or stepdown fix to the TCH. Pilots can use the published angle and estimated or actual ground speed to find a target rate of descent using the rate of descent table in the back of the TPP.

9. Explain how you will use the published VDA on a non-precision approach chart to fly a stabilized descent to the MDA? (AIM 5-4-5, TPP)

a. Determine the published vertical descent angle on the approach chart (e.g., 3.1 degrees).

b. Determine your estimated or actual ground speed (i.e., 90 knots GS).

c. Locate the Rate of Climb/Descent Table (inside the back cover of TPP).

d. The table indicates that a VDA of 3.1 degrees equates to a descent rate of 329 ft/NM.

e. 329 ft/NM converts to a descent rate of 494 fpm at 90 knots ground speed.

To fly the VDA, at the FAF or stepdown fix, descend at the required descent rate and maintain your airspeed/ground speed.

10. Does the VDA guarantee an obstacle protection below the MDA? (AIM 5-4-5)

A VDA does not guarantee obstacle protection below the MDA in the visual segment. The presence of a VDA does not change any non-precision approach requirements. Pilots must be aware that the published VDA is for advisory information only and not to be considered instrument procedure derived vertical guidance. The VDA solely offers an aid to help pilots establish a continuous, stabilized descent during final approach.

11. Will standard instrument approach procedures always have a final approach fix (FAF)? (FAA-H-8083-16)

No. When a FAF is not designated, such as on an approach that incorporates an on-airport VOR or NDB, a final approach point is designated and is typically where the procedure turn intersects the final approach course inbound.

12. If no FAF is published, where does the final approach segment begin on a nonprecision approach? (FAA-H-8083-16)

The final approach segment begins where the procedure turn intersects the final approach course inbound.

13. Certain conditions are required for an instrument approach procedure to have "straight-in" minimums published. What are they? (AIM 5-4-20)

Straight-in minimums are shown on the IAP when the final approach course is within 30 degrees of the runway alignment (15 degrees for GPS IAPs) and a normal descent can be made from the IFR altitude shown on the IAP to the runway surface.

14. What is a stepdown fix? (P/CG)

A stepdown fix permits additional descent within a segment of an instrument approach procedure by identifying a point at which a controlling obstacle has been safely overflown.

15. What does a VASI system provide? (AIM 2-1-2)

A visual approach slope indicator (VASI) system provides visual descent guidance during an approach to a runway; safe obstruction clearance within ±10° of extended runway centerline up to 4 NM from the runway threshold. Two-bar VASI installations normally provide a 3° visual glide path.

16. What are the major differences between SDF and LDA approaches? (FAA-H-8083-15)

In an SDF approach procedure, the SDF course may or may not be aligned with the runway; usable off-course indications are limited to 35° either side of course centerline. The SDF signal emitted is fixed at either 6° or 12°.

The LDA compares in utility and accuracy to a localizer, but it is not part of a complete ILS. The LDA course width is between 3° and 6° and thus provides a more precise approach course than an SDF installation. Some LDAs are equipped with a GS. The LDA course is not aligned with the runway, but straight-in minimums may be published where the angle between the runway centerline and the LDA course does not exceed 30°. If this angle exceeds 30°, only circling minimums are published.

17. What criteria determines whether or not you may attempt an approach? (14 CFR 91.175)

No regulation states that you cannot attempt an approach, if operating under Part 91 regulations. But if you reach MDA or DA/DH and decide to descend to land, flight visibility must be at least equal to that published.

18. What regulations require use of specified procedures by all pilots approaching for landing under IFR? (14 CFR Part 97)

Specified procedures are required by 14 CFR Part 97.

19. What self-announced radio calls should you make when conducting an instrument approach to an airport without a control tower? (FAA-H-8083-16)

a. Initial call within 5–10 minutes of the aircraft's arrival at the IAF with aircraft location and approach intentions.

b. Departing the IAF, stating the approach that is being initiated.

c. Procedure turn (or equivalent) inbound.

d. FAF inbound, stating intended landing runway and maneuvering direction if circling.

e. Short final, giving traffic on the surface notification of imminent landing.

D. RNAV (GPS) Approaches

1. **Describe the following lines of minima found on area navigation RNAV (GPS) instrument approach charts: LNAV, LP, LNAV/VNAV, LPV, and GLS.** (AIM 5-4-5)

   LNAV—Lateral navigation only; non-precision approach; requires TSO-C129 (non WAAS) or C145/C146 (WAAS) equipment. Minimums shown as MDA.

   LP—Localizer Performance; non-precision approach; requires TSO C145/C146 (WAAS) equipment; minimums shown as MDA.

   LNAV/VNAV—Lateral Nav/Vertical Nav; APV approach; requires approach approved Baro-VNAV or TSO-C145/C146 (WAAS) equipment; minimums are shown as DA.

   LPV—Localizer performance with vertical guidance; APV approach; requires TSO-C145/C146 (WAAS) equipment; minimums are shown as DA.

   GLS—GBAS landing system; U.S. version of GBAS is Local Area Augmentation System (LAAS); provides lateral and vertical guidance; requires an aircraft GBAS receiver; relatively new category of approach. Most RNAV (GPS) approach charts have had the GLS minima line replaced by a WAAS LPV line of minima.

2. **What are APV approaches? Give several examples of this type of approach.** (AIM 5-4-5)

   An approach with vertical guidance (APV) is an instrument approach based on a navigation system that is not required to meet the precision approach standards of ICAO Annex 10 but that provides course and glidepath deviation information. Examples are Baro-VNAV, LDA with glidepath, LNAV/VNAV, and LPV approaches.

3. **What is indicated when a letter suffix is added to the approach title (i.e., RNAV (GPS) Z RWY 13C)?** (FAA-H-8083-16)

   When two or more straight-in approaches with the same type of guidance exist for a runway, a letter suffix is added to the title of the approach so that it can be more easily identified. These approach charts start with the letter Z and continue in reverse alphabetical order.

4. Will there be any significant differences when two straight-in approaches with the same type of guidance exist for a runway—i.e., RNAV (GPS) Z RWY 13C and RNAV (RNP) Y RWY 13C? (FAA-H-8083-16)

Yes; The approach procedure labeled Z will have lower landing minimums than Y (some older charts may not reflect this). Although both of these approaches can be flown with GPS to the same runway, they can be significantly different—e.g., one may be a "SPECIAL AIRCRAFT & AIRCREW AUTHORIZATION REQUIRED (SAAAR)"; one can have circling minimums and the other no circling minimums; the minimums are different; and the missed approaches may not be the same.

5. What is an LPV approach? (AIM 1-1-18)

Localizer performance with vertical guidance (LPV) is a type of approach with vertical guidance (APV) that takes advantage of the high accuracy guidance and increased integrity provided by WAAS. This WAAS-generated angular guidance allows the use of the same TERPS approach criteria used for ILS approaches. LPV minima may have a decision altitude (DA) as low as 200 feet height above touchdown with visibility minimums as low as ½ mile, when the terrain and airport infrastructure support the lowest minima.

6. How can you determine if your aircraft is equipped to fly an LPV approach procedure? (AIM 1-1-18)

GPS/WAAS operation must be conducted in accordance with the FAA-approved aircraft flight manual (AFM) and flight manual supplements. Flight manual supplements will state the level of approach procedure that the receiver supports. IFR-approved WAAS receivers support all GPS only operations as long as lateral capability at the appropriate level is functional.

7. What does the acronym "LP" indicate in the minimums section of an RNAV (GPS) approach chart? (AIM 5-4-5)

LP is the acronym for localizer performance. Approaches to LP lines of minima take advantage of the improved accuracy of WAAS to provide approaches with lateral and angular guidance. Angular guidance does not refer to a glideslope angle but rather to the increased lateral sensitivity as the aircraft gets closer to the

runway, similar to localizer approaches. LP minimums are only
published if terrain, obstructions, or some other reason prevents
publishing a vertically guided procedure. LP lines of minima are
minimum descent altitudes (MDAs). Also, LP is not a fail-down
mode for an LPV. LP and LPV are independent.

8. **After selecting the approach procedure at your
destination airport, what method will the GPS receiver
use to select the appropriate minimums for the
approach?** (AIM 1-1-18)

When an approach procedure is selected and active, the receiver
will notify the pilot of the most accurate level of service supported
by the combination of the WAAS signal, the receiver, and the
selected approach, using the naming conventions on the minima
lines of the selected approach procedure. For example, if an
approach is published with LPV minima and the receiver is only
certified for LNAV/VNAV, the equipment would indicate "LNAV/
VNAV available," even though the WAAS signal would support
LPV.

9. **What is the significance of temperature limitations
published on an approach procedure chart?** (AIM 5-4-5)

A minimum and maximum temperature limitation is published
on procedures which authorize Baro-VNAV operation. These
temperatures represent the airport temperature above or below
which Baro-VNAV is not authorized to LNAV/VNAV minimums.

Note: Temperature limitations do not apply to flying the LNAV/
VNAV line of minima using approach certified WAAS receivers
when LPV or LNAV/VNAV are annunciated to be available.

10. **What is the WAAS Channel Number/Approach ID found
on the upper left corner of an approach procedure chart
used for?** (AIM 5-4-5)

The WAAS Channel Number is an optional equipment capability
that allows the use of a 5-digit number to select a specific final
approach segment without using the menu method.

11. You are flying an LPV approach in an aircraft with a
    WAAS-certified GPS receiver and have passed the FAF.
    If your GPS receiver is no longer meeting GPS accuracy
    requirements, will it fail-down to LNAV minimums? Are
    you allowed to continue the approach or should you
    execute a missed approach? (AFM, AIM 1-1-18)

    Receivers do not "fail down" to lower levels of service once the
    approach has been activated. If only the vertical off flag appears,
    the pilot may elect to use the LNAV minima if the rules under
    which the flight is operating allow changing the type of approach
    being flown after commencing the procedure. If the lateral integrity
    limit is exceeded on an LP approach, a missed approach will be
    necessary since there is no way to reset the lateral alarm limit
    while the approach is active.

12. What are the possible reasons your GPS receiver would
    fail to sequence from the "Armed" to the "Approach"
    mode prior to the final approach waypoint (FAWP)?
    (AIM 1-1-17)

    The receiver performs a RAIM prediction by 2 NM prior to the
    FAWP to ensure that RAIM is available at the FAWP as a condition
    for entering the approach mode. Failure to sequence may be an
    indication of the detection of a satellite anomaly, failure to arm
    the receiver (if required), or other problems which preclude
    completing the approach. The pilot should always ensure that the
    receiver has sequenced from "Armed" to "Approach" prior to the
    FAWP (normally occurs 2 NM prior to the FAWP).

13. If the GPS receiver does not sequence from "Armed" to
    "Approach" mode or a RAIM failure/status annunciation
    occurs prior to the FAWP, what procedure should the
    pilot follow? (AIM 1-1-17)

    If a RAIM failure/status annunciation occurs prior to the final
    approach waypoint (FAWP), the approach should not be completed
    since GPS may no longer provide the required accuracy. The pilot
    should not descend to minimum descent altitude (MDA) but should
    proceed to the missed approach waypoint (MAWP) via the FAWP,
    perform a missed approach, and contact ATC as soon as practical.

14. If a RAIM flag/status annunciation appears after you have passed the FAWP, should you continue the approach? (AIM 1-1-17)

No, you should initiate a climb and execute the missed approach. The GPS receiver may continue to operate after a RAIM flag/status annunciation appears, but the navigation information should be considered advisory only. Refer to the receiver operating manual for operating mode information during a RAIM annunciation.

15. What is the significance of the presence of a gray shaded line from the MDA to the runway in the profile view of a RNAV (GPS) approach? (FAA-H-8083-16)

It is an indication that the visual segment below the MDA is clear of obstructions on the 34:1 slope. Absence of the gray shaded area indicates the 34:1 OCS is not free of obstructions.

16. What is indicated when a GPS receiver provides the annunciation "LNAV+V"? (AC 90-107)

Advisory vertical guidance is being provided. Depending on the manufacturer, some GPS receivers will provide advisory vertical guidance when associated with LP or LNAV lines of minima. The system creates an artificial advisory glide path to assist the pilot in flying a constant descent to the MDA. Barometric altimeter information remains the primary altitude reference for complying with any altitude restrictions.

Note: It is the pilot's responsibility to use the barometric altimeter to ensure compliance with altitude restrictions, particularly during approach operations. *Advisory* vertical guidance is *not* the same thing as *approved* vertical guidance, such as the type found on approaches with LNAV/VNAV, LPV or ILS lines of minima.

17. How will rising terrain be depicted in the plan view of an IAP chart? (USRGD)

Terrain will be depicted with contour lines in shades of brown in the plan view portion of all IAPs at airports that meet the following criteria:

- If the terrain within the plan view exceeds 4,000 feet above the airport elevation, or
- If the terrain within a 6.0 nautical mile radius of the airport reference point (ARP) rises to at least 2,000 feet above the airport elevation.

18. What is a computer navigation fix (CNF)? (AIM 1-1-17, P/CG)

A CNF is a point defined by a latitude/longitude coordinate and is required to support performance-based navigation (PBN) operations. A five-letter identifier denoting a CNF can be found next to an "x" on enroute charts and on some approach charts. Pilots should not use CNFs for point-to-point navigation (e.g., proceed direct), filing a flight plan, or in aircraft/ATC communications.

19. What is the significance of the "negative W" ☒ symbol placed on some RNAV (GPS) approach charts? (AIM 1-1-18)

When the approach chart is annotated with the W symbol, site specific WAAS UNRELIABLE NOTAMs or air traffic advisories are not provided for outages in WAAS LNAV/VNAV and LPV vertical service. Vertical outages may occur daily at these locations due to being close to the edge of WAAS system coverage. Use LNAV or circling minima for flight planning at these locations, whether as a destination or alternate. For flight operations at these locations, when the WAAS avionics indicate that LNAV/VNAV or LPV service is available, then the vertical guidance may be used to complete the approach using the displayed level of service. If an outage occurs during the procedure, reversion to LNAV minima may be required.

20. If a discrepancy exists between the information provided by a GPS navigation database and the information published on an approach chart, which one takes precedence? (AIM 1-1-17)

If significant differences arise between the approach chart and the GPS avionics' application of the navigation database, the published approach chart, supplemented by NOTAMs, holds precedence.

21. When flying an RNAV (GPS) approach, most FMS require the pilot to choose whether to "load" or "load and activate" an instrument approach procedure. Explain the difference. (FAA-H-8083-16)

Loading an approach adds its component waypoints to the end of the flight plan, but it does not make them active. Activating an approach will cause the FMS to immediately give course guidance to the initial approach fix or closest fix outside the final fix, depending on the unit's programming.

22. What does the performance-based navigation (PBN) box indicate on an approach chart? (AIM 5-4-5)

For procedures with PBN elements, the PBN box will contain the procedure's navigation specification(s) and, if required, specific sensors or infrastructure needed for the navigation solution, any additional or advanced functional requirements, the minimum required navigation performance (RNP) value, and any amplifying remarks. Items listed in this PBN box are required for the procedure's PBN elements. For example, an ILS with an RNAV missed approach would require a specific capability to fly the missed approach portion of the procedure. That required capability will be listed in the PBN box. The separate Equipment Requirements box will list ground-based equipment requirements. On procedures with both PBN elements and equipment requirements, the PBN requirements box will be listed first. The publication of these notes will continue incrementally until all charts have been amended to comply with the new standard.

23. Some approaches are listed as "RNP" approaches in their title. An example might be the RNAV (RNP) Z RWY 28L at Columbus, OH (KCMH). These approaches will typically also have a note in their minimums that indicates "AUTHORIZATION REQUIRED." What is the significance of this to an IFR pilot? (AIM 5-4-5, AC 90-101)

RNP AR procedures require authorization analogous to the special authorization required for Category II or III ILS procedures. All operators require specific authorization from the FAA to fly any RNP AR approach or departure procedure. The FAA issues RNP AR authorization via operations specifications (ops specs), management specification (MSpec), or letter of authorization (LOA). There are no exceptions. Operators can find comprehensive information on RNP AR aircraft eligibility, operating procedures, and training requirements in FAA AC 90-101, *Approval Guidance for Required Navigation Performance (RNP) Procedures with Authorization Required (AR)*.

E. Circling Approaches

1. What are circle-to-land approaches? (P/CG)

A circle-to-land approach is not technically an approach, but a maneuver initiated by a pilot to align the aircraft with the runway for landing when a straight-in landing from an instrument approach is not possible or desirable. At tower-controlled airports, this maneuver is made only after ATC authorization has been obtained and the pilot has established required visual reference to the airport.

2. What is indicated when an approach procedure title (e.g., VOR-A) is followed only by a letter (no runway designation)? (FAA-H-8083-15)

The type of approach followed by a letter identifies approaches that do not have straight-in landing minimums and only have circling minimums. The first approach of this type created at the airport is labeled with the letter A, and the lettering continues in alphabetical order (e.g., "VOR-A or "LDA-B").

3. Why do certain airports have only circling minimums published? (AIM 5-4-20)

When either the normal rate of descent or the runway alignment factor of 30 degrees (15 degrees for GPS IAPs) is exceeded, a straight-in minimum is not published, and a circling minimum applies.

4. Can a pilot make a straight-in landing if using an approach procedure having only circling minimums? (AIM 5-4-20)

Yes; the fact that a straight-in minimum is not published does not preclude pilots from landing straight-in, if they have the active runway in sight and have sufficient time to make a normal approach to landing. Under such conditions and when ATC has cleared them for landing on that runway, pilots are not expected to circle, even though only circling minimums are published.

5. If cleared for a "straight-in VOR-DME 34 approach," can a pilot circle to land, if needed? (P/CG)

Yes. A "straight-in approach" is an instrument approach wherein final approach is begun without first having executed a procedure turn. Such an approach is not necessarily completed with a straight-in landing or made to straight-in minimums.

6. When can you begin your descent to the runway during a circling approach? (14 CFR 91.175)

Three conditions are required before descent from the MDA can occur:

a. The aircraft is continuously in a position from which a descent to a landing on the intended runway can be made at a normal rate of descent using normal maneuvers.

b. The flight visibility is not less than the visibility prescribed in the standard instrument approach being used.

c. At least one of the specific runway visual references for the intended runway is distinctly visible and identifiable to the pilot.

7. While circling to land, you lose visual contact with the runway environment. At the time visual contact is lost, your approximate position is a base leg at the circling MDA. What procedure should be followed? (AIM 5-4-21)

If visual reference is lost while circling to land from an instrument approach, the pilot should make an initial climbing turn toward the landing runway and continue the turn until established on the missed approach course. Since the circling maneuver may be accomplished in more than one direction, different patterns will be required to become established on the prescribed missed approach course, depending on the aircraft position at the time visual reference is lost. Adherence to the procedure will ensure that an aircraft will remain within the circling and missed approach obstacle clearance areas.

8. How can a pilot determine the approach category minimums applicable to a particular aircraft? (AIM 5-4-7)

Minimums are specified for various aircraft approach categories based on a speed of V_{REF}, if specified, or if V_{REF} is not specified, 1.3 V_{S0} at the maximum certified landing weight.

9. What are the different aircraft approach categories and speeds? (AIM 5-4-7)

Category A—Speed less than 91 knots.
Category B—Speed 91 knots or more but less than 121 knots.
Category C—Speed 121 knots or more but less than 141 knots.
Category D—Speed 141 knots or more but less than 166 knots.
Category E—Speed 166 knots or more.

10. **What clearance is guaranteed to a pilot based on category of approach speed when conducting a circling approach?** (FAA-H-8083-16, TPP)

In all circling approaches, the circling minimum provides 300 feet of obstacle clearance within the circling approach area. The size of this area depends on the category in which the aircraft operates.

Category A—1.3-mile radius
Category B—1.5-mile radius
Category C—1.7-mile radius
Category D—2.3-mile radius
Category E—4.5-mile radius

11. **Beginning In 2012, the FAA began developing circling approaches with expanded approach maneuvering airspace radius. What radius apply when circling for an approach based on the category of approach speed with expanded approach category minimums?** (FAA-H-8083-16, TPP)

Circling MDA in feet MSL	Approach Category and Circling Radius (NM)				
	CAT A	CAT B	CAT C	CAT D	CAT E
1,000 or less	1.3	1.7	2.7	3.6	4.5
1,001–3,000	1.3	1.8	2.8	3.7	4.6
3,001–5,000	1.3	1.8	2.9	3.8	4.8
5,001–7,000	1.3	1.9	3.0	4.0	5.0
7,001–9,000	1.4	2.0	3.2	4.2	5.3
9,001 and above	1.4	2.1	3.3	4.4	5.5

12. **What is the significance of the presence of a "negative C" C symbol on the circling line of minima?** (AIM 5-4-20)

Circling approach protected areas developed after late 2012 use the radius distance dependent on aircraft approach category *and* the altitude of the circling MDA which accounts for true airspeed increase with altitude. The approaches using expanded circling approach areas can be identified by the presence of the "negative C" symbol on the circling line of minima.

Note: The increase in size of the circling protected area is particularly beneficial for pilots of CAT C and CAT D turbine-powered, transport category aircraft in that it provides greater lateral obstacle clearance and additional maneuvering room to properly align and stabilize for final approach and landing.

13. **An aircraft operating under 14 CFR Part 91 has a 1.3 times V$_{S0}$ speed of 100 KIAS, making Category B minimums applicable. If it becomes necessary to circle at a speed in excess of this category, what minimums should be used?** (AIM 5-4-7)

A pilot must use the minima corresponding to the category determined during certification, or higher. If it is necessary to operate at a speed in excess of the upper limit of the speed range for an aircraft's category, the minimums for the higher category must be used.

F. Missed Approaches

1. **When must a pilot execute a missed approach?** (AIM 5-4-21, 5-5-5)

A missed approach must be executed when one of the following conditions occurs:

a. Arrival at the missed approach point and the runway environment is not yet in sight;

b. Arrival at DA on the glide slope with the runway not yet in sight;

c. Anytime a pilot determines a safe landing is not possible;

d. When circling-to-land visual contact is lost; or

e. When instructed by ATC.

2. **On a nonprecision approach procedure, how is the missed approach point (MAP) determined?** (FAA-H-8083-15)

In nonprecision procedures, the pilot determines the MAP by timing from FAF when the approach aid is well away from the airport, by a fix or NAVAID when the navigation facility is located on the field, or by waypoints as defined by GPS.

3. **If no final approach fix is depicted, how is the MAP determined?** (FAA-H-8083-15)

The MAP is at the airport (NAVAID on airport).

4. Where is the MAP on a precision approach?
(FAA-H-8083-15)

For the ILS, the MAP is at the decision altitude/decision height (DA/DH).

5. Under what conditions are missed approach procedures published on an approach chart not followed?
(FAA-H-8083-15)

They are not followed when ATC has assigned alternate missed approach instructions.

6. Some approach plates list an "Alternate Missed APCH FIX". What is the purpose of having this on an approach plate? (AIM 5-4-21)

Some locations may have a preplanned alternate missed approach procedure for use in the event the primary NAVAID used for the missed approach procedure is unavailable. To avoid confusion, the alternate missed approach instructions are not published on the chart. However, the alternate missed approach holding pattern will be depicted on the instrument approach chart for pilot situational awareness and to assist ATC by not having to issue detailed holding instructions. The alternate missed approach may be based on NAVAIDs not used in the approach procedure or the primary missed approach. When the alternate missed approach procedure is implemented by NOTAM, it becomes a mandatory part of the procedure. The NOTAM will specify both the textual instructions and any additional equipment requirements necessary to complete the procedure. Air traffic may also issue instructions for the alternate missed approach when necessary, such as when the primary missed approach NAVAID fails during the approach.

Pilots may reject an ATC clearance for an alternate missed approach that requires equipment not necessary for the published approach procedure when the alternate missed approach is issued after beginning the approach. However, when the alternate missed approach is issued prior to beginning the approach, the pilot must either accept the entire procedure (including the alternate missed approach), request a different approach procedure, or coordinate with ATC for alternative action to be taken (i.e., proceed to an alternate airport, etc.).

7. If, during the execution of an instrument approach procedure, you determine a missed approach is necessary due to full-scale needle deflection, what action is recommended? (AIM 5-4-21)

Protected obstacle clearance areas for a missed approach are predicated on the assumption that the missed approach is initiated at the decision altitude/height (DA/H) or at the missed approach point, and not lower than minimum descent altitude (MDA). Reasonable buffers are provided for normal maneuvers. However, no consideration is given to an abnormally early turn. Therefore, when an early missed approach is executed, pilots should (unless otherwise cleared by ATC) fly the IAP as specified on the approach plate to the missed approach point at or above the MDA or DA/H before executing a turning maneuver.

8. You have arrived at decision altitude on a precision approach and only have the approach light system in sight. Must you execute a missed approach or can you continue? (14 CFR 91.175)

A pilot is authorized to descend below the DA when the approach light system is visible, except that the pilot may not descend below 100 feet above the touchdown zone elevation using the approach lights as a reference unless the red terminating bars or the red side row bars are also distinctly visible and identifiable.

9. How do you determine flight visibility when transitioning from IMC to visual on an instrument approach procedure? (FAA-H-8083-15)

According to 14 CFR Part 91, no pilot may land when the flight visibility is less than the visibility prescribed in the standard IAP being used. ATC provides the pilot with the current visibility reports appropriate to the runway in use. This may be in the form of prevailing visibility, runway visual value (RVV), or runway visual range (RVR). However, only the pilot can determine if the flight visibility meets the landing requirements indicated on the approach chart. If the flight visibility meets the minimum prescribed for the approach, then the approach may be continued to a landing. If the flight visibility is less than that prescribed for the approach, then the pilot must execute a missed approach regardless of the reported visibility.

10. Are the required visibility figures in the instrument minimums sections on approach charts in statute or nautical miles? (FAA-H-8083-15)

The reported ground visibility on an approach is in statute miles.

11. What action should a pilot take in the event a balked (rejected) landing occurs at a position other than the published missed approach point? (AIM 5-4-21)

The pilot should contact ATC as soon as possible to obtain an amended clearance. If unable to contact ATC for any reason, the pilot should attempt to re-intercept a published segment of the missed approach and comply with route and altitude instructions. If unable to contact ATC, and in the pilot's judgment it is no longer appropriate to fly the published missed approach procedure, then the pilot should consider either maintaining visual conditions if practicable and reattempt a landing, or a circle-climb over the airport. Contact ATC when able to do so.

12. What are several factors a pilot should consider (prior to the approach) when assessing options available if it becomes necessary to execute a missed approach from beyond the MAP or below the MDA or DA/DH? (AIM 5-4-21)

The pilot should consider factors such as the aircraft's geographical location with respect to the prescribed missed approach point, direction of flight, and/or minimum turning altitudes in the prescribed missed approach procedure. The pilot must also consider aircraft performance, visual climb restrictions, charted obstacles, availability of a published obstacle departure procedure, takeoff visual climb requirements as expressed by nonstandard takeoff minima, other traffic expected to be in the vicinity, or other factors not specifically expressed by the approach procedures.

13. What is a low approach? (AIM 4-3-12)

A low approach (sometimes referred to as a low pass) is the go-around maneuver following an approach. Instead of landing or making a touch and go, a pilot may wish to go-around (low approach) in order to expedite a particular operation (for example, a series of practice instrument approaches). Unless otherwise authorized by ATC, the low approach should be made straight ahead, with no turns or climb made until the pilot has made a thorough visual check for other aircraft in the area.

14. What does the phrase "Cleared for the Option" mean?
(AIM 4-3-22)

The "Cleared for the Option" procedure will permit an instructor, flight examiner, or pilot the option to make a touch-and-go, low approach, missed approach, stop-and-go, or full stop landing. The pilot should make a request for this procedure passing the final approach fix inbound on an instrument approach.

15. What is an "overhead approach" maneuver, and when would it be utilized by an IFR pilot? (AIM 5-4-27)

Pilots operating in accordance with an IFR flight plan in visual meteorological conditions (VMC) may request ATC authorization for an overhead maneuver. An overhead maneuver is not an instrument approach procedure. Overhead maneuver patterns are developed at airports where aircraft have an operational need to conduct the maneuver. An aircraft conducting an overhead maneuver is considered to be VFR, and the IFR flight plan is canceled when the aircraft reaches the initial point on the initial approach portion of the maneuver. The existence of a standard overhead maneuver pattern does not eliminate the possible requirement for an aircraft to conform to conventional rectangular patterns if an overhead maneuver cannot be approved. Aircraft operating to an airport without a functioning control tower must initiate cancellation of an IFR flight plan prior to executing the overhead maneuver. Cancellation of the IFR flight plan must be accomplished after crossing the landing threshold on the initial portion of the maneuver or after landing.

G. Landing Procedures

1. Is it legal to land a civil aircraft if the actual visibility is below the minimums published on the approach chart?
(14 CFR 91.175)

No, 14 CFR Part 91 states that no pilot operating an aircraft, except a U.S. military aircraft, may land that aircraft when the flight visibility is less than the visibility prescribed in the standard instrument approach procedure being used.

2. **When landing at an airport with an operating control tower following an IFR flight, must the pilot call FSS to close the flight plan?** (AIM 5-1-15)

   No, if operating on an IFR flight plan to an airport with a functioning control tower, the flight plan will automatically be closed upon landing.

3. **If a pilot lands at an airport without an operating control tower, how should they close their flight plan if they were not able to do so prior to landing in the air?** (AIM 5-1-15)

   If operating on an IFR flight plan to an airport where there is no functioning control tower, the pilot must initiate cancellation of the IFR flight plan. This can be done after landing if there is a functioning FSS or other means of direct communications with ATC. In most instances, this can be done through calling the controlling agency directly or through contacting Flight Service via phone.

4. **You are operating on an IFR flight plan into an airport without an operating control tower, and you have forgotten to close your flight plan after landing. Discuss the effect this will have on ATC.** (AIM 5-1-15)

   The airspace surrounding that airport cannot be released for use by other IFR aircraft until the status of your flight has been determined.

5. **If the visibility provided by ATC is less than that prescribed for the approach, can a pilot legally continue an approach and land?** (FAA-H-8083-15)

   According to 14 CFR Part 91, no pilot may land when the *flight visibility* is less than the visibility prescribed in the standard IAP being used. ATC will provide the pilot with the current visibility reports appropriate to the runway in use. This may be in the form of prevailing visibility, runway visual value (RVV), or runway visual range (RVR). However, only the pilot can determine if the flight visibility meets the landing requirements indicated on the approach chart. If the flight visibility meets the minimum prescribed for the approach, then the approach may be continued to a landing. If the *flight visibility* is less than that prescribed for the approach, then the pilot must execute a missed approach, regardless of the reported visibility.

6. How will you determine flight visibility when coming out of the clouds on an approach? (FAA-P-8740-09)

If the approach has a lighting system, there are a number of clues in the system itself:

a. *Decision bar*—Every approach lighting system has a decision bar located 1,000 feet from the runway threshold. These lights (or bar) are perpendicular to the approach lighting system.

b. *Sequenced flashing lights*—These provide another 1,000-foot clue, known to pilots as the "rabbit." The sequenced flashing lights stop at the decision bar.

If you are at the middle marker or DA(H) on glide slope and you cannot see the runway threshold, look for the decision bar. Assume that you spot the decision bar. If you know that the MM is six tenths of a nautical mile (0.6) from the threshold, then you have 3,650 feet from the runway. Subtract the 1,000 feet from the threshold, which you cannot see, to the decision bar, which you have spotted, and that leaves 2,650 feet—just under ½ mile. If the minimum visibility for this approach is ½ mile, then you have the required visibility.

7. The acronym LAHSO refers to what specific ATC procedure? (AIM 4-3-11)

LAHSO is an acronym for Land and Hold Short Operations. These operations include landing and holding short of an intersecting runway, an intersecting taxiway, or some other designated point on a runway other than an intersecting runway or taxiway.

8. What is a side-step maneuver? (FAA-H-8083-15)

ATC may authorize a side-step maneuver to either one of two parallel runways that are separated by 1,200 feet or less, followed by a straight-in landing on the adjacent runway. Aircraft executing a side-step maneuver are cleared for a specified nonprecision approach and landing on the adjacent parallel runway. For example, "Cleared ILS runway 7 left approach, side-step to runway 7 right." The pilot is expected to commence the side-step maneuver as soon as possible after the runway or runway environment is in sight. Landing minimums to the adjacent runway are based on nonprecision criteria and therefore higher than the precision minimums to the primary runway, but they are normally lower than the published circling minimums.

H. Instrument Approach Procedure Charts: General

All questions in this section reference FAA Aeronautical Information Services charts.

1. **While flying a night instrument approach, you begin to experience several types of optical illusions (rain on windshield, bright lights), increasing overall risk. What procedures can you use to mitigate this risk?** (AIM 8-1-5, FAA H-8083-15)

   To prevent these illusions and their potentially hazardous consequences, pilots can:

   a. Anticipate the possibility of visual illusions during approaches to unfamiliar airports, particularly at night or in adverse weather conditions. Consult airport diagrams and the *Airport/ Facility Directory* (A/FD) for information on runway slope, terrain, and lighting.

   b. Make frequent reference to the altimeter, especially during all approaches, day and night.

   c. If possible, conduct an aerial visual inspection of unfamiliar airports before landing.

   d. Use visual approach slope indicator (VASI) or precision approach path indicator (PAPI) systems for a visual reference, or an electronic glide slope, whenever they are available.

   e. Utilize the visual descent point (VDP) found on many nonprecision instrument approach procedure charts.

   f. Recognize that the chances of being involved in an approach accident increase when some emergency or other activity distracts from usual procedures.

   g. Maintain optimum proficiency in landing procedures.

2. **How can a pilot determine the position of the highest obstacle on an instrument approach procedure chart?** (FAA-H-8083-15)

   The largest dot and number combination indicates the highest elevation. An inverted "V" with a dot in the center depicts an obstacle: ⩗. The highest obstacle is indicated with a bolder, larger version of the same symbol.

3. **When the approach procedure title contains more than one navigational system separated by a slash (e.g., VOR/ DME 31), what does this indicate?** (AIM 5-4-5)

   It indicates that more than one type of equipment must be used to execute the final approach.

4. **When the approach procedure title contains more than one navigational system separated by the word "or" (e.g., VOR or GPS RWY 15), what does this indicate?** (AIM 5-4-5)

   It indicates that either type of equipment may be used to execute the final approach (e.g., VOR or GPS RWY 15).

5. **With no FAF available, when would final descent to the published MDA be started?** (FAA-H-8083-15)

   For non-precision approaches, a final descent is initiated and the final segment begins at either the FAF or the final approach point (FAP). When no FAF is depicted, the final approach point is the point at which the aircraft is established inbound on the final approach course.

6. **If a black triangle with a white "A" appears in the notes section of an approach chart, what significance does this have to a pilot?** (FAA-H-8083-15, Order 8260.3)

   It indicates that nonstandard IFR alternate minimums exist for the airport. If an "NA" appears after the "A," alternate minimums are not authorized. This information is found in the beginning of the *Terminal Procedures Publication* (TPP). Approved terminal weather observation and reporting facilities, or a general area weather report, must be available before an airport may serve as an alternate.

7. What is the significance of the term "radar required" found on some approach charts? (P/CG)

"Radar Required" is terminology used to indicate to a pilot that the approach procedure includes segments that are not navigable without assistance from ATC providing radar services. Typically, this will include vectoring onto the approach course. The pilot can expect to be provided radar navigational guidance while transiting segments labeled with this term. A pilot would not be able to conduct such an approach if they were not in radar contact and receiving ATC guidance services.

8. Define the term *final approach point*. (P/CG)

The final approach point (FAP) is the point, applicable only to a nonprecision approach with no depicted FAF (such as an on airport VOR), where the aircraft is established inbound on the final approach course from the procedure turn and where the final approach descent may be commenced. The FAP serves as the FAF and identifies the beginning of the final approach segment.

For questions in the following sections I–L, refer to the ILS or LOC RWY 16 approach chart for Fort Worth, Texas, depicted on page 195.

I. Instrument Approach Procedure Charts: Plan View

1. What are the MSAs for this approach? (FAA-H-8083-15)

2,200 feet—180° through 270°
3,600 feet—270° through 360°
2,800 feet—360° through 180°

2. On which facility is the MSA centered, and what does it provide? (AIM 5-4-5)

The MSA is centered on the MUFIN LOM; the altitude shown provides at least 1,000 feet of clearance above the highest obstacle within the defined sector up to a distance of 25 NM from the facility. Navigational course guidance is not assured at the MSA.

3. What is the IAF for this procedure? (FAA-H-8083-15)

The IAF is MUFIN LOM.

4. What significance does the bold arrow extending from Bowie VOR have? (FAA-H-8083-15)

It represents a feeder route or flyable route utilized when transitioning from the enroute structure to the initial approach fix.

5. When intercepting the localizer from procedure turn inbound, what will be the relative bearing on the ADF indicator as the localizer needle begins to center? (FAA-H-8083-15)

Assuming a 45° intercept angle, the relative bearing will be 315°.

6. What are the frequencies for the locator outer marker and middle marker beacons? (FAA-H-8083-15)

The locator frequency is 365 kHz. All marker beacons transmit on a frequency of 75 MHz.

7. Explain the difference between a "Note" such as RADAR REQUIRED or DME REQUIRED being charted in the plan view of an approach procedure, and a note being charted in the "Notes" box of the pilot briefing portion of the approach chart. (AIM 5-4-5)

When radar or other equipment is required for procedure entry from the enroute environment, a note will be charted in the plan view of the approach procedure chart. When radar or other equipment is required on portions of the procedure outside the final approach segment, including the missed approach, a note will be charted in the notes box of the pilot briefing portion of the approach chart. Notes are not charted when VOR is required outside the final approach segment. Pilots should ensure that the aircraft is equipped to receive the required NAVAID(s) in order to execute the approach, including the missed approach.

8. Where does the final approach segment begin for the ILS 16 approach? (FAA-H-8083-15)

On all precision approaches, the final approach segment begins when the glide slope is intercepted at glide slope altitude. For nonprecision approaches such as the straight-in LOC 16 approach, the final approach segment begins at the Maltese cross which is the MUFIN LOM.

J. Instrument Approach Procedure Charts: Profile

1. **Within what distance from the MUFIN LOM must the procedure turn be executed?** (FAA-H-8083-15)

   The procedure turn must be executed within 10 NM.

2. **If a procedure turn is required, what would be the minimum altitude while flying this segment?** (FAA-H-8083-15)

   The minimum altitude for the initial approach segment and while executing the procedure turn is 2,400 feet MSL.

3. **To what altitude may a pilot descend after the procedure turn?** (FAA-H-8083-15)

   When established inbound after the procedure turn, the pilot may descend to 2,000 MSL.

4. **What does the number "1992" located at the outer marker indicate?** (FAA-H-8083-15)

   1992 indicates the altitude of the glide slope at the outer marker.

5. **What is the glide slope angle for this approach?** (FAA-H-8083-15)

   The glide slope angle is 3°.

6. **What is the altitude at which the electronic glide slope crosses the threshold of runway 16?** (FAA-H-8083-15)

   The threshold crossing height (TCH) is 57 feet.

7. **If the glide slope became inoperative, could you continue this approach if established on the localizer at the time of the malfunction? Why?** (FAA-H-8083-15)

   Yes, provided ATC is notified and approves a localizer-only approach. Since the procedure indicates a localizer-only minimum, a localizer-only approach can be authorized. The minimum is now an MDA, and the approach is now a nonprecision procedure with MAP being a time or DME point.

8. **If you discovered your marker beacon receiver was inoperative, what are the authorized substitutes for the MUFIN outer marker?** (FAA-H-8083-15)

   Substitutes for the outer marker are:

   a. The compass locator (365 kHz)

   b. 5.3 DME I-FTW

   c. Maverick VORTAC (TTT) radial 269

9. **What DME distance is indicated in the profile view for the MUFIN LOM and the runway threshold?** (FAA-H-8083-15)

   The MUFIN LOM is 5.3 NM, and the runway threshold is 1.5 NM from the localizer antenna site.

10. **Where is the MAP for the precision and nonprecision approach in this procedure?** (FAA-H-8083-15)

    a. For the precision approach procedure, the MAP is upon reaching the DA(H) of 910 feet MSL on the glide slope.

    b. For the nonprecision procedure, the MAP is:

       • 1.5 DME from IFTW; or

       • Time from MUFIN.

K. Instrument Approach Procedure Charts: Minimums

1. **What is the minimum visibility for a Category A full ILS 16 approach?** (FAA-H-8083-15)

   Minimum visibility is ½ mile or RVR of 2,400 feet. RVR of 1,800 feet is authorized with the use of FD or AP or HUD to DA.

2. **If the approach light system became inoperative, how would you determine the minimum visibility for a Category A full ILS 16 approach?** (FAA-H-8083-15)

   To determine landing minimums, consult the "Inoperative Components or Visual Aids Table" found in the *U.S. Terminal Procedures Publication* (TPP) for a complete description of the effect of inoperative components on approach minimums.

3. **Convert the following RVR values to meteorological visibility: 1,600; 2,400; 3,200; 4,000; 4,500; 5,000; and 6,000 feet.** (14 CFR 91.175)

RVR (feet)	Visibility (statute miles)
1,600	1/4
2,400	1/2
3,200	5/8
4,000	3/4
4,500	7/8
5,000	1
6,000	1-1/4

4. **Are takeoff minimums standard or nonstandard for Ft. Worth Meacham Field?** (FAA-H-8083-15)

   Nonstandard; takeoff minimums are not standard and/or departure procedures are published as indicated by the triangle with a "T" printed in the notes area. IFR Takeoff Minimums and (Obstacle) Departure Procedures Section, Section L, of the *Terminal Procedures Publications* (TPPs) should be consulted.

5. **For the localizer approach 16, what are the minimums for a Category A airplane if a circling maneuver is desired?** (FAA-H-8083-15)

   The circling MDA is 1,260 MSL; the visibility requirement increases to 1 mile for the circling maneuver.

6. **What significance do the numbers in parentheses (200-½) have?** (FAA-H-8083-15)

   Any minimums found in parentheses are not applicable to civil pilots. These minimums are directed at military pilots who should refer to appropriate regulations.

7. **When established at the MDA on the final approach course inbound for the straight-in LOC 16 approach, is the MDA expressed as height above touchdown (HAT) or as height above airport (HAA)?** (FAA-H-8083-15)

   The MDA of 530 feet for a straight-in landing always represents height above touchdown (HAT) since the approach is for a specific runway. MDAs for circling approaches will always represent height above airport (HAA) since a specific runway will not be used for landing.

8. **If the current weather reports indicate ceilings 100 overcast and visibility ½ mile, can a pilot legally make an approach to ILS 16, and can the pilot land?** (FAA-H-8083-15)

Under 14 CFR Part 91, the approach may be attempted regardless of the ceiling and visibility. At the DA (DH), the pilot must have the runway environment in sight and have the prescribed flight visibility to land. If these conditions are met, the approach may be continued to a landing.

L. Instrument Approach Procedure Charts: Aerodrome

1. **What types of lighting are available for runway 16?** (FAA-H-8083-15)

HIRL—High-intensity runway lighting

MALSR—Medium-intensity approach lighting system with sequenced flashing lights; denoted by the circled A5 on the approach to runway 16.

2. **What is the touchdown zone elevation for runway 16?** (FAA-H-8083-15)

The TDZE is 710 MSL.

3. **What is the bearing and distance of the MAP from the FAF?** (FAA-H-8083-15)

The MAP is 164°, 3.8 NM from FAF for the localizer approach, and approximately the same distance for the full ILS approach.

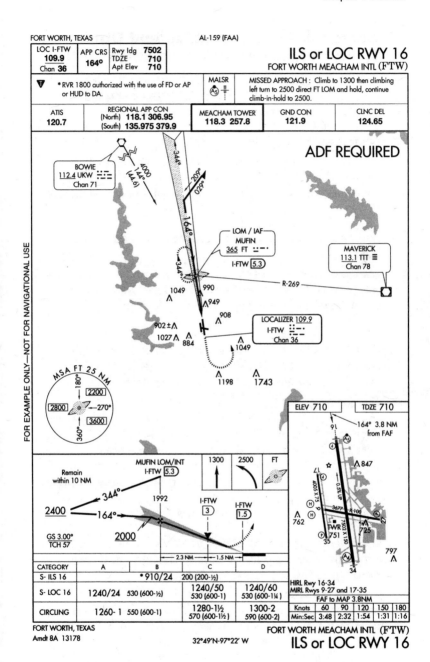

M. Approach Plate Examples and Other Types of Instrument Approaches

For the following questions 1–6, refer to the ILS or LOC RWY 4 approach plate for the Kansas City Charles B Wheeler Downtown Airport (KMKC) depicted on page 198.

1. What is an ILS approach? (AIM 1-1-9)

An ILS is designed to provide an approach path for exact alignment and descent of an aircraft on final approach to a runway. It provides both vertical and horizontal alignment and operates on VHF frequencies from 108.1 to 111.95 MHz.

2. What are the basic components of an ILS approach? (AIM 1-1-9)

The basic components of an ILS are the localizer, glide slope, and outer marker (OM) and, when installed for use with Category II or Category III instrument approach procedures, an inner marker (IM).

3. If a pilot had to execute the missed approach on the ILS or LOC 4 at KMKC and was assigned the "alternate missed," what would the pilot be expected to do?

This approach plate lists a primary missed approach procedure that takes a pilot to the NAPOLEAN (ANX) VOR, but it also lists an alternate missed approach procedure that would take a pilot to the LYMES waypoint for a hold. If the pilot was assigned the alternate missed approach waypoint to hold, the pilot would proceed to this waypoint, which is a cross radial from the MCI and ANX VOR. It could be identified using the VOR cross radials, using DME at 29.2 miles from the MCI VOR, or using an IFR GPS system.

4. When flying the ILS or LOC 4 at KMKC as an ILS, what minimum would a pilot be able to descend to if they were flying the approach at 100 knots?

A pilot flying an approach at 100 knots would be flying the approach to Category B minimums and, with the full ILS system being used, would also be receiving vertical guidance. This would allow the pilot to descend to 1,001 feet MSL, which would take the aircraft down to 257 feet AGL at which point the pilot would reach the decision altitude.

5. **If a pilot were flying the ILS or LOC 4 at KMKC and not receiving radar services, could they still fly the approach?**

   In the approach notes, it is indicated that "DME or RADAR required for procedure entry." This is an indication that a pilot who is not receiving radar vectoring services from ATC would be required to have DME functionality in their aircraft to be able to fly the entry to this approach. If they did, they would be able to conduct this approach as a full approach without ATC vectoring services.

6. **A pilot flying the ILS or LOC 4 at KMKC intends to circle to land on runway 19. To what minimums would the pilot be able to descend to do this, and how would they conduct their circles?**

   A pilot flying the ILS or LOC 4 at KMKC cannot descend to the lowest available minimums for the ILS if they plan to circle to land on a different runway. In this case, the circling minimums would be 1,560 feet MSL for all categories (with different visibility requirements for faster aircraft). A note in the top of the chart also indicates to the pilot that "circling NA east of Rwy 1-19," which indicates that the pilot would have to enter a circling to the airport to the west of that runway, flying right turns through the traffic pattern to a landing on runway 19 if it was their runway of choice for landing. A further note indicates that circling to runway 22 is not authorized.

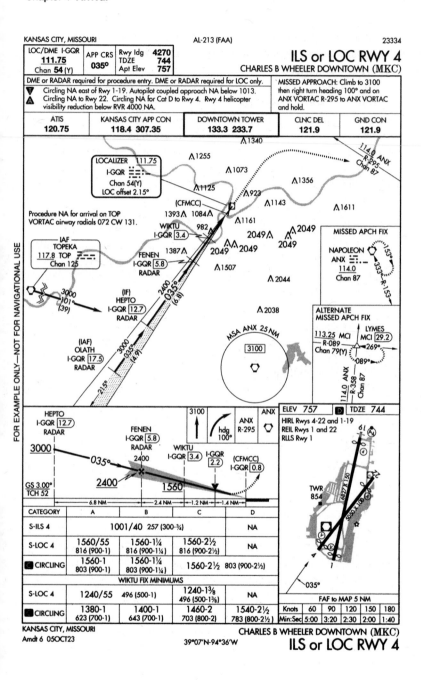

For the following questions 7–10, refer to the LDA/DME RWY 25 approach plate for the Columbia Gorge RGNL/The Dalles MUNI airport (KDLS) depicted on page 201.

7. What is an LDA approach? (AIM 1-1-9)

The localizer directional aid (LDA) is of comparable use and accuracy to a localizer but is not part of a complete ILS. The LDA course usually provides a more precise approach course than the similar simplified directional facility (SDF) installation, which may have a course width of 6 or 12 degrees.

The LDA is not aligned with the runway. Straight-in minimums may be published where alignment does not exceed 30 degrees between the course and runway. Circling minimums only are published where this alignment exceeds 30 degrees.

A very limited number of LDA approaches also incorporate a glide slope. These are annotated in the plan view of the instrument approach chart with a note, "LDA/Glideslope." These procedures fall under a newly defined category of approaches called *approach with vertical guidance* (APV) described in FAA *AIM* ¶5-4-5(a)(7) (b). LDA minima for with and without glide slope is provided and annotated on the minima lines of the approach chart as S-LDA/GS and S-LDA. Because the final approach course is not aligned with the runway centerline, additional maneuvering will be required compared to an ILS approach.

8. When approaching the airport flying the LDA/DME RWY 25 approach, what approach direction would the pilot be flying when inbound to the airport?

While the approach is to runway 25, a pilot flying the LDA/DME RWY 25 approach will be flying an inbound course of 238 degrees using the localizer frequency of 109.35. In the airport layout view in the lower left of the chart, it shows that the 238-degree approach path does not align directly with runway 25, which is why this approach is a LDA approach instead of a straight in localizer approach.

9. **When flying the LDA/DME RWY 25 approach to KDLS, what minimums are available for a pilot?**

   On this approach, "straight in" minimums are the only minimums offered as denoted in the minimums box by "S-LDA/GS 25" for a pilot. The fact that there are no alternative minimums given for a localizer only (assuming a glide slope was inoperative) or circling minimums is an indication that a pilot may only use this approach for a straight-in landing on runway 25.

10. **How does a pilot know if the LDA/DME RWY 25 approach at KDLS has a glide slope?**

    While many LDA approaches do not have glide slopes associated with them, a note in the upper left of the plan view of the chart indicates "LDA/GLIDE SLOPE" which is an indication to a pilot that they could expect to have a glide slope on this approach procedure.

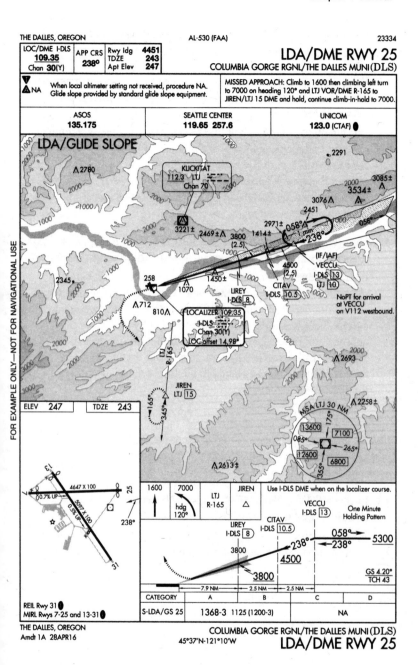

THE DALLES, OREGON   AL-530 (FAA)   23334

LOC/DME I-DLS	APP CRS	Rwy ldg	4451
109.35	**238°**	TDZE	**243**
Chan 30(Y)		Apt Elev	**247**

LDA/DME RWY 25
COLUMBIA GORGE RGNL/THE DALLES MUNI (DLS)

▼ NA — When local altimeter setting not received, procedure NA. Glide slope provided by standard glide slope equipment.

MISSED APPROACH: Climb to 1600 then climbing left turn to 7000 on heading 120° and LTJ VOR/DME R-165 to JIREN/LTJ 15 DME and hold, continue climb-in-hold to 7000.

ASOS	SEATTLE CENTER	UNICOM
135.175	**119.65 257.6**	**123.0** (CTAF) ●

FOR EXAMPLE ONLY—NOT FOR NAVIGATIONAL USE

LDA/GLIDE SLOPE

KLICKITAT
112.3 LTJ
Chan 70

LOCALIZER 109.35
I-DLS
Chan 30(Y)
LOC offset 14.98°

(IF/IAF)
VECCU
I-DLS [13]
LTJ [10]

NoPT for arrival at VECCU on V112 westbound.

CITAV
I-DLS [10.5]

LIREY
I-DLS [8]

JIREN
LTJ [15]

MSA LTJ 30 NM

ELEV	247		TDZE	243

Use I-DLS DME when on the localizer course.

1600	7000	LTJ R-165	JIREN △			VECCU I-DLS [13]	One Minute Holding Pattern

4647 X 100
0.7% UP
5597 X 100
0.5% UP
238°

REIL Rwy 31 ●
MIRL Rwys 7-25 and 13-31 ●

LIREY I-DLS [8]
CITAV I-DLS [10.5]
3800
4500
3800

058°
238°
5300
GS 4.20°
TCH 43

CATEGORY	A	B	C	D
S-LDA/GS 25	1368-3 1125 (1200-3)		NA	

THE DALLES, OREGON
Amdt 1A 28APR16

COLUMBIA GORGE RGNL/THE DALLES MUNI (DLS)
45°37'N-121°10'W
LDA/DME RWY 25

*For the following questions 11–12, refer to the RNAV (GPS) RWY 28
approach plate for Albany INTL (KALB) depicted on page 203.*

**11. When approaching the KALB airport and selecting
a point to start the approach, what points would be
considered initial approach fixes (IAFs)?**

The Cambridge CAM VOR and the CANAN waypoint are both
denoted as starting points for the approach by the "IAF" indication
next to them. A pilot flying the approach should expect to start the
approach at one of these waypoints unless otherwise sequenced
to an intermediate fix (IF) by ATC when in contact with ATC and
receiving radar services.

**12. How would a pilot flying the KALB RNAV (GPS) RWY 28
approach know to what minimums they could descend?**

Four minimums are offered for this approach. If a pilot was
intending to circle to land, they would use the circling minimums.
If the pilot was flying an aircraft with a non-WAAS-equipped GPS
system, they would be limited to either LNAV/VNAV or LNAV
approach minimums. If the pilot was flying an aircraft that had a
WAAS-certificated GPS system, they could fly the approach to
the lowest minimums as listed in the LPV section of the approach
minimums.

*For the following questions 13–16, refer to the VOR/DME-A approach
plate for the Savannah/Hilton Head International Airport (KSAV)
depicted on page 205.*

**13. Is the KSAV VOR/DME-A approach considered a
precision or non-precision approach?**

A VOR approach does not offer a glide slope for vertical guidance
to the airport, so it cannot be considered a precision approach.

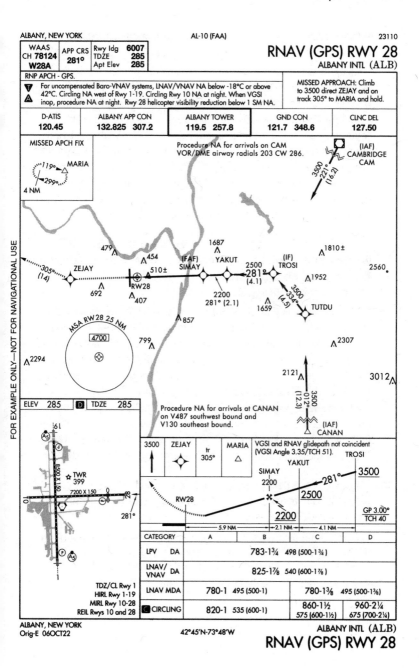

ALBANY, NEW YORK — AL-10 (FAA) — 23110

RNAV (GPS) RWY 28
ALBANY INTL (ALB)

WAAS CH 78124 W28A	APP CRS 281°	Rwy Idg 6007 TDZE 285 Apt Elev 285

RNP APCH - GPS.

For uncompensated Baro-VNAV systems, LNAV/VNAV NA below -18°C or above 42°C. Circling NA west of Rwy 1-19. Circling Rwy 10 NA at night. When VGSI inop, procedure NA at night. Rwy 28 helicopter visibility reduction below 1 SM NA.

MISSED APPROACH: Climb to 3500 direct ZEJAY and on track 305° to MARIA and hold.

D-ATIS 120.45	ALBANY APP CON 132.825 307.2	ALBANY TOWER 119.5 257.8	GND CON 121.7 348.6	CLNC DEL 127.50

MISSED APCH FIX

MARIA 119° / 299° 4 NM

Procedure NA for arrivals on CAM VOR/DME airway radials 203 CW 286.

(IAF) CAMBRIDGE CAM 3500 221° (16.2)

479 Λ 454 Λ 510± 1687 Λ (FAF) SIMAY YAKUT 2500 281° (4.1) (IF) TROSI 1810± Λ 2560 •

ZEJAY 305° (14) RW28 692 Λ 407 Λ 2200 281° (2.1) 1659 Λ 1952 Λ 3500 334° (4.5) TUTDU

MSA RW28 25 NM 4700

857 Λ 799 Λ 2307 Λ

2294 Λ 2121 Λ 3012 Λ 3500 012° (12.3)

Procedure NA for arrivals at CANAN on V487 southwest bound and V130 southeast bound.

(IAF) CANAN

ELEV 285 D TDZE 285

| 3500 ↑ | ZEJAY ✦ | tr 305° | MARIA △ | VGSI and RNAV glidepath not coincident (VGSI Angle 3.35/TCH 51). |

SIMAY 2200 YAKUT 2500 TROSI 3500 281°

RW28 2200 2200 GP 3.00° TCH 40

5.9 NM — 2.1 NM — 4.1 NM

CATEGORY	A	B	C	D
LPV DA	783-1¾ 498 (500-1¾)			
LNAV/ VNAV DA	825-1⅞ 540 (600-1⅞)			
LNAV MDA	780-1 495 (500-1)		780-1⅜ 495 (500-1⅜)	
CIRCLING	820-1 535 (600-1)		860-1½ 575 (600-1½)	960-2¼ 675 (700-2¼)

TDZ/CL Rwy 1
HIRL Rwy 1-19
MIRL Rwy 10-28
REIL Rwys 10 and 28

TWR 399

7200 X 150
8500 X 150
281°

ALBANY, NEW YORK
Orig-E 06OCT22

42°45'N-73°48'W

ALBANY INTL (ALB)
RNAV (GPS) RWY 28

FOR EXAMPLE ONLY—NOT FOR NAVIGATIONAL USE

14. **When flying the KSAV VOR/DME-A approach, what runway will the approach be aligned with for landing?**

    This approach does not indicate a particular runway for alignment. It can be initially identified as a circling only approach by the fact that the heading indicates it is the VOR/DME-A approach instead of noting a runway where the "A" is in the approach heading. A secondary point that indicates that it is not to a specific runway is the fact that only circling minimums are offered in the minimums section. This is an approach that broadly approaches the airport. A pilot can see in the airport layout view in the bottom right of the chart that the arrow indicates a general approach to the airport from the southwest between runways 10 and 1.

15. **If a pilot establishes their aircraft onto the KSAV VOR/ DME-A approach by starting at the SAV VOR, what would the pilot do next to establish themself back inbound on the approach course?**

    The SAV VOR is an initial approach fix (IAF) from which a pilot could establish themself onto this approach. The pilot would then proceed outbound on the 204 radial past the UVITE waypoint at 4 DME from the SAV VOR and no further than 15 NM from the VOR, where they would conduct a procedure turn. The procedure turn would be to a 159-degree heading from which they would turn back around to 339 degrees and intercept the 024 degree inbound course. Once established inbound on that course, the pilot could descend below 3,000 feet MSL until reaching the final approach fix (FAF), after which they could descend below 1,200 feet MSL.

16. **How would a pilot flying the KSAV VOR/DME-A approach know when to execute a missed approach if the airport environment was not visible?**

    A DME point at the RUYOL waypoint is noted at 1.7 DME from the SAV VOR. This could be identified using DME on the SAV VOR frequency of 115.95 or substituting an IFR-capable GPS system to identify the RUYOL waypoint.

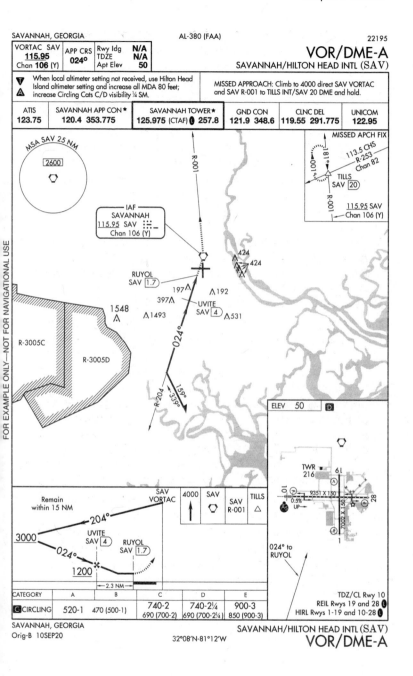

*For the following questions 17–19, refer to the LOC BC RWY 27L
approach plate for Pontiac, Michigan, Oakland County International
Airport (KPTK) depicted on page 207.*

17. What is a "back course" approach? (AIM 1-1-9)

A back course approach is a localizer-type approach that utilizes
a localizer frequency either associated with a localizer or ILS
approach that approaches the runway from the other side. Unless
the aircraft's ILS equipment includes reverse sensing capability,
when flying inbound on the back course it is necessary to steer
the aircraft in the direction opposite the needle deflection when
making corrections from off-course to on-course. This "flying
away from the needle" is also required when flying outbound on
the front course of the localizer. Do not use back course signals for
approach unless a back course approach procedure is published for
that particular runway and the approach is authorized by ATC.

18. When flying the LOC BC RWY 27L approach at KPTK, what would a pilot in an aircraft without reverse sensing navigation equipment need to know regarding course deflection corrections?

Unless the aircraft's ILS equipment includes reverse sensing
capability, when flying inbound on the back course, it is necessary
to steer the aircraft in the direction opposite the needle deflection
when making corrections from off-course to on-course.

19. What should a pilot approaching the KPTK airport using the LOC BC RWY 27L approach do with respect to glide slope indications?

A note in the profile view of the chart indicates that a pilot should
"Disregard GS indications." This approach should be considered
a non-precision approach on which a pilot will descend to a
minimum descent altitude, not a decision height with the assistance
of a glide slope as they might on an ILS approach.

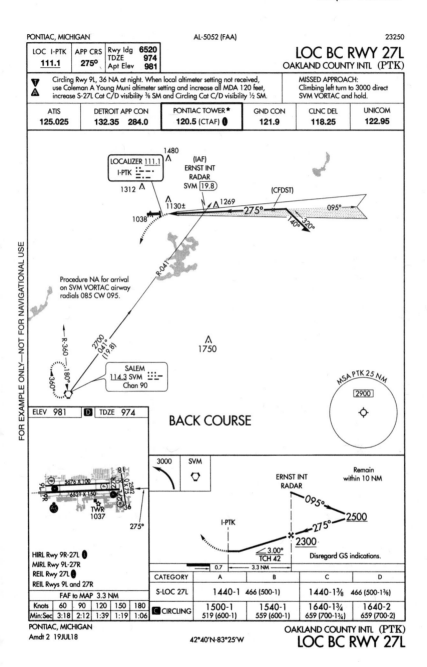

PONTIAC, MICHIGAN
AL-5052 (FAA)
23250

LOC I-PTK	APP CRS	Rwy Idg	**6520**
111.1	**275°**	TDZE	**974**
		Apt Elev	**981**

LOC BC RWY 27L
OAKLAND COUNTY INTL (PTK)

▼⚠ Circling Rwy 9L, 36 NA at night. When local altimeter setting not received, use Coleman A Young Muni altimeter setting and increase all MDA 120 feet, increase S-27L Cat C/D visibility ⅜ SM and Circling Cat C/D visibility ½ SM.

MISSED APPROACH: Climbing left turn to 3000 direct SVM VORTAC and hold.

ATIS	DETROIT APP CON	PONTIAC TOWER *	GND CON	CLNC DEL	UNICOM
125.025	**132.35 284.0**	**120.5** (CTAF) ⬤	**121.9**	**118.25**	**122.95**

FOR EXAMPLE ONLY—NOT FOR NAVIGATIONAL USE

LOCALIZER 111.1
I-PTK

(IAF)
ERNST INT
RADAR
SVM 19.8

(CFDST)

275°   095°
140° 320°

R-041°

Procedure NA for arrival on SVM VORTAC airway radials 085 CW 095.

R-360°   180°
2700 041°
(19.8)
360°

SALEM
114.3 SVM
Chan 90

MSA PTK 25 NM
2900

BACK COURSE

ELEV 981	Ⅾ	TDZE 974

HIRL Rwy 9R-27L ⬤
MIRL Rwy 9L-27R
REIL Rwy 27L ⬤
REIL Rwys 9L and 27R

5676 X 100
6521 X 150
TWR 1037
275°

3000   SVM

ERNST INT
RADAR
Remain within 10 NM
095°
2500
275°
I-PTK
2300
3.00°
TCH 42
Disregard GS indications.
0.7   3.3 NM

CATEGORY	A	B	C	D
S-LOC 27L	1440-1 466 (500-1)		1440-1⅜ 466 (500-1⅜)	
Ⓒ CIRCLING	1500-1 519 (600-1)	1540-1 559 (600-1)	1640-1¾ 659 (700-1¾)	1640-2 659 (700-2)

FAF to MAP 3.3 NM					
Knots	60	90	120	150	180
Min:Sec	3:18	2:12	1:39	1:19	1:06

PONTIAC, MICHIGAN
Amdt 2 19JUL18

42°40'N-83°25'W

OAKLAND COUNTY INTL (PTK)
LOC BC RWY 27L

Scenario-Based Training

Training

5

by Arlynn McMahon

Introduction

During the oral portion of the instrument practical exam, expect the questions to include scenarios focused on the flight environment that instrument pilots are authorized to fly in. The examiner/inspector will expect you to be able to anticipate weather changes during flight and how the flight handling characteristics of an aircraft may change with changes in meteorological conditions. You should also expect questions that find you unexpectedly in conditions that you must escape from—primarily icing, fog, and thunderstorms.

Often there is more than one correct answer for a scenario-based question; therefore, ensure that your answers to the examiner include the content identified as the "must" items listed in the answers given below. Additionally, be generous in displaying to the examiner your aeronautical decision making by sharing your thought process aloud as you analyze the elements involved.

As a pilot with an instrument rating, you are expected by the FAA, the industry, and your future passengers to handle the unexpected as well as routine procedures. You must see the "big picture" in addition to the details. In answering oral exam questions, you must look for and recognize the underlying elements presented by the scenarios. Be prepared to include risk management aspects in your answers whenever possible.

Scenario-Based Questions

1. **On a beautiful clear, sunny, VMC day, you are flying on an IFR flight plan. Are you required to be instrument current?**

   In this question, the examiner is testing your knowledge of meteorological conditions versus the rules under which you are flying.

   Regardless of the meteorological conditions, if I am flying under instrument rules, then I must be instrument current.

2. **Thirty minutes after takeoff you enter the clouds. The climb through a cloud layer requires 10 minutes. The enroute phase is 50 minutes and is above the overcast layer, at night. Descent requires 30 minutes through the clouds before breaking out into clear VMC. How much of this flight will you log as "actual instruments"?**

Your answer must include the regulation pertaining to logging time. In this scenario, the flight through the clouds obviously should be logged; however, the examiner has allowed you to judge if the flight above an overcast layer at night is "by reference to instruments."

I would log as "actual instruments" all of the time that I was flying by reference to instruments. This would obviously include the time flying through the cloud layer, but also any other time that I was flying by reference to instruments. *[See page 9, Chapter 1 questions A18 and A19.]*

3. **Your aircraft is equipped with a certified GPS, but during the VOT preflight check, both VORs failed to be accurate. You have no other means of navigation. How will this affect your flight?**

Your answer must demonstrate your knowledge of a VOT check and the accuracy requirements (see page 89), as well as your knowledge of GPS requirements.

I will not be able to file an IFR flight plan. To file an IFR flight plan, I must have an alternate (non-GPS) means of navigation unless my GPS is WAAS certified.

4. **The airport that you desire to use as a required alternate airport offers only RNAV IAPs. How will this affect you?**

If an alternate airport is required and that airport offers only RNAV IAPs, then my aircraft must be equipped with a WAAS-certified GPS. If there are IAPs that use other NAVAIDs, in addition to the RNAV IAP, then I can file it as a required alternate with a GPS that is not WAAS certified.

The following questions refer to the enroute low-altitude chart for the Lexington, Kentucky, area shown on the next page.

5. On a flight departing from the Cynthiana Harrison Co Airport to Georgetown Scott County Field, when do FARs require you to be on an IFR flight plan?

I must be on an IFR flight plan when conditions are less than VMC and when in controlled airspace, which in the Cynthiana area is 1,200 feet AGL, and in the vicinity of Georgetown is 700 feet AGL.

6. During the preflight run-up, you find the transponder is INOP. How does this affect your IFR flight from Cynthiana to Georgetown?

- Transponder requirements are not specific to flights under IFR.

- Technically, the flight from Cynthiana to Georgetown is not in airspace that requires a transponder: it's not in or above Class C or Class B airspace and I'm flying below 10,000 feet MSL. So from that perspective I am legal to fly.

- However, the inoperative equipment regulation would require me to placard the transponder INOP.

- With the unit INOP, I will leave the transponder unit OFF.

7. Your flight plan is a round-robin: Depart KLEX, direct to HYK, V53 IRVIN, V517 LOGIC, V178 HYK, landing KLEX. You filed 3,000 feet MSL. Your ATC clearance is: "Cleared as filed, climb to and maintain 2,500' expect 3,000' 10 minutes after..." Immediately after takeoff, you are IMC with no ground contact and very shortly after that all calls to ATC go unanswered. You hear no other traffic on the frequency. What will you do?

Your answer must demonstrate your understanding of IFR 2-way communications loss. It should demonstrate your ability to diagnose routine radio problems. Your answer could include:

- I will climb to 2,500 feet MSL and proceed direct to HYK. After 10 minutes or upon crossing HYK, I will climb to 3,000 feet. At IRVINE I'll climb to 3,300 feet, and at LOGIC I'll descend to 3,000 feet to HYK.

- I'll change my transponder code to 7600 and I'll continue to make radio calls into the blind.

(continued)

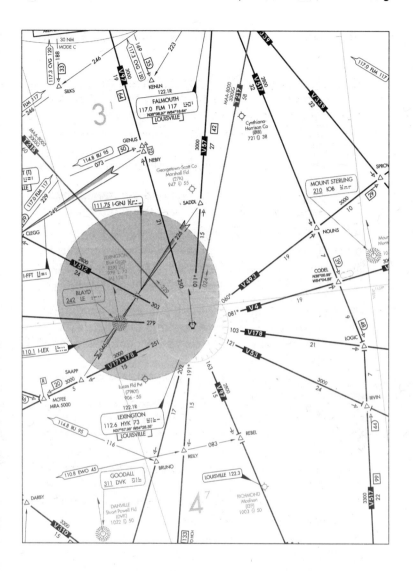

- In the meantime, I'll try to correct or work around the problem by:
  1. Verifying the volume control.
  2. Verifying the audio panel receive/transmit selector.
  3. Verifying the headset is fully connected.
  4. Attempting to call ATC using the other COM.
  5. Attempting to call ATC using the co-pilot PTT.
  6. Attempting to call Louisville FSS using the HYK RCO and relaying to ATC.
  7. Attempting to use my cell phone to call FSS, who may be able to relay to ATC for me.
- Considering what I think is the active runway and the IAP most likely to result in seeing the runway, I'll choose an appropriate approach procedure, and if necessary, I will hold in order to depart the IAP as close to my flight plan time as possible.

8. When using VOR as the primary source for navigation, how will you set up your NAVs along this flight (i.e., Which NAV will you set up to identify each intersection)?

Good instrument pilots have "standard operating procedures" that they use consistently. The examiner would like to know you have developed SOPs. Your answer could be:

My flight deck standard operating procedure is to always use NAV #1 to navigate along and NAV #2 to identify intersections. So I'd put:

- HYK in #1 and the NAVAID 44 NM south in #2 to identify IRVINE.
- Then turning to navigate along V517: The NAVAID 44 NM south in #1 and HYK in #2 to identify LOGIC.
- Make a turn at LOGIC: The NAVAID 48 NM north in #1 and HYK in #2 to identify CODEL and NOUNS.
- Then turning to navigate along V493, I'd probably put HYK in #2 in anticipation of using #1 for the IAP.

9. **When using GPS as a primary source for navigation, you would enter each intersection as a waypoint into the GPS Flight Plan: KLEX, HYK, IRVIN, LOGIC, CODEL, NOUNS, HYK, KLEX. What is the button sequence to remove CODEL from the flight plan?**

   Your answer will depend on your specific GPS unit; you should demonstrate your understanding of your GPS unit by describing the particular button sequence required to remove the CODEL waypoint.

10. **During this flight, what tasks are needed to properly prepare for an IAP?**

    Your answer should demonstrate your understanding of the tasks to prepare for an IFR arrival, and your ability to prioritize and manage tasks. Your specific answer will depend on your airplane, but should include specific tasks and the timing for each. For example:

    To properly prepare for an IAP, I would:

    • Listen to the ATIS.

    • Self-brief the approach procedure by reviewing the IAP in detail.

    • Reduce speed.

    • Set up avionics and identify NAVAIDs.

    • Perform the pre-landing checklist and configure the aircraft for landing.

11. **Will the length of runway required for a landing from an IAP be different than a landing from a VFR approach?**

    Most pilots configure the aircraft and fly an IAP differently than a VFR approach. The examiner is testing your standard operating procedure and your understanding of how that may affect your runway requirements. Your answer could include:

    • The landing should be a full-stall touchdown, especially from an IAP when snow or standing water may be present on the runway.

    • If I fly an IAP at a speed that is higher than the manufacturer's recommended VFR approach speed, it will require more runway to land to give the plane time to dissipate the excess speed.

    • If I have a stabilized approach set up, I might land from an IAP with less than full flaps, which will require more runway to land.

12. The ACS calls for our IAPs to be "stabilized approaches." Why is that important and what does having a stabilized approach mean to you?

Your answer must demonstrate your knowledge of the elements of the stabilized approach for your specific airplane and the relationship between a stabilized approach and CFIT-related accidents. Your answer could include:

It's important to have a stabilized approach during final descent because I don't want last-minute configuration changes or distractions. This is important in preventing CFIT accidents. My stabilized approach means that I'll achieve by 1,000 feet AGL (or nearly after) the FAF and continue to touchdown with:

- proper configuration for landing.
- an appropriate power setting.
- a consistent 500–700 fpm rate of descent (if nonprecision approach).
- stabilized approach airspeed for the lowest possible landing category.
- tracking on-course, within one dot.
- on or within one-dot-above glideslope (if precision approach).
- only minor corrections. If large corrections are necessary, then I'll miss the approach rather than continue a descent or attempt to salvage a risky situation.

13. If you encounter unforecasted freezing rain, would you allow the autopilot to control the plane or would you hand-fly it?

There is no "right" answer to this question. The examiner wants to know that you have given thought to how you will handle this situation. Possible answers:

AGAINST using the autopilot: I would hand fly. The largest hazard in freezing rain is that ice accumulates quickly on the aircraft surface and results in a loss of lift. If flying with the autopilot on, I won't receive tactile inputs on the effectiveness of control surfaces and may not perceive the loss of lift.

FOR using the autopilot: I would turn on the autopilot. This represents a busy time in the flight deck. I have to alter plans and reprogram technology. I want the autopilot to relieve some of the workload tasks.

14. **If you were concerned about freezing rain developing along your flight, what specific weather reports or forecasts would you look at to determine the likelihood of freezing rain developing?**

    Several of the forecasts may mention freezing rain. However, I know that freezing rain is the result of a temperature inversion. The Winds and Temperatures Aloft Forecast shows air temperatures at various altitudes; I could use this forecast to detect a temperature inversion—to see if there is warm air over colder air and temperatures near freezing.

15. **If you inadvertently encounter freezing rain, what would be your preferred escape method?**

    Your answer must demonstrate your understanding of the impact of operating in freezing rain. It could include:

    - An immediate escape is necessary—I would not wait.

    - The best and fastest escape from freezing rain is a 180-degree turn back to where I came from.

    - The next best escape method is to try to change altitudes to find warmer air.

16. **Do you have any anti-ice or deice equipment installed on your airplane?**

    Your answer must be specific to your airplane; demonstrate that you know what equipment is installed on your airplane as well as when to use it.

    - Alternate air control—used when primary air input is blocked; allows entry of heated air.

    - Carburetor heat—used to keep fuel and air flowing to the engine. I would turn it on after the first sign of possible carburetor icing.

    - Pitot heat—used to keep the pilot/static instrument operational. I would turn it on in advance of a possible icing situation.

    - Windshield defrost—used to keep the windshield clear. I would turn it on in advance of a possible icing situation.

17. If you encounter icing during a lost-com situation, what will you do?

This is not a question about lost-com procedures. Your answer must demonstrate your awareness of a possible emergency situation forming and how you will handle it.

- This is no longer just a lost-com situation, but is now a possible emergency.
- I will change the transponder code from 7600 to 7700.
- I will use my pilot's emergency prerogative. I will do whatever I feel I need to do—including changing altitudes to get out of the clouds or to find warm air, changing route segment, and/or initiating an IAP to the nearest airport.

18. If you are concerned about fog, what specific weather reports/forecasts would you look at to determine the likelihood of fog developing?

Your answer should demonstrate your knowledge of the contents of specific reports and forecasts. (Refer to Chapter 1, Section H.) Specifically:

- I would review all of the reports for current temperatures and dewpoints.
- I would consider how the setting sun (if flying in the evening) or rising sun (early in the morning) might change the temperature.
- If the temperature and dewpoint spread is becoming small, then I know to expect fog.

19. If you inadvertently encounter thick fog, what would be your preferred escape method?

Your answer should demonstrate your understanding of fog.

Flying in fog is not usually a problem until it becomes time for an IAP and landing. Depending on the type of fog:

- I would look for an airport at a higher elevation, or if it's upslope fog, I might look for an airport at a lower elevation.
- If flying near the coast, I would look for an airport further inland.
- If all else fails, I would lean the engine for best economy and fly to an area with improved conditions.

20. A VOR IAP has a published MSA. An RNAV IAP has a published TAA? How do you correctly use these altitudes?

Your answer must demonstrate an understanding of the difference between these altitudes.

- A minimum safe altitude (MSA) is advisory information used as an emergency quick reference. Pilots normally don't use the MSA during normal operations. An MSA may be published on any IAP.

- A terminal arrival area (TAA) is only associated with an RNAV IAP. The TAA is part of the IAP. If I am in a TAA and have been cleared for the IAP, I am considered to be on a published portion of the IAP and am authorized to descend to that altitude without further ATC instructions.

21. While conducting a nonprecision IAP, you decide that you are too high. At what point can you initiate a missed approach procedure?

Your answer must demonstrate your understanding of the missed approach procedure.

I can arrest my descent at any time. However, I must continue the IAP to the missed approach point before maneuvering.

22. You are flying an airway that has three altitudes published for that segment:

8,000

5,000G

4,500*

What does this mean to you?

- 8,000 is the minimum enroute altitude (MEA) if the aircraft is not GPS equipped.

- 5,000G is the altitude that may be used as the MEA when navigating via GPS.

- 4,500* is the minimum obstruction clearance altitude (MOCA); ATC may assign this altitude when I'm within 22 NM of the VOR.

23. About 25 NM from your destination, you determine that the aircraft has been using more fuel than planned. You think you should have adequate fuel to reach your destination as long as there are no delays. Is this something that you should report to ATC?

Yes, I should inform ATC so that they can be a resource for me. Additionally:

- I should report "minimum fuel" when I'm concerned about the time in my tanks.

- I would declare a "fuel emergency" if I need priority handling to the airport.

- I would not hesitate to declare an emergency. I would not be concerned about possible repercussions, because it's better to be safe than sorry.

24. You have checked out in the flight school's new C172; how will you conduct an IFR preflight instrument flight deck check?

- I would verify that all needed flight deck equipment (charts, flashlight, etc.) is on board and accessible in the flight deck. Verifying means touching everything, and not just assuming that items are in my flight bag.

- I would verify the instruments are reading correctly for ground operations:

  1. Magnetic compass is full of fluid and free. During taxi, it swings appropriately to known headings.
  2. Airspeed indicator reads zero.
  3. Attitude indicator is stable and horizon bar is set correctly.
  4. Altimeter reads field elevation when set to current barometric pressure.
  5. Baro setting may also be needed in GPS, autopilot or other technology.
  6. Turn coordinator indicates correctly during taxi and the ball rolls away from the turn.
  7. HI/HSI/RMI is set correctly and moves correctly during taxi.
  8. VSI indicates near zero.

25. **During the instrument flight deck check, you note the following:**
    - **The turn coordinator does not indicate a turn during taxi.**
    - **With the correct barometric pressure set, the altimeter reads 60 feet above the field elevation.**
    - **Vertical speed is showing a 100-foot climb on the ground.**

    Which of the indications listed represent a no-go item and which are acceptable?

    No-go:

    - The turn coordinator does not indicate a turn during taxi.

    Acceptable:

    - With the correct barometric pressure set, the altimeter reads 60 feet above the field elevation.

    - Vertical speed is showing a 100-foot climb on the ground.

26. **During your first flight in the flight school's new C172, what equipment checks will you perform for an IFR flight that you normally don't do on a VFR flight?**

    Your answer should demonstrate your knowledge of the equipment checks that are appropriate for your plane.

    I would perform the following equipment checks:

    - Verify that the pitot-static check has been completed in the previous 24 months.

    - During preflight inspection, check the pitot heat.

    - Turn on all equipment. Make sure that it powers up correctly.

    - During run-up, in addition to all normal checklist items, I would:
      1. Perform an autopilot check.
      2. Verify that the VOR(s) have been checked and appropriately noted in the previous 30 days.
      3. Set the clock and confirm its operation.
      4. Verify the outside air temperature.
      5. Follow the proper GPS startup and check procedures. Verify the database expiration date and RAIM.

27. What action would you take if you encounter unforecasted rime ice?

Your answer must include an understanding of the formation of rime ice, as well as strategies you would use to escape the icing conditions and improve your situation.

Rime ice forms when flying in visible moisture and the outside air temperature is at or below freezing. My highest priority is to get to conditions that remove one of these factors. Specifically, I would consider:

- Doing something immediately. I would not delay; rime ice forms quickly.
- Inform ATC that I'm encountering ice. Then based on my knowledge of current weather conditions:
  1. Change altitudes to get out of the clouds.
  2. Change altitudes to get to warmer air.
  3. Make a 180-degree turn. If I was not picking up ice where I came from, then I would go back there.
  4. Land as soon as possible.

I would use additional strategies to improve my situation:

- Turn on anti-ice equipment (pitot heat, windshield defrost, carb heat, etc.).
- As time permits: Solicit PIREPs from ATC from other pilots in my vicinity regarding their icing conditions.

28. After inadvertently encountering icing conditions, your engine begins to run rough, with a loss of engine RPM. What is the likely cause and solution?

Your answer must include an understanding of the engine and symptoms associated with engine roughness in icing conditions. Specifically:

- Probability is high that my engine air intake has become blocked.
- If my engine is equipped with carb heat, I would apply it to access outside air through a different inlet.
- If my engine is equipped with alternate air, I would turn it on to access outside air through a different inlet.
- I would exit icing conditions as soon as possible.

29. On a day IMC flight, about 50 miles from your destination, you notice the ammeter is discharging. What will you do?

Your answer must include an understanding of the electrical system and the underlying implication of an ammeter discharging.

I am about to lose electrical power and with it, electrical accessories. If faced with this situation, I would:

- Recycle the master switch (alternator side on a split switch) to reset a possible overvoltage relay problem.

- Prepare for possible complete electrical failure.

- Turn off all unnecessary electrical equipment.

- Inform ATC, if I still have communications.

- Not count on making my destination. I would select the closest airport with an IAP that will assure a successful approach.

- Navigate to the closest IAF.

- Obtain the POH and review electrical system checklists.

- Inform passengers of the situation and how they may be of assistance to me.

30. When I say that I want to see strong SRM habits in the flight deck during this flight, specifically what does that mean I want you to do?

Your answer must demonstrate your understanding of SRM and its six components.

Single-pilot resource management (SRM) consists of six components that are closely affected by each other. Specifically:

1. *Aeronautical decision making (ADM)*—you want to know that I have looked at all the available options and made a decision based on facts and my personal limitations.

2. *Risk management (RM)*—you want to know that my decisions are made in such a way to mitigate risks.

3. *Task management (TA)*—you want to see me prioritize and plan flight deck workload so that I don't become saturated with tasks and fail to aviate, navigate and communicate.

4. *Situational awareness (SA)*—you want to see that I have an awareness of what is going on inside and outside of the airplane, presently as well as how the situation may develop during the remainder of the flight.

(continued)

5. *Controlled flight into terrain (CFIT)*—you want to see me flying in such a way that reduces the likelihood that we'll fly into terrain. This probably means that I have demonstrated good ADM, RM, TA and SA.

6. *Automation management (AM)*—you want to see me managing a current level of automation and being aware of automation modes, alerts and programming.

31. Give me a few specific examples of how you use good task management skills on an IFR flight?

Your answer should demonstrate your understanding of how to plan for and prioritize tasks.

- I'll prioritize tasks in a way that doesn't distract from flying the airplane. Overall, this means that I will Aviate first; Navigate second; Communicate third.

- I'll execute tasks (such as checklists) so as not to increase workload during critical phases of flight.

- I'll think ahead and set up NAVAIDs in advance.

- I'll complete tasks, appropriate for the phase of flight, without getting distracted from the job of flying the airplane.

- When necessary, I'll slow down the aircraft to give me more time to complete required tasks.

32. You've had a busy business trip, with 18 IFR IAPs in the past three days. On this IAP, you break out of the clouds at 1,500 feet AGL to find a blanket of snow completely covering the ground and runway at Tiny City Airport. What will you do?

Your answer must discuss risk factors and possible mitigations, and should include the soft-field landing procedure for your aircraft.

I would attempt to mitigate the risk factors associated with this landing by:

- Attempting to call UNICOM to see if the attendant can tell me how deep the snow is.

- Considering a low approach over the runway to see what I can see and look for possible drifts or snow banks.

- Calling ATC to inquire about runway conditions at nearby airports for a possible diversion.

- Giving myself plenty of time to evaluate alternatives and set up the airplane properly. I would not hesitate to fly out of my way to where runway and services are better.

- If I proceed with landing at Tiny City Airport, I would follow the soft-field landing procedure for my aircraft. This includes keeping the nose wheel off the ground as long as possible, and minimizing braking.

This scenario reveals insufficient preflight planning. By making a phone call to the FBO to learn about local airport conditions before takeoff, I could have avoided this situation. Perhaps the reason for this poor planning is my fatigue—I've flown a lot in the past three days. Did I pass the "I'M SAFE" checklist?

33. Give me a few examples of situations that might result in a CFIT accident?

Your answer must show an understanding of controlled flight into the ground and how it occurs.

Controlled flight into terrain (CFIT) could result from situations such as:

- When the pilot descends below published minimums on an approach.

- When the pilot does not follow the prescribed Obstacle Departure Procedure.

- When the pilot does not perceive a change in terrain height and initiate a suitable climb.

- When the pilot becomes distracted and loses situational awareness.

For the following questions 34–35, use the low altitude enroute chart depicting the Iron Mountain and Sawyer VOR navigation sources, shown on pages 228–229.

34. You are flying at 7,000 feet MSL along a route from the Ironwood (IWD) VOR along V430 through the Iron Mountain (IM) VOR and then using V78-430 to an intended landing location at Escanaba (KESC). While flying along this route, you experience a loss of RAIM on your GPS. After querying ATC, you learn that GPS interference is being experienced across the route. What would be the best course of action that you might consider in this scenario?

A first course of action would be to transition any navigation to a non-GPS-based navigation source. In this case, flying the Victor airways as filed or cleared would be acceptable.

If in VFR conditions, I could continue navigating using VFR practices. If in IFR conditions, a change of navigation source would be required.

Considering the loss of GPS navigation source, I might need to consider diverting to an airport at which an approach could be flown that did not require GPS functionality or potentially DME if the source of DME in my aircraft is GPS-based.

I could determine that the Marquette/Sawyer Regional Airport where the SAW VOR is located is an airport that reliably could be depended on in the case of a loss of GPS services based on the "MON" note above the airport indicating that the airport provides at least one approach that is available as a part of the minimum operational network in the event of loss of GPS coverage.

I could choose to proceed directly to the SAW VOR from my route if I am within service volume radius and receiving the VOR signal, or I could proceed along the route to one of the other VORs available and then follow a victor airway to the SAW VOR. Since this VOR is depicted as a (H)(H) VOR, I would know by referring to service volumes that above 5,000 feet MSL, I could expect a reliable signal from this VOR out to 70 nautical miles.

35. **You are flying a route from between the SAW VOR along V316 to the IWD VOR in a non-icing equipped aircraft, and you experience icing at your cruising altitude of 8,000 feet. Bases of the clouds are reported as ranging from 1,200 feet AGL to 2,000 feet AGL across the route, and tops have been reported to be above 14,000 feet MSL. The temperature is –4 degrees Celsius at 8,000 feet MSL. What options might you consider to remedy the icing?**

In this situation, I would be looking for an option to get out of the icing conditions, since my aircraft is not capable of getting rid of the ice once it has accumulated.

Since I know the standard lapse rate of 2 degrees Celsius per 1,000 feet, this might allow me to determine how far they would need to descend to get out of the icing conditions and back into warmer non-freezing conditions. Dividing the –4 degrees by 2 and multiplying by 1,000, I find that I would need to descend to at least 6,000 feet to get to where the temperature is zero.

Finding the freezing level, I would want to descend to a lower altitude to get to temperatures above freezing. In this case, a descent below 6,000 feet would be desired. An appropriate next IFR altitude that I might select could be 4,000 feet for direction of flight.

Considering the route, I can see that there is a MEA along V316 between these VORs at 6,000 feet MSL and a MOCA of 3,700 feet MSL.

While it would be more desirable to stay at the MEA, I might choose to descend to 4,000 feet, which is an altitude that the MOCA guarantees will offer guaranteed obstacle clearance.

I might choose this as I understand that the MOCA only guarantees navigation equipment signal coverage within 22 nautical miles of either VOR along the route, which is a total of 92 nautical miles. This leaves me with a middle section of the route that is 48 nautical miles where VOR coverage could not be relied upon. I might choose to transition to navigation using GPS along this route (if equipped) to allow me to fly the lower altitude and avoid icing conditions.

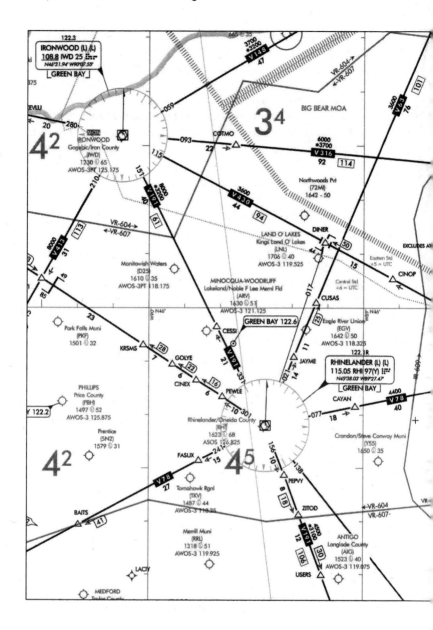

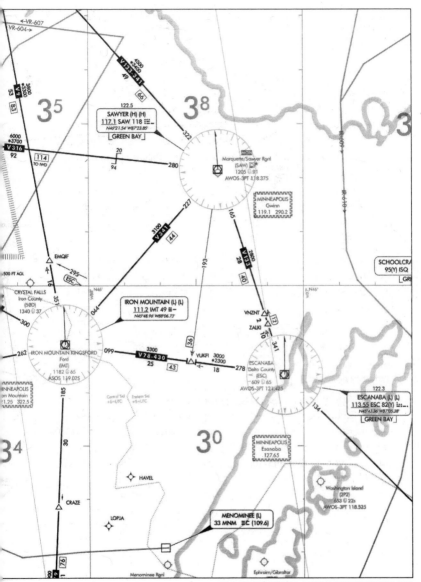

FOR EXAMPLE ONLY—NOT FOR NAVIGATIONAL USE

For the following questions 36–37, use the example low altitude enroute chart that shows a course between the SAW and RHI VOR navigation sources, shown on pages 232–233.

36. **If you are navigating off of a Victor airway between the SAW and RHI VORs using VORs for navigation, you would need to determine if the route is able to be flown within the service volumes of the VOR sources. With a distance of 96.5 nautical miles between the VORs, what applications of VOR service volumes might you apply across this route?**

The SAW VOR is a (H)(H) VOR and would have a service as a very high frequency VOR and a range from 1,000 feet MSL to 5,000 feet MSL over 40 NM and from 5,000 feet MSL to 14,500 feet MSL out to 70 NM.

The RHI VOR is a (L)(L) VOR and would have service as a Low VOR and would have a range from 1,000 feet MSL to 5,000 feet MSL over 40 NM and from 5,000 feet MSL to 18,000 feet MSL out to 70 NM.

Knowing this about the two VORs, I would be able to determine that a flight below 5,000 feet MSL would offer only 80 nautical miles of service, leaving a gap of 16.5 nautical miles where coverage would not be guaranteed.

I could apply these VOR service volumes to know that a flight above 5,000 feet MSL would offer a total range of coverage of 140 nautical miles (applying 70 nautical miles out from each VOR respectively) and would allow for overlap of signal and greater signal coverage distance than the distance between the two VORs (96.5 NM).

37. If you were flying the route from the SAW VOR to the RHI VOR not following a Victor airway, what minimum altitude would be applicable if you were operating on an IFR flight plan while also applying appropriate direction of flight altitude considerations?

Considering the route is generally a westerly direction, 244 degrees, I would fly at an even altitude along this route.

Reviewing off-route (OROCA) minimum sector altitudes in this area, I note that near SAW VOR, an altitude of 3,800 feet MSL would be required, and as I transition along the route and get closer to the RHI VOR, a sector altitude of 4,500 feet MSL is noted. Considering this, while I might start the route at 4,000 feet MSL on the westerly heading, I should expect to be flying into an area where required obstacle clearances are higher and I might need to climb to 6,000 feet MSL for proper terrain and obstacle clearance and correct altitude for direction of flight on an IFR flight plan.

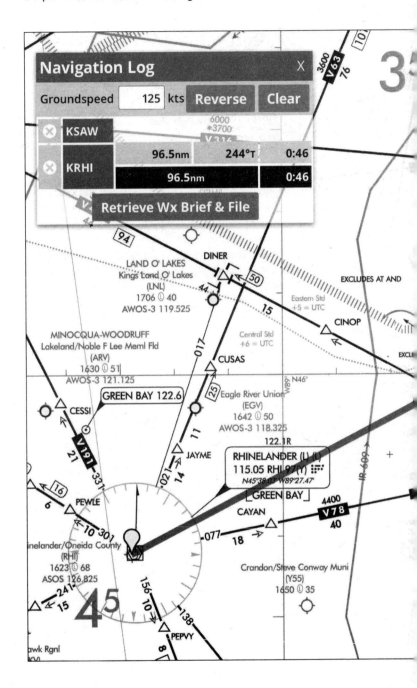

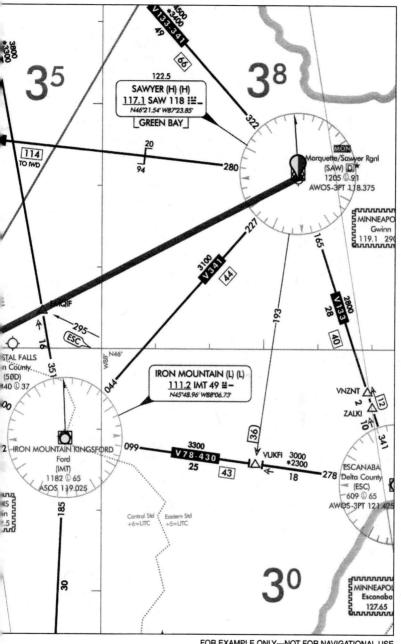

FOR EXAMPLE ONLY—NOT FOR NAVIGATIONAL USE

Appendix 1

Applicant's Practical Test Checklist

Applicant's Practical Test Checklist

Appointment with Examiner

Examiner's Name: _____

Location for test (airport): _____

Date of test: _____

Start time for test: _____

Examiner's fee: _____

Documents to Bring to the Practical Test

___ *Aircraft Maintenance Records*
Logbook record of airworthiness and inspections for engine, aircraft, propeller, and AD compliance:
- Annual inspection
- 100-hour inspection (if applicable)
- VOR test (if applicable)
- Altimeter, pitot static test
- Transponder test
- ELT inspection and battery
- AD compliance documentation
- Current GPS database (if applicable)

___ *Aircraft Required Documents:*
- Supplemental documents
- Placards
- Airworthiness certificate
- Current aircraft registration
- Radio station license
- Owner's manual (AFM/POH)
- Weight and balance documentation

Personal Documents
___ Government-issued photo identification
___ Pilot certificate
___ Aviation Medical Certificate or BasicMed qualification (when applicable)
___ FAA Knowledge Test results
___ Completed FAA Form 8710-1, Airman Certificate and/or Rating Application, with instructor's signature, or completed IACRA form (a best practice is to have both in case of an IACRA system outage)

Training Documentation

___ Log of ground training meeting FAR requirements*

___ Log of flight training meeting FAR requirements

___ Log of experience requirements meeting FAR requirements

___ Endorsements signed by instructor for practical test eligibility

___ Graduation certificate if test will be conducted based on graduation from a Part 141 approved training provider

___ Log of experience indicating currency for flight (flight review endorsement or current solo endorsement; complex, high-performance, or tailwheel endorsement if applicable)

___ Copy of previous Notice of Disapproval (if the test is a retest)

___ Endorsement for retest (if the test is a retest)

A best practice is to have all of these items tabbed or identified to be able to demonstrate eligibility for the practical test to the examiner. The examiner is required to determine and confirm eligibility prior to beginning the test. If they are unable to determine eligibility or you are missing documentation, they may be unable to begin the test and it may need to be rescheduled.

Equipment and Materials to Bring to the Test

___ View-limiting device

___ Current aeronautical charts (printed or electronic)

___ Flight computer, calculator, and/or plotter

___ Flight plan form and flight logs (printed or electronic)

___ *Chart Supplement*, airport diagrams, or other charting resources

___ Current FAR/AIM

* Note that ground training as logged by an online ground school for the FAA Knowledge Test typically does not meet the requirements for ground training for a certificate or rating. Be sure that you have logged ground training for the practical test and that you have it documented and available for review for the practical test.

Appendix 2

Flight Instructor–Instrument
Airplane Supplement

This Flight Instructor–Instrument appendix has been designed for use in conjunction with the material presented in Chapters 1–4 of this guide, for one comprehensive outline and reference. A review of this guide should provide the Flight Instructor–Instrument applicant with aid for preparation and accomplishment of the Flight Instructor Instrument Airplane practical check. This appendix may be supplemented with other study materials as noted in parentheses after each question.

A. Flight by Reference to Instruments

1. Define basic attitude instrument flying. (FAA-H-8083-15)

Attitude instrument flying may be defined as the control of an aircraft's spatial position by using instruments rather than outside visual references.

2. What are the two basic methods for learning attitude instrument flying? (FAA-H-8083-15)

The two basic methods used for learning attitude instrument flying are "control and performance" and "primary and supporting." Both methods involve the use of the same instruments, and both use the same responses for attitude control. They differ in their reliance on the attitude indicator and interpretation of other instruments.

3. Explain the control and performance method of attitude instrument flying. (FAA-H-8083-15)

Aircraft performance is achieved by controlling the aircraft attitude and power (angle of attack and thrust-to-drag relationship). Aircraft attitude is the relationship of its longitudinal and lateral axes to the Earth's horizon. An aircraft is flown in instrument flight by controlling the attitude and power, as necessary, to produce the desired performance. This is known as the control and performance method of attitude instrument flying and can be applied to any basic instrument maneuver. The three general categories of instruments are control, performance, and navigation instruments.

4. What are the control instruments? (FAA-H-8083-15)

The control instruments display immediate attitude and power indications and are calibrated to permit attitude and power adjustments in precise amounts. In this discussion, the term "power" is used in place of the more technically correct term "thrust or drag relationship." Control is determined by reference to the attitude indicator and power indicators. These power indicators vary with the aircraft and may include manifold pressure, tachometers, fuel flow, etc.

5. What are the performance instruments? (FAA-H-8083-15)

The performance instruments indicate the aircraft's actual performance. Performance is determined by reference to the altimeter, airspeed indicator, or vertical speed indicator (VSI).

6. What are the navigation instruments? (FAA-H-8083-15)

The navigation instruments indicate the position of the aircraft in relation to a selected navigation facility or fix. This group of instruments includes various types of course indicators, range indicators, glideslope indicators, and bearing pointers. Technologically advanced aircraft can provide all of these instruments and GPS in one electronic display, giving the pilot more accurate positional information.

7. What are the procedural steps used in the control and performance method of attitude instrument flying? (FAA-H-8083-15)

a. *Establish* an attitude and power setting on the control instruments that will result in the desired performance. Known or computed attitude changes and approximate power settings will help to reduce the pilot's workload.

b. *Trim* until control pressures are neutralized. Trimming for hands-off flight is essential for smooth, precise aircraft control. It allows pilots to divert their attention to other flight deck duties with minimum deviation from the desired attitude.

c. *Cross-check* the performance instruments to determine if the established attitude or power setting is providing the desired performance. The cross-check involves both seeing and interpreting. If a deviation is noted, determine the magnitude and direction of adjustment required to achieve the desired performance.

d. *Adjust* the attitude or power setting on the control instruments as necessary.

8. How is attitude control accomplished? (FAA-H-8083-15)

Proper control of aircraft attitude is the result of maintaining a constant attitude, knowing when and how much to change the attitude, and smoothly changing the attitude a precise amount. Aircraft attitude control is accomplished by properly using the attitude indicator. The attitude reference provides an immediate, direct, and corresponding indication of any change in aircraft pitch or bank attitude.

9. How is pitch control accomplished? (FAA-H-8083-15)

Pitch changes are made by changing the "pitch attitude" of the miniature aircraft or fuselage dot by precise amounts in relation to the horizon. These changes are measured in degrees or fractions thereof, or bar widths depending upon the type of attitude reference. The amount of deviation from the desired performance will determine the magnitude of the correction.

10. How is bank control accomplished? (FAA-H-8083-15)

Bank changes are made by changing the "bank attitude" or bank pointers by precise amounts in relation to the bank scale. The bank scale is normally graduated at 0°, 10°, 20°, 30°, 60°, and 90° and may be located at the top or bottom of the attitude reference. Normally, use a bank angle that approximates the degrees to turn, not to exceed 30°.

11. How is power control accomplished? (FAA-H-8083-15)

Proper power control results from the ability to smoothly establish or maintain desired airspeeds in coordination with attitude changes. Power changes are made by throttle adjustments and reference to the power indicators. Power indicators are not affected by such factors as turbulence, improper trim, or inadvertent control pressures. Therefore, in most aircraft little attention is required to ensure the power setting remains constant. From experience in an aircraft, you know approximately how far to move the throttles to change the power a given amount. Therefore, you can make power changes primarily by throttle movement and then cross-check the indicators to establish a more precise setting. The key is to avoid fixating on the indicators while setting the power. A knowledge of approximate power settings for various flight configurations will help you avoid overcontrolling power.

12. Explain the primary and supporting method of attitude instrument flying. (FAA-H-8083-15)

For any maneuver or condition of flight, the pitch, bank, and power control requirements are most clearly indicated by certain key instruments. The instruments that provide the most pertinent and essential information will be referred to as primary instruments. Supporting instruments back up and supplement the information shown on the primary instruments.

13. What instruments are used to determine and control pitch? (FAA-H-8083-15)

Attitude indicator, altimeter, airspeed indicator, and vertical speed indicator. The attitude indicator displays a direct indication of the aircraft's pitch attitude while the other pitch attitude control instruments indirectly indicate the pitch attitude of the aircraft.

14. What instruments are used to determine and control bank? (FAA-H-8083-15)

Attitude indicator, heading indicator, magnetic compass, and turn coordinator.

15. What instruments are used to determine and control power? (FAA-H-8083-15)

The airspeed indicator and engine instruments, which are the manifold pressure gauge (MP) and tachometer/RPM.

16. What instruments are used for trim control? (FAA-H-8083-15)

Attitude indicator, airspeed indicator, turn coordinator, and heading indicator.

17. What are the two fundamental flight skills that must be developed during attitude instrument training? (FAA-H-8083-15)

These two skills are instrument cross-check and instrument interpretation, and use of both result in positive aircraft control. Although these skills are learned separately and in deliberate sequence, a measure of proficiency in precision flying is the ability to integrate these skills into unified, smooth, positive control responses to maintain any prescribed flight path.

18. What does the first fundamental skill of instrument cross-checking consist of? (FAA-H-8083-15)

Cross-checking is the continuous and logical observation of instruments for attitude and performance information. In attitude instrument flying, the pilot maintains an attitude by reference to instruments that will produce the desired result in performance. Due to human error, instrument error, and airplane performance differences in various atmospheric and loading conditions, it is impossible to establish an attitude and have performance remain constant for a long period of time. These variables make it necessary for the pilot to constantly check the instruments and make appropriate changes in airplane attitude.

19. What are some of the common cross-check errors students make? (FAA-H-8083-15)

Fixation—Staring at a single instrument; this may be related to difficulties with one or both of the other fundamental skills. A student may be fixating because of uncertainty about reading the heading indicator (interpretation) or because of inconsistency in rolling out of turns (control).

Omission of an instrument from their cross-check; this may be caused by failure to anticipate significant instrument indications following attitude changes.

Emphasis on a single instrument, instead of on the combination of instruments necessary for attitude information; students naturally tend to rely on the instrument they understand most readily, even when it provides erroneous or inadequate information. Reliance on a single instrument is poor technique.

20. What does the second fundamental skill of instrument interpretation consist of? (FAA-H-8083-15)

The second fundamental skill, instrument interpretation, requires the most thorough study and analysis. You must understand each instrument's construction and operating principles. Then you must apply this knowledge to the performance of the aircraft you are flying, the particular maneuvers to be executed, the cross-check and control techniques applicable to that aircraft, and the flight conditions in which you are operating.

21. What are the four components of aircraft control? (FAA-H-8083-15)

a. *Pitch control*—Controlling the rotation of the aircraft about the lateral axis by movement of the elevators. After interpreting the pitch attitude from the proper flight instruments, you exert control pressures to effect the desired pitch attitude with reference to the horizon.

b. *Bank control*—Controlling the angle made by the wing and the horizon. After interpreting the bank attitude from the appropriate instruments, you exert the necessary pressures to move the ailerons and roll the aircraft about the longitudinal axis.

c. *Power control*—Used when interpretation of the flight instruments indicates a need for a change in thrust.

d. *Trim*—Used to relieve all control pressures held after a desired attitude has been attained. An improperly trimmed aircraft requires constant control pressures, produces tension, distracts your attention from cross-checking, and contributes to abrupt and erratic attitude control. The pressures you feel on the controls must be those you apply while controlling a planned change in aircraft attitude, not pressures held because you let the aircraft control you.

22. Are there any differences in the method you would use to scan the instruments in an aircraft equipped with a primary flight display? (FAA-H-8083-16)

The PFD is not intended to change the fundamental way in which you scan your instruments during attitude instrument flying. The PFD supports the same familiar control and performance, or primary and supporting methods you use with conventional flight instruments. However, you need to train your eyes to find and interpret these instruments in their new formats and locations.

23. How would you define a technically advanced aircraft (TAA), and what would you do differently when training a pilot in a TAA? (FAA-H-8083-16, 14 CFR 61.129)

A technically advanced aircraft is an airplane equipped with an electronic PFD and an MFD that includes, at a minimum, GPS moving map navigation and an integrated two-axis autopilot. A pilot transitioning to a TAA should receive instruction with more emphasis on knowledge of advanced avionics, including flight automation such as a flight management system (FMS) and a coupled autopilot; at the very least, they should receive instruction in how to operate the advanced systems, which advanced systems to use and when, and how advanced avionic systems affect the pilot and the way the pilot flies.

B. Instrument Certification Regulations

1. What conditions must exist for an instrument instructor who is conducting a flight lesson to log instrument time? (14 CFR 61.51)

An authorized instructor may log instrument time when conducting instrument flight instruction in actual instrument flight conditions.

2. What time is considered *training time* and how should this be logged? (14 CFR 61.51)

a. A person may log training time when that person receives training from an authorized instructor in an aircraft, full flight simulator, flight training device, or aviation training device.

b. The training time must be logged in a logbook, or record of training, and must be endorsed in a legible manner by the authorized instructor; and include a description of the training given, the length of the training lesson, and the authorized instructor's signature, certificate number, and certificate expiration date.

3. Concerning instructional flights with both an authorized flight instructor and a certified pilot on board, which person is allowed to log pilot-in-command time? (14 CFR 61.51)

Both the flight instructor and private pilot will log PIC time. Provided the private pilot is the sole manipulator of the controls of an aircraft for which the pilot is rated, that pilot may log the time as PIC.

4. For the purposes of meeting the recent instrument experience requirements, what information must be recorded in the person's logbook? (14 CFR 61.51)

a. The location and type of each instrument approach accomplished; and

b. The name of the safety pilot, if required.

5. What does an instrument proficiency check consist of? (14 CFR 61.57, FAA-S-ACS-8)

Section 61.57(d) sets forth the requirements for an instrument proficiency check (IPC). Instructors and evaluators conducting an IPC must ensure the pilot meets the standards established in the *Instrument Rating–Airplane Airman Certification Standards* (FAA-S-ACS-8), which includes a useful "Instrument Proficiency Check" table in that guide's Appendix 5, "Practical Test Roles, Responsibilities, and Outcomes." At a minimum, the applicant must demonstrate the ability to perform the tasks listed in that table. The person giving the check should develop a scenario that incorporates as many required tasks as possible to assess the pilot's ADM and risk management skills.

Exam Tip: Guidance on how to conduct an IPC can be found in Appendix 3 of this book and also in FAA Advisory Circular 61-98, *Currency Requirements and Guidance for the Flight Review and Instrument Proficiency Check.*

6. Who can give an instrument proficiency check? (14 CFR 61.57)

14 CFR §61.57 states that the instrument proficiency check must be given by—

a. An examiner;

b. A person authorized by the U.S. Armed Forces to conduct instrument flight tests, provided the person being tested is a member of the U.S. Armed Forces;

c. A company check pilot who is authorized to conduct instrument flight tests under 14 CFR Part 121, 125, 135, or Part 91 Subpart K, and provided that both the check pilot and the pilot being tested are employees of that operator or fractional ownership program manager;

d. An authorized instructor; or

e. A person approved by the Administrator to conduct instrument practical tests.

7. The instrument proficiency check required by 14 CFR §61.57 can be accomplished by flying with an authorized flight instructor. Does that flight instructor have to be an instrument instructor? (14 CFR 61.193, 61.195, AC 61-98)

The flight instructor must hold an Instrument Rating on his or her Pilot and Flight Instructor Certificate appropriate to the category and class of aircraft used for the IPC. For example, an IPC conducted in a multi-engine airplane requires that the flight instructor hold both Multi-Engine and Instrument Ratings on his or her Pilot and Flight Instructor Certificate. The basis for flight instructor privileges and limitations are found in §§61.193 and 61.195. The flight instructor should also meet currency requirements for his or her Pilot and Flight Instructor Certificate.

Note: In addition to having the appropriate instructor ratings, the flight instructor should consider other factors relating to his or her ability to conduct an IPC, including those discussed for the flight review, as well as the instructor's own instrument currency.

8. Can the instrument proficiency check be given in a full flight simulator or flight training device? (AC 61-98, AC 61-136)

A flight instructor may conduct all or part of the IPC in an FAA-approved full flight simulator (FFS), flight training device (FTD), or aviation training device (ATD) as appropriate. If the IPC is accomplished in an FFS or FTD qualified under 14 CFR Part 60, that IPC checking program must receive approval by the FAA Administrator (14 CFR §61.4). Guidance on what IPC instrument tasks can be accomplished in an FFS, FTD, or ATD is located in the current instrument PTS or ACS, as appropriate.

Note: Advanced aviation training devices (AATD) and basic aviation training devices (BATD) collectively make up the two categories of FAA-approved ATDs. Only AATDs may be used for the IPC. The flight instructor should review the ATD letter of authorization (LOA) for the specific credit allowances provided for that training device model.

9. What are several pre-check considerations a flight instructor should think about prior to conducting an IPC? (AC 61-98)

The flight instructor should—

a. Structure an IPC in a manner similar to that of the flight review, tailoring the check to the needs of the pilot.

b. Discuss with the pilot the operating conditions under which the check will occur If the check is in an aircraft. (VFR or IFR in simulated IMC or under IFR in actual IMC). If the flight instructor conducts the check under IFR, or while under VFR conditions simulating IMC with a view-limiting device, it is the flight instructor's responsibility to constantly remain vigilant to other aircraft throughout all phases of the flight.

c. Develop a plan of action that uses realistic scenarios to organize and sequence the required tasks and maneuvers.

d. Discuss crewmember roles and responsibilities with the pilot.

Note: Guidance on how to structure an IPC can be found in Appendix 3 of this book and also in FAA Advisory Circular 61-98, *Currency Requirements and Guidance for the Flight Review and Instrument Proficiency Check.*

10. What standards shall be used to determine satisfactory completion of the IPC? (14 CFR 61.57, AC 61-98, FAA-S-ACS-8)

14 CFR §61.57(d) sets forth the requirements for an IPC. The maneuvers and procedures selected for the IPC must include those listed in the Rating Task Table in FAA-S-ACS-8 or FAA-S-8081-4, as applicable. The flight instructor conducting the IPC has the discretion to require any other maneuver(s) necessary to determine that the pilot can safely operate under IFR in a broad range of conditions appropriate to the aircraft flown and the ATC environment selected. Regardless of the maneuvers and procedures selected, the flight instructor should ensure that the pilot demonstrates satisfactory basic attitude instrument flying skills.

Note: As an aid to the flight instructor, FAA AC 61-98, Appendix J, contains a sample flight instructor IPC checklist for conducting the IPC.

11. When conducting an instrument proficiency check, what emergency approach procedures must be covered when the IPC is conducted in a single-engine airplane? (FAA-S-ACS-8)

When referring to the Instrument Proficiency Check task table in the appendix of the ACS, a CFI will find that Area of Operation VII parts B, C, and D are required. Since Tasks B and C are only applicable to multi-engine aircraft, those would not be required. Task D is required and would require the CFI to include an "approach with loss of primary flight instrument indicators" on the IPC. Worth noting in this practice is that under the skills section it specifically notes that the approach shall be a "nonprecision instrument approach." A CFI should select appropriately an approach that is not a precision approach such as an ILS for this demonstration purpose.

12. What areas of knowledge should be reviewed by the flight instructor when conducting the knowledge portion of an IPC? (AC 61-98)

The flight instructor should determine whether the pilot has adequate knowledge and understanding of 14 CFR Part 91, especially Subpart B, Flight Rules; Subpart C, Equipment, Instrument, and Certificate Requirements; and Subpart E, Maintenance, Preventive Maintenance, and Alterations; and also the following areas:

a. Instrument enroute and approach chart interpretation, including departure procedures (SIDs and ODPs), standard terminal arrival routes (STAR), and area navigation (RNAV)/global positioning system (GPS)/wide area augmentation system (WAAS) procedures.

b. Obtaining and analyzing weather information, including knowledge of hazardous weather phenomena, such as icing and convective activity.

c. Preflight planning, including aircraft performance, Notices to Air Missions (NOTAM) information (including temporary flight restrictions [TFR]), fuel requirements, alternate requirements, and use of appropriate FAA publications such as the *Chart Supplement*.

d. Aircraft systems related to IFR operations, including appropriate operating methods, limitations, and emergency procedures due to equipment failure.

e. Aircraft flight instruments and navigation equipment, including characteristics, limitations, operating techniques, and emergency procedures due to malfunction or failure, such as lost communications and automation failure procedures.

f. Determining the airworthiness status of the aircraft for instrument flight, including required inspections and documents.

g. Air Traffic Control (ATC) procedures pertinent to flight under IFR with emphasis on elements of ATC clearances and pilot/controller responsibilities.

h. A general, working knowledge of aerodynamic principles relating to angle of attack (AOA) and the purpose, operation, and limitations of AOA indicators (if installed).

13. **After conducting the knowledge portion of an IPC, what actions should the flight instructor request the pilot to complete prior to conducting the flight skill portion of the check?** (AC 61-98)

The flight instructor should ask the pilot to prepare for the skill portion of the proficiency check by completing the necessary flight planning, obtaining current weather data, filing a flight plan, and conducting the preflight inspection. In order to fully evaluate the pilot's skills under normal operating conditions, the flight instructor may wish to have the pilot conduct a short IFR cross-country flight with at least part of the flight conducted "in the system" under IFR.

14. **What are some of the general considerations a flight instructor should have in determining the specific maneuvers and procedures for an IPC?** (14 CFR 61.57, AC 61-98)

The maneuvers and procedures selected for the IPC must include those listed in the Instrument Proficiency Check table in the *Instrument Rating–Airplane ACS* (FAA-S-ACS-8). The flight instructor conducting the IPC has the discretion to require any other maneuver(s) necessary to determine that the pilot can safely operate under IFR in a broad range of conditions appropriate to the aircraft flown and the ATC environment selected. The flight instructor should emphasize proper adherence to ATC clearances. Regardless of the maneuvers and procedures selected, the flight instructor should ensure that the pilot demonstrates satisfactory basic attitude instrument flying skills.

15. **What postflight actions and logbook entries should occur upon completion of an IPC?** (AC 61-98)

Upon completion of the proficiency check, the flight instructor should complete the plan and checklist (if used) and debrief the pilot on the results of the check (satisfactory or unsatisfactory). Regardless of the determination, the flight instructor should provide the pilot with a comprehensive analysis of his or her performance, including suggestions for improving any weak areas. If the proficiency check was unsatisfactory, the flight instructor should not endorse the pilot's logbook, but should sign the logbook to record the instruction given. If the proficiency check was satisfactory, the endorsement for a satisfactory proficiency check should be in accordance with the current issue of AC 61-65. If a lesson plan and checklist was used, the flight instructor may wish to retain the plan as a record of the scope and content of the competency check, even though not required.

16. May a CFI-I who conducts an IPC for a pilot also log that IPC as a flight review? (14 CFR 61.56, 61.57)

While an IPC is a currency validation event, it does not necessarily meet the requirements of a flight review. Since an IPC does not require ground training, it would not necessarily meet the requirements of the ground portion of a flight review. A flight review additionally requires more than an hour of flight in the air, and it is possible that an IPC may be completed in less time than the requisite hour for a flight review. So, an IPC does not automatically count for a flight review. A CFI and the student might choose to conduct an IPC that does include ground training and more than an hour of flight training that could additionally meet the requirements of a flight review concurrently. If this is done, the CFI would need to give each endorsement (a flight review and an IPC) separately.

17. What are the general requirements for a person to be eligible for an Instrument Rating? (14 CFR 61.65)

a. Hold at least a current Private Pilot Certificate, or be concurrently applying for a Private Pilot Certificate, with an Airplane, Helicopter, or Powered-Lift Rating appropriate to the instrument rating sought;

b. Be able to read, speak, write, and understand the English language. If the applicant is unable to meet any of these requirements due to a medical condition, the Administrator may place such operating limitations on the applicant's pilot certificate as are necessary for the safe operation of the aircraft;

c. Receive and log ground training from an authorized instructor or accomplish a home-study course of training on the aeronautical knowledge areas that apply to the instrument rating sought;

d. Receive a logbook or training record endorsement from an authorized instructor certifying that the person is prepared to take the required knowledge test;

e. Receive and log training on the areas of operation from an authorized instructor in an aircraft, full flight simulator, or flight training device that represents an airplane, helicopter, or powered-lift appropriate to the instrument rating sought;

f. Receive a logbook or training record endorsement from an authorized instructor certifying that the person is prepared to take the required practical test;

g. Pass the required knowledge test on the aeronautical knowledge areas; however, an applicant is not required to take another knowledge test when that person already holds an instrument rating; and

h. Pass the required practical test on the areas of operation in an airplane, helicopter, or powered-lift appropriate to the rating sought; or a full flight simulator or a flight training device appropriate to the rating sought and for the specific maneuver or instrument approach procedure performed. If an approved flight training device is used for the practical test, the instrument approach procedures conducted in that flight training device are limited to one precision and one nonprecision approach, provided the flight training device is approved for the procedure performed.

18. What are the aeronautical knowledge requirements for a person to be eligible for an Instrument Rating? (14 CFR 61.65)

A person who applies for an Instrument Rating must have received and logged ground training from an authorized instructor or accomplished a home-study course on the following aeronautical knowledge areas that apply to the instrument rating sought:

a. Federal Aviation Regulations that apply to flight operations under IFR;

b. Appropriate information that applies to IFR operations in the *Aeronautical Information Manual*;

c. Air traffic control system and procedures for instrument flight operations;

d. IFR navigation and approaches by use of navigation systems;

e. Use of IFR en route and instrument approach procedure charts;

(continued)

f. Procurement and use of aviation weather reports and forecasts and the elements of forecasting weather trends based on that information and personal observation of weather conditions;

g. Safe and efficient operation of aircraft under instrument flight rules and conditions;

h. Recognition of critical weather situations and windshear avoidance;

i. Aeronautical decision making and judgment; and

j. Crew resource management, including crew communication and coordination.

19. What are the flight proficiency requirements for a person to be eligible for an Instrument Rating? (14 CFR 61.65)

A person who applies for an Instrument Rating must receive and log training from an authorized instructor in an aircraft, or in a full flight simulator or flight training device that includes the following areas of operation:

a. Preflight preparation;

b. Preflight procedures;

c. Air traffic control clearances and procedures;

d. Flight by reference to instruments;

e. Navigation systems;

f. Instrument approach procedures;

g. Emergency operations; and

h. Postflight procedures.

20. What are the aeronautical experience requirements for a person to be eligible for an Instrument Rating? (14 CFR 61.65)

A person who applies for an Instrument–Airplane Rating must have logged the following:

a. 50 hours of cross-country flight time* as PIC, of which 10 hours must have been in an airplane.

b. 40 hours of actual or simulated instrument time in the areas of operation listed in 14 CFR §61.65(c), of which 15 hours must have been received from an authorized instructor who holds an Instrument–Airplane Rating, and the instrument time includes:

- 3 hours of instrument flight training from an authorized instructor in an airplane that is appropriate to the Instrument–Airplane Rating within 2 calendar months before the date of the practical test;
- Instrument flight training on cross-country flight procedures, including one cross-country flight in an airplane with an authorized instructor, that is performed under IFR, when a flight plan has been filed with an air traffic control facility, and that involves a flight of 250 NM along airways or ATC-directed routing, an instrument approach at each airport, and 3 different kinds of approaches with the use of navigation systems.

*Notes:

- An applicant for a combined Private Pilot Certificate with an Instrument–Airplane Rating may satisfy the cross-country flight time requirements by crediting up to 45 hours of cross-country flight time performing the duties of pilot-in-command with an authorized instructor.

- A recent legal interpretation change was made by the FAA that allow for the three approaches in the cross-country qualifying event for Instrument Rating experience to be three different approaches, but not require that they be of three differing approach systems. For example, this could allow a pilot to fly a GPS approach at Airport A, a different GPS approach at Airport B, and a third GPS approach at Airport C. This is a change from previous legal interpretation and allows more flexibility in the IFR long cross-country flights for pilots seeking an Instrument Rating. (For more information, see the FAA Memorandum from February 28, 2022: www.faasafety.gov/files/notices/2022/Mar/61.65_Recission_memo.pdf.)

- A commonly missed part of the qualification requirement for the IFR long cross-country is that an instrument approach must be flown at *each* airport along the route. A pilot should terminate their IFR cross-country from an approach to an airport. If the pilot then would be returning to another airport without flying an approach or to which one was not available, it should be logged as a separate activity.

21. What regulations apply if full flight simulators or flight training devices are used for some of the training required for the Instrument Rating? (14 CFR 61.65)

If the instrument time was provided by an authorized instructor in a full flight simulator or flight training device:

a. A maximum of 30 hours may be performed in that full flight simulator or flight training device if the instrument time was completed in accordance with 14 CFR Part 142; or

b. A maximum of 20 hours may be performed in that full flight simulator or flight training device if the instrument time was not completed in accordance with 14 CFR Part 142.

c. A maximum of 10 hours of instrument time received in a basic aviation training device or a maximum of 20 hours of instrument time received in an advanced aviation training device (FAA approved and authorized) may be credited for the instrument time requirements of 14 CFR Part 61.

22. What is the minimum length of time a flight instructor is required to retain a record of their flight instruction activity? (14 CFR 61.189)

Each flight instructor must retain the records required by 14 CFR Part 61 for at least 3 years.

23. What are the required records a flight instructor must retain? (14 CFR 61.189)

A flight instructor must maintain a record in a logbook or a separate document that contains the following:

a. The name of each person whose logbook that instructor has endorsed for solo flight privileges, and the date of the endorsement; and

b. The name of each person that instructor has endorsed for a knowledge test or practical test, and the record shall also indicate the kind of test, the date, and the results.

24. What qualifications must a flight instructor possess before instruction may be given for the issuance of an Instrument Rating? (14 CFR 61.195)

A flight instructor who provides instrument training for the issuance of an Instrument Rating, a type rating not limited to

VFR, or the instrument training required for Commercial Pilot and Airline Transport Pilot Certificates, must hold an Instrument Rating on his or her Pilot Certificate and Flight Instructor Certificate that is appropriate to the category and class of aircraft used for the training he or she is providing.

25. Can an instrument instructor give instrument instruction in a multi-engine airplane if the instructor does not possess a Multi-Engine Instructor Rating or a Multi-Engine Rating on his/her pilot certificate? (14 CFR 61.195)

No. A flight instructor who provides instrument training for the issuance of an Instrument Rating, a type rating not limited to VFR, or the instrument training required for Commercial Pilot and Airline Transport Pilot Certificates must hold an Instrument Rating on his or her Pilot Certificate and Flight Instructor Certificate that is appropriate to the category and class of aircraft used for the training he or she is providing.

26. What should a CFI-I know about the allowance of electronic flight bag tools as a source for charting and data during a practical test (or IPC)? (FAA-S-8081-9, FAA-S-ACS-8)

The evaluator is expected to test the applicant's knowledge of the systems that are available or installed and operative during both the ground and flight portions of the practical test. If the applicant has trained using a portable EFB to display charts and data and wishes to use the EFB during the practical test, the applicant is expected to demonstrate appropriate knowledge, risk management, and skill appropriate to its use.

An examiner may not require an applicant to use paper charts but may test the applicant's ability to manage scenarios such as a battery failure of the EFB device. An instrument pilot should be ready to manage such a situation with backup devices, charging options, or alternative available ATC services.

27. What should a CFI-I know about the requirement for an applicant with respect to demonstration of DME ARC procedures on a practical test (or while conducting an IPC)? (FAA-S-8081-9, FAA-S-ACS-8)

The evaluator may not select DME arcs, unless charted and available (including use of RNAV substitution techniques, if appropriate).

28. What should a CFI-I know about the requirement for conducting an approach using an installed IFR GPS (RNAV) system for applicants on practical tests? (FAA-S-8081-9, FAA-S-ACS-8)

For practical tests conducted in an aircraft equipped with an installed, instrument flight rules (IFR)-approved RNAV or required navigational performance (RNP) system, or in a flight simulation training device (FSTD) equipped to replicate an installed, IFR-approved RNAV or RNP system, the applicant must demonstrate approach proficiency using that system. The applicant may use a suitable RNAV system on conventional procedures and routes as described in the *Aeronautical Information Manual* (AIM) to accomplish ACS tasks on conventional approach procedures, as appropriate.

29. When conducting an IPC, or for a student on a practical test, what must be completed when meeting the task requirement for a "precision approach?" (FAA-S-8081-9, FAA-S-ACS-8)

The applicant must accomplish a precision approach to the decision altitude (DA) using aircraft navigational equipment for centerline and vertical guidance in simulated or actual instrument meteorological conditions. A precision approach is a standard instrument approach procedure to a published decision altitude using provided approved vertical guidance.

This could be a ground-based approach such as an ILS or a GPS WAAS or LNAV/VNAV approach as long as a decision altitude (DA) is charted for the approach procedure.

Recent instrument ACS and CFI-I PTS updates removed a previous restriction that a precision approach needed to bring a pilot to 300 feet or lower to be eligible to meet the "precision-like" approach conditions.

This is no longer the case.

C. Logbook Entries Related to Instrument Certification

1. What advisory circular contains recommended sample endorsements for use by authorized instructors when endorsing airmen pilot logbooks? (AC 61-65)

AC 61-65—*Certification: Pilots and Flight and Ground Instructors*

2. Each instructor endorsement should include what information? (AC 61-65)

Each endorsement should include—

a. Instructor signature

b. Date of signature

c. Instructor certificate number

d. Certificate expiration date

3. Give examples of the endorsements you would use when endorsing a logbook for a pilot applying for an Instrument Rating. (AC 61-65)

Aeronautical knowledge test: §§61.35(a)(1) and 61.65(a), (b)
I certify that (First name, MI, Last name) has received the required training of §61.65(b). I have determined that he/she is prepared for the (name the knowledge test).

/s/   [date]   J.J. Jones   987654321CFI   Exp. 12-31-26

Flight proficiency/practical test: §61.65(a)(6)
I certify that (First name, MI, Last name) has received the required training of §61.65(c) and (d). I have determined he/she is prepared for the Instrument–(Airplane, Helicopter, or Powered-lift) practical test.

/s/   [date]   J.J. Jones   987654321CFI   Exp. 12-31-26

Prerequisites for instrument practical tests: §61.39(a)
I certify that (First name, MI, Last name) has received and logged the required flight time/training of §61.39(a) in preparation for the practical test within 2 calendar-months preceding the date of the test and has satisfactory knowledge of the subject areas in which he/she was shown to be deficient by the FAA Airman Knowledge

Test Report. I have determined he/she is prepared for the Instrument–(Airplane, Helicopter, or Powered lift) practical test.

/s/   [date]   J.J. Jones   987654321CFI   Exp. 12-31-26

4. Give an example of the endorsement you would use for a pilot who has just completed an instrument proficiency check. (AC 61-65)

I certify that (First name, MI, Last name), (pilot certificate), (certificate number), has satisfactorily completed the instrument proficiency check of §61.57(d) in a (list make and model of aircraft) on (date).

/s/   [date]   J.J. Jones   987654321CFI   Exp. 12-31-26

D. Fundamentals of Instructing

1. Briefly define the term *learning*. (FAA-H-8083-9)

Learning can be defined as a change in behavior as a result of experience.

2. What are the basic characteristics of learning?
(FAA-H-8083-9)

Learning is:

*P*urposeful—Each learner is a unique individual whose past experience affects readiness to learn and understanding of the requirements involved. Learners have fairly definite ideas about what they want to do and achieve.

*E*xperience—Learning is an individual process from individual experience. Previous experience conditions a person to respond to some things and to ignore others. Knowledge cannot be poured into the learner's head.

*M*ultifaceted—Learning may include verbal elements, conceptual elements, perceptual elements, emotional elements, and problem-solving elements all taking place at once.

*A*ctive process—Learners do not soak up knowledge like a sponge absorbs water. For learners to learn, they must react and respond—perhaps outwardly, perhaps only inwardly, emotionally, or intellectually.

3. What are the six principles (laws) of learning?
(FAA-H-8083-9)

These are rules and principles that generally apply to the learning process. The first three are the basic laws; the last three laws are the result of experimental studies.

Readiness—individuals learn best when they are ready to learn, and they do not learn if they see no reason for learning.

Exercise—those things most often repeated are best remembered. It is the basis of practice and drill.

Effect—learning is strengthened when accompanied by a pleasant or satisfying feeling, and that learning is weakened when associated with an unpleasant feeling.

Primacy—the state of being first, often creates a strong, almost unshakable, impression. What is taught must be right the first time.

Intensity—a vivid, dramatic, or exciting learning experience teaches more than a routine or boring experience.

Recency—the things most recently learned are best remembered.

4. How do people learn? (FAA-H-8083-9)

All learning involves the following:

a. *Perception*—Initially all learning comes from perceptions that are directed to the brain by one or more of the five senses (sight, hearing, touch, smell, and taste).

b. *Insight*—The grouping of perceptions into meaningful wholes.

c. *Motivation*—The most dominant force governing the learner's progress and ability to learn.

5. What are the factors that affect an individual's perception? (FAA-H-8083-9)

Both internal and external factors affect an individual's ability to perceive:

a. *Physical organism*—Provides individuals with the perceptual apparatus for sensing the world around them; the ability to see, hear, feel, and respond.

b. *Goals and values*—Every experience and sensation that is funneled into one's central nervous system is colored by the individual's own beliefs and value structures.

(continued)

c. *Self-concept*—A learner's self-image, described in such terms as "confident" or "insecure," has a great influence on the total perceptual process.

d. *Time and opportunity*—Learning some things depends on other perceptions that have preceded those learnings, and on the availability of time to sense and relate those new things to the earlier perceptions.

e. *Element of threat*—Confronted with threat, learners tend to limit their attention to the threatening object or condition. Fear adversely affects perception by narrowing the perceptual field.

6. What are the four levels of learning? (FAA-H-8083-9)

Rote learning—The ability to repeat back something that one has been taught, without understanding or being able to apply what has been learned.

Understanding—To comprehend or grasp the nature or meaning of something.

Application—Achieving the skill to apply what has been learned and to perform correctly.

Correlation—Associating what has been learned, understood, and applied with previous or subsequent learning; this level is the overall objective of aviation instruction.

7. Why do individuals forget what has been learned? (FAA-H-8083-9)

Several theories exist about why people forget what they have learned, including:

a. *Fading*—A person forgets information that is not used for an extended period of time.

b. *Interference*—People forget because a certain experience has overshadowed it or the learning of similar things has intervened.

c. *Repression or suppression*—A memory is pushed out of reach because the individual does not want to remember feelings associated with it.

d. *Retrieval failure*—The inability to retrieve information.

8. **What actions can the instructor take to assist individuals in remembering what has been learned?** (FAA-H-8083-9)

   Praise stimulates remembering; responses that give a pleasurable return tend to be repeated.

   Recall is prompted by association. Each bit of information or action that is associated with something to be learned tends to facilitate its later recall by the learner.

   Favorable attitudes aid retention; people learn and remember only what they wish to know. Without motivation, there is little chance for recall.

   Learning with all senses is most effective. Although we generally receive what we learn through the eyes and ears, other senses also contribute to most perceptions.

   Meaningful repetition aids recall; each repetition gives the learner an opportunity to gain a clearer and more accurate perception of the subject to be learned, but mere repetition does not guarantee retention.

9. **What are defense mechanisms?** (FAA-H-8083-9)

   Certain behavior patterns are called defense mechanisms because they are subconscious defenses against the realities of unpleasant situations.

10. **What are several common defense mechanisms?** (FAA-H-8083-9)

   Repression—A person places uncomfortable thoughts into inaccessible areas of the unconscious mind.

   Denial—A refusal to accept external reality because it is too threatening.

   Compensation—A process of psychologically counterbalancing perceived weaknesses by emphasizing strength in other areas.

   Projection—An individual places his or her own unacceptable impulses onto someone else.

   Rationalization—A subconscious technique for justifying actions that otherwise would be unacceptable.

   Reaction formation—A person fakes a belief opposite to the true belief because the true belief causes anxiety.

   (continued)

Fantasy—Occurs when a learner engages in daydreams about how things should be rather than doing anything about how things are.

Displacement—Results in an unconscious shift of emotion, affect, or desire from the original object to a more acceptable, less threatening substitute.

11. How can an instructor minimize learner frustrations during training? (FAA-H-8083-9)

a. *Motivate learners*—They will gain more if they want to learn than if they are forced to learn.

b. *Keep learners informed*—Tell learners what is expected of them and what they can expect in return.

c. *Approach learners as individuals*—Each individual has a unique personality.

d. *Give credit when due*—Praise and credit from the instructor provides incentive to do better.

e. *Criticize constructively*—It is important to identify mistakes and failures and explain how to correct them.

f. *Be consistent*—The instructor's philosophy and actions must be consistent.

g. *Admit errors*—No one, including learners, expects an instructor to be perfect.

12. What are the basic steps involved in the teaching process? (FAA-H-8083-9)

The teaching of new material can be broken down into the steps of:

a. *Preparation*—Determining the scope of the lesson, the objectives, and the goals to be attained, and ensuring the necessary supplies are available.

b. *Presentation*—Consists of delivering information or demonstrating the skills that make up the lesson. The delivery could be through the lecture method, guided discussion method, demonstration-performance method, etc.

c. *Application*—The learner performs the procedure or demonstrates the knowledge required in the lesson.

d. *Review and evaluation*—Consists of a review of all material and an evaluation of the learner's performance.

13. What are the three most common teaching methods? (FAA-H-8083-9)

a. Lecture method

b. Guided discussion method

c. Demonstration/performance method

14. Discuss the lecture method of teaching. (FAA-H-8083-9)

The lecture is used primarily to introduce learners to a new subject, but it is also a valuable method for summarizing ideas, showing relationships between theory and practice, and re-emphasizing main points.

15. What is the guided discussion method of teaching? (FAA-H-8083-9)

In contrast to the lecture method, where the instructor provides information, the guided discussion method relies on the learners to provide ideas, experiences, opinions, and information. Through the skillful use of "lead-off" type questions, the instructor draws out what the learners know rather than spending the class period telling them.

16. What is the demonstration/performance method of teaching? (FAA-H-8083-9)

This method of teaching is based on the simple yet sound principle that people learn by doing. The instructor first shows the learner the correct way to perform an activity and then has the learner attempt the same activity. Learners observe the skill and then try to reproduce it.

17. What are the five essential phases of the demonstration/ performance method of teaching? (FAA-H-8083-9)

a. Explanation

b. Demonstration

c. Learner performance

d. Instructor supervision

e. Evaluation

18. What are the three main steps used in the organization of material for a particular lesson? (FAA-H-8083-9)

a. Introduction
b. Development
c. Conclusion

19. The "introduction" step of a lesson should contain which basic elements? (FAA-H-8083-9)

Attention—Gain the learner's attention and focus it on the subject involved.

Motivation—Appeal to each learner personally and accentuate his or her desire to learn.

Overview—Tell the learners what is to be covered; provide a clear, concise presentation of the objectives and key ideas, which serves as a road map of the route to be followed.

20. Discuss the "development" step of a presentation. (FAA-H-8083-9)

This is the main part of the lesson. The instructor develops the subject matter in a manner that helps the learner achieve desired learning outcomes. The instructor must logically organize the material to show the relationships of the main points.

21. Define the term *integrated flight instruction*. (FAA-H-8083-9)

Integrated flight instruction is flight instruction during which learners are taught to perform flight maneuvers both by outside visual references and by reference to flight instruments, from the first time each maneuver is introduced.

22. What are the general characteristics of an effective assessment? (FAA-H-8083-9)

An assessment should be:

a. *Objective*—An effective critique is focused on learner performance and should not reflect the personal opinions, likes, dislikes, and biases of the instructor.

b. *Flexible*—An instructor must fit the tone, technique, and content of the critique to the occasion and the learner.

c. *Acceptable*—Before learners willingly accept their instructor's criticism, they must first accept the instructor. Effective critiques are presented with authority, conviction, sincerity, and from a position of recognizable competence.

d. *Comprehensive*—Effective critiques will cover a few major points or a few minor points as well as cover the overall strengths and weaknesses of the learner.

e. *Constructive*—The instructor should provide positive guidance for correcting the faults and strengthening the weaknesses.

f. *Well organized*—Unless a critique follows some pattern of organization, a series of valid comments may lose their impact.

g. *Thoughtful*—An instructor should always be thoughtful toward the learner's need for self-esteem, recognition, and approval from others.

h. *Specific*—The instructor's comments and recommendations should be specific, not so general that the learner can find nothing to hold on to.

23. Control of human behavior involves understanding human needs. Name the six basic needs. (FAA-H-8083-9)

a. Physiological
b. Security
c. Belonging
d. Esteem
e. Cognitive and aesthetic
f. Self-actualization

24. What are the basic steps in planning a course of learning? (FAA-H-8083-9)

Before any important instruction can begin, the following must be considered:

a. Determination of standards and objectives.
b. Development and assembly of blocks of learning.
c. Identification of the blocks of learning.

25. What is a training syllabus? (FAA-H-8083-9)

A training syllabus is an outline of the course of training. It uses a step-by-step, building block progression of learning, with provisions for regular review and evaluations at prescribed stages of learning. The syllabus defines the unit of training, states objectives as to what the learner is expected to accomplish during the unit, shows an organized plan for instruction, and dictates the evaluation process for either the unit or stages of learning.

26. What is a lesson plan? (FAA-H-8083-9)

A lesson plan is an organized outline or "blueprint" for a single instructional period and should be prepared in written form for each ground school and flight period. A lesson plan should tell

a. what to do;
b. what order to do it in; and
c. what procedure to use in teaching it.

27. What items will a lesson plan always contain? (FAA-H-8083-9)

The lesson objectives, included elements, schedule, equipment, instructor's actions, learner's actions, and completion standards.

28. Describe the steps necessary in preparing a lesson plan. (FAA-H-8083-9)

a. Determine the objective of the lesson.

b. Research the subject as defined by the objective.

c. Determine the method of instruction and lesson plan format.

d. Decide on how to organize the lesson and select suitable supporting material.

e. Assemble training aids.

f. Write the lesson plan outline.

E. Preflight Lesson on a Maneuver to be Performed in Flight

An FAA examiner will determine that the applicant exhibits instructional knowledge of the elements related to the planning of instructional activity. This will be accomplished by requiring the applicant to develop a lesson plan for any one of the required maneuvers. The following is an example of a lesson plan for a 90-minute instructional flight period.

Date _____

Lesson _____

Straight-and-Level Flight by Student _____

Reference to Instruments

Objective

To determine that the pilot:

1. Exhibits adequate knowledge of the elements related to attitude instrument flying during straight-and-level flight.
2. Maintains straight-and-level flight in the configuration specified by the examiner.
3. Maintains the heading within 10 degrees, altitude within 100 feet (30 meters), and airspeed within 10 knots.
4. Uses proper instrument cross check and interpretation, and applies the appropriate pitch, bank, power, and trim corrections.

Elements

1. Instrument cross-check
2. Instrument interpretation
3. Aircraft control (pitch, bank, power, and trim)

Schedule

1. Preflight—discuss lesson objective   :20
2. Inflight instructor demonstration   :20
3. Inflight student practice   :25
4. Postflight critique   :15
5. Assignment next lesson   :10

Equipment

1. Instrument panel mockup
2. Chalkboard/notebook
3. View limiting device
4. *Instrument Flying Handbook*

Instructor's Actions

1. Discuss lesson objective.
2. Discuss concept of attitude instrument flying.
3. Present straight-and-level flight on mockup from standpoint of pitch, bank, power, and trim.
4. Inflight—Demonstrate straight-and-level flight by reference to instruments.
5. Inflight—Direct student practice of straight-and-level flight by reference to instruments.
6. Postflight—Critique student performance.
7. Make reading assignments for next lesson.

Student's Actions

1. Discuss lesson objective.
2. Listen, take notes, ask pertinent questions.
3. Inflight—Observe instructor demonstration of straight-and-level flight by reference to instruments.
4. Inflight—Practice of straight-and-level flight by reference to instruments.
5. Postflight—Ask appropriate questions.
6. Obtain reading assignments for next lesson.

Completion

The student should demonstrate that they have an understanding of the concept of attitude instrument flying and of the performance of straight-and-level flight by reference to instruments.

Common Errors

1. Slow or improper cross-check during straight-and-level flight.
2. Improper power control.
3. Failure to make smooth, precise corrections, as required.
4. Uncoordinated use of controls.
5. Improper trim control.

Appendix 3

FAA Instrument Proficiency Check (IPC) Guidance

The following are excerpts from the FAA's Instrument Proficiency Check (IPC) Guidance document (available at www.faasafety.gov) and FAA Advisory Circular 61-98, *Currency Requirements and Guidance for the Flight Review and Instrument Proficiency Check*. Visit asa2fly .com/oegi to download the complete documents, which include additional information and helpful worksheets for both the Instrument Instructor and IPC applicant.

Instrument Proficiency Check Guidance

Introduction

The flight instructor performs one of the most vital and influential roles in aviation, because the aviation educator's work matters not just for the individual pilot, but for every passenger who entrusts his or her life to that pilot's knowledge, skill, and judgment.

The instrument flight instructor—the so-called "double-I"—carries an even greater responsibility. Weather is still the factor most likely to result in aviation accidents with fatalities. Notwithstanding the common reminder that the instrument rating is not an "all weather license," the Instrument Instructor's endorsement for instrument privileges attests that the pilot has the knowledge and skill to operate safely in instrument meteorological conditions (IMC) during all phases of flight.

Two special challenges arise for the Instrument Instructor who administers the instrument proficiency check (IPC) described in 14 CFR §61.57(d). The Instrument Instructor who trains a pilot for the initial instrument rating can develop a comprehensive picture of that pilot's instrument flying knowledge, skills, and judgment, usually in an aircraft familiar to both the Instrument Instructor and the trainee. By contrast, an IPC more often requires short-term evaluation of an unknown pilot, possibly with the added challenge of an unfamiliar aircraft and/or avionics, particularly in technically advanced aircraft. In addition, the IPC is not always conducted in the "real-world" IMC flying environment.

To ensure that the IPC serves the purpose for which it was intended, the current version of the Airman Certification Standards for the Instrument Rating (FAA-S-ACS-8) stipulates that the flight portion of an IPC must include a representative number of tasks, as determined by the examiner/instructor, to assure the competence of the applicant to operate in the IFR environment. This guide offers additional (optional) guidance, with special emphasis on conducting a thorough ground review and on administering IPCs in aircraft with advanced avionics. The goal is to help the Instrument Instructor determine that a pilot seeking an IPC endorsement has both the knowledge and skills for safe operation in all aspects of instrument flying.

Step 1: Preparation

Expectations: Regulations for the flight review (14 CFR §61.56) require a minimum of one hour of ground training and one hour of flight training. While 14 CFR §61.57(d) does not stipulate a minimum time requirement for the IPC, a good rule of thumb is to plan at least 90 minutes of ground time and at least two hours of flight time for a solid evaluation of the pilot's instrument flying knowledge and skills. Depending on the pilot's level of instrument experience and currency, you may want to plan on two or more separate sessions to complete an IPC. For pilots with little or no recent instrument flying experience, it is a good idea to schedule an initial session in an appropriate aircraft training device (ATD).

Regulatory Review: The regulations (14 CFR §61.57[d]) state that an IPC shall consist of the areas of operation and instrument tasks required in the instrument rating airman certification standards. A thorough IPC should cover general operating and flight rules for IFR as set out in 14 CFR Part 91 and in the *Aeronautical Information Manual* (AIM). To make the best use of ground time, ask the pilot to review the *Instrument Procedures Handbook* (FAA-H-8083-16), *Instrument Flying Handbook* (FAA-H-8083-15), and *Aviation Weather Handbook* (FAA-H-8083-28) in advance of your session. Remind the pilot to bring current copies of documents such as the instrument rating ACS, FAR/AIM, charts (en route and instrument approach procedures), *Chart Supplement U.S.*, and Pilot's Operating Handbook (POH) or Airplane Flight Manual (AFM) for the aircraft to be used.

As part of the IPC preparation process, you may want to ask the pilot to complete the IPC Prep Course available in the Aviation Learning Center at www.faasafety.gov. This online course lets the pilot review material at his or her own pace and focus attention on areas of particular interest.

Cross-Country Flight Plan Assignment: Because IFR flying is almost always for transportation purposes, structuring the IPC as an IFR cross-country—ideally one representative of the pilot's typical IFR flying—is an excellent way to evaluate real world instrument flying skills. The airport(s) to be used should have published instrument approach procedures. The flight plan should include consideration of all preflight planning elements required by 14 CFR §91.103, as well as appropriate instrument departure, arrival, and approach procedures. It should be based on a standard weather briefing for the day of the discussion and flight. If the ground and flight portions take place on different days, the pilot should have current weather for each session.

To ensure a thorough evaluation of the pilot's weather interpretation and analysis skills—especially if the weather for the actual IPC is MVFR or better—your own advance preparation might include obtaining a weather briefing for the assigned route on an IFR or low IFR (LIFR) day. You can either provide this IFR briefing to the pilot for advance analysis, or present it during the session for an on-the-spot review and evaluation.

Step 2: Ground Review

Knowledge is key to safe instrument operation, but it needs to be much deeper than the ability to recite rules and regulations. Scenario-based training is a very effective way to test a pilot's knowledge in the context of real-world IFR flying, so consider using the pre-assigned XC flight plan as a basis for both the ground review and the actual flight. A good ground review technique is to work through rules and "real world" procedures related to each phase of flight from departure to the destination airport. Topics to cover include the following:

Preflight (14 CFR §91.103)

For a flight under IFR, the pilot must become familiar with "all available information." For the pre-assigned flight plan, the pilot should be able to address the following topics:

Weather (standard briefing)

- **Describe** weather for departure, en route, and arrival, to include discussion of forecast convective activity or freezing levels/cloud bases along the intended route. For example: "Conditions for departure are VFR, but we will encounter MVFR and IFR conditions en route. Conditions for ETA at destination are IFR. There is no convective activity in the forecast, but the freezing level is expected to be just above the filed altitude."
- **Evaluate** current/forecast weather in terms of:
  - Personal minimums
  - Aircraft equipment
  - Terrain/obstacle avoidance
  - Distance, time, and fuel to nearest VFR conditions

Expected performance and equipment required (airworthiness)

- **Determine** that aircraft is appropriately equipped for proposed flight (14 CFR §§91.205(d), 91.171, Kinds of Operations Equipment List (KOEL) if provided in the Aircraft Flight Manual (AFM)).
- **Calculate** expected aircraft performance (takeoff/landing distances and cruise performance) under known and forecast conditions.
- **Describe** operation and failure modes of installed equipment (e.g., GPS, autopilot, avionics), and appropriate pilot response (including the requirement to report failures to ATC).

Alternatives

- **Determine** if weather requires filing an alternate and, if so:
- **Designate** alternates that are not only "legal," but also appropriate to conditions, pilot experience, needs, etc. If planning to fly a GPS approach to the destination, consider the need to have a non-GPS approach at the alternate unless there is a WAAS-capable GPS. Can the pilot identify viable alternatives for every 25–30 nm along the route? Does he or she establish "tripwire" conditions related to personal minimums as triggers for diversion?

Length/lighting of runways to be used

- **Determine** that available runway length is at least 150% of values shown in the POH/AFM, or at least 200% of the POH/AFM numbers for a wet, icy, or otherwise contaminated runway.
- **Explain** LAHSO procedures (AIM 4-3-11), if in effect at the airport(s) to be used.
- **Describe** expected lighting, including lighting as it applies to descent below MDA or DA (14 CFR §91.175).

Traffic delays

- **Determine** whether traffic delays might require holding, and
- **Describe** holding procedures (AIM 5-3-8). During this part of the review, you may want to give the pilot a practice holding clearance and have him or her explain how the entry would be made from the en route heading to the holding fix. For aircraft equipped with GPS moving map navigators, does the pilot understand how to set up and use this equipment to fly a non-published ("random") holding pattern?

How much fuel is required

- **Calculate** fuel requirements sufficient to fly approaches at both the destination and alternate, and
- **Decide** on the amount of reserve fuel (e.g., legal reserve plus safety margin appropriate to reported and forecast weather conditions).

Risk Management and Personal Minimums

The ground discussion should include all risk factors that affect the planned flight, as well as the types of trips the pilot typically flies. The PAVE checklist is one way to make a structured identification and analysis. For example:

Pilot: general health, physical/mental/emotional state; proficiency, currency

Aircraft: airworthiness, equipment, performance capability

en**V**ironment: weather hazards, terrain, airports/runways to be used, conditions

External pressures: meetings, people waiting at destination, etc.

For each risk factor identified, ask the pilot what strategies can be used to mitigate or eliminate the hazards. This part of the IPC also offers an excellent opportunity to discuss personal minimums, and to help the pilot complete a personal minimums worksheet if he or she has never done so.

Personal Minimums Checklist: One of the most important concepts to convey is that safe pilots understand the difference between what is "legal" in terms of the regulations, and what is "smart" or "safe" in terms of pilot experience and proficiency. For this reason, assistance in completing a Personal Minimums Checklist tailored to the pilot's individual circumstances is perhaps the single most important "takeaway" item you can offer. Use the Personal Minimums Development Worksheet in Appendix 3 to help the pilot work through some of the questions that should be considered in establishing "hard" personal minimums, as well as in preflight and in-flight decision-making for flight under IFR.

It may also be helpful to include key findings from accident data. For example, instrument pilots should be aware that non-precision approaches have an accident rate five times greater than precision approaches. Circling approaches, particularly at night, also increase risk, so the pilot should consider such factors as how much of a tailwind can be acceptable in lieu of a circling approach.

Taxi, Takeoff and Departure

Even at a familiar airport, departure under instrument meteorological conditions can be challenging. Topics to cover in this part of the review include:

Taxi Procedures and Runway Incursion Avoidance

One of the FAA's top priorities is to reduce the frequency of runway incursions and the risk of a runway collision, so be sure that the pilot can correctly identify airport markings. Give the pilot a practice taxi clearance from ramp to runway, and ask him or her to show you on the airport diagram how to execute it. If the airports to be used have only a single runway, give the pilot taxi instructions for a more complex airport.

The FAA's Runway Safety Office (www.faa.gov/airports/runway_safety/) offers links to a number of resources available to help pilots operate safely on the airport surface. Sections 4-3-18 and 4-3-19 of the *Aeronautical Information Manual* (AIM) also offer guidance on safe taxi procedures, including taxi during low-visibility conditions.

Instrument Departures (AIM 5-2-9)

All departure procedures (DPs) provide a way to depart the airport and transition safely to the en route structure, but proficient instrument pilots need to understand the difference between obstacle departure procedures (ODPs) and standard instrument departure procedures (SIDs). If the airport to be used has a SID, ask the pilot to explain how he or she would file and fly that specific procedure. Other questions to ask:

Obstacle Departure Procedures:
- What is an ODP, and where do you find it?
- What functions does the ODP serve?
- Do you need an ATC clearance to fly an ODP?
- Can ATC assign an ODP for departure from a non-towered airport?
- When should you fly an ODP?
- When departing from an airport without an ODP or SID, how will you ensure terrain/obstacle clearance until reaching a published MEA?

Standard Instrument Departure Procedures:

- What is a SID, and where do you find it?
- What functions does the SID serve?
- Can you fly a SID without ATC clearance?
- How do you file a SID (e.g., how is it stated in the flight plan)?

En Route

Topics to review in connection with en route IFR operations include the following:

Airways and Route Systems

Using the proposed route of flight on the appropriate IFR en route chart, ask the pilot to talk you through the journey. Be sure that the pilot is familiar with standard terms and symbols (e.g., MEA, MOCA, MORA, COP). Most pilots are familiar with the airway system defined by VOR facilities, but if your client flies with area navigation (RNAV) equipment, be sure to review the material in AIM 5-3-4 and AIM 5-1-9 on RNAV routes. Questions to ask:

- What is a published RNAV (Q) route, and who can use it?
- What is an "unpublished" RNAV route, and when can you fly it?
- What is the Magnetic Reference Bearing (MRB), and what are the limitations on its use?

En Route Navigation (AIM 1-1-17)

This portion of the ground review should focus on use of the specific navigational equipment installed in the aircraft to be used for the IPC. For IPCs in aircraft equipped with GPS moving map navigators, special emphasis topics include:

- What requirements must your GPS meet before you can use it for IFR (e.g., equipment/installation approvals; operation in accordance with approved AFM or flight manual supplement, etc.).
- Under what conditions can you use GPS in place of ADF or DME equipment?
- Under what circumstances must you have (and use) means of navigation other than GPS?
- What is RAIM, and when is it required?
- What are GPS NOTAMs (1-1-17), and how do you find them?
- Must your database be current?

- How and where are GPS database updates logged?
- How does course and distance information on a GPS navigation display differ from data presented on navigational charts and conventional instrumentation?

En Route Weather

Since weather is at the heart of IFR flying, no IPC ground review can be complete without ensuring that the pilot is thoroughly familiar with sources of inflight weather information, including those available via datalink or on handheld devices. Pilots should be familiar with AIM guidance on ATC Inflight Weather Avoidance Assistance, including ATC descriptive terminology for convective activity and weather radar echoes. Be sure to note that there have been recent changes to the terminology that ATC uses to describe weather radar echoes.

Whether via approved installation or a portable handheld unit, weather datalink (AIM 7-1-9) provides both textual and graphical information that can help improve pilot situational awareness. While datalink has significant potential to improve GA safety, realization of these safety benefits depends heavily upon the pilot's understanding of the specific system's capabilities and limitations. With datalink, IFR pilots should pay particular attention to such system limitations as:

- *Latency.* Where would you find the time stamp or "valid until" time on the particular datalink weather information displayed in the cockpit? (*Note:* since initial processing and transmission of NEXRAD data can take several minutes, pilots should assume that datalink weather information will always be a minimum of seven to eight minutes older than shown on the time stamp and use datalink weather radar images for broad strategic avoidance of adverse weather.)
- *Coverage.* What coverage limitations are associated with the type of datalink network being used? (For example, ground-based systems that require a line-of-sight may have relatively limited coverage below 5,000 feet AGL. Satellite-based datalink weather systems can have limitations stemming from whether the network is in geosynchronous orbit or low earth orbit (LEO). Also, National Weather Service coverage has numerous gaps, especially in the western states.)
- *Content/format.* Since service providers often refine or enhance datalink products for cockpit display, pilots must be familiar with the content, format, and meaning of symbols and displays in the specific system.

Abnormal Procedures and Emergencies

An IPC ground review of abnormal/emergency procedures for IFR operations should include the following topics:

- *Loss of two-way radio communications* (AIM 6-4-1): As stated in the AIM, a pilot who experiences a radio communications failure in VFR conditions should remain VFR and land as soon as practicable. In IFR conditions, the pilot should continue via the route assigned, vectored, expected, filed and at the highest of the following altitudes or flight levels for the route segment being flown: MEA, assigned, expected. Be sure to review the AIM guidance on clearance limits.

- *Loss of avionics/equipment* (AIM 5-3-3; 14 CFR §§91.185, 91.187): Any loss of navigational capability (e.g., loss of one VOR in a dual VOR installation) during operations in controlled airspace should be reported to ATC, along with information on the degree to which the problem affects the aircraft's ability to operate under IFR in the ATC system.

- *Loss of PFD/MFD/Autopilot:* Many pilots today operate with the situational awareness advantage of moving map navigators, "glass cockpit" avionics, and capable autopilots. If your client uses such equipment, or if it is installed in the aircraft to be used for the IPC, have the pilot describe failure modes and recommended procedures for each piece of equipment. The pilot should also be able to describe how one failure may affect other installed components (e.g., how would failure of the AHRS or ADC affect the autopilot?).

Arrival and Approach Procedures

Check for the pilot's understanding of the ways to fly an instrument approach:

- Via pilot navigation ("own nav"):
  - Where are the IAFs?
  - Which IAFs require a course reversal, and how should it be flown?
- Via vectors
  - What are minimum vectoring altitudes?
  - How can you maintain position awareness relative to nearby terrain?
- Via direct to IF (intermediate fix)
  - Is a course reversal required if a racetrack is depicted at the IF?
  - What are the requirements for a controller to issue a clearance direct to the IF?

Standard Terminal Arrival Procedures (AIM 5-4-1)

In reviewing the basics of flying a standard terminal arrival procedure (STAR), points to cover include the following:

- How do you file a STAR?
- When navigating a STAR, when may you descend?
- What does it mean if ATC instructs you to "descend via" the STAR?
- Do you need the approved chart in order to fly a STAR?
- What is an RNAV STAR?

Terminal Arrival Areas (AIM 5-4-5)

Some pilots may not be familiar with the concept of terminal arrival areas, which have been designed to provide a seamless transition from the en route structure to the terminal environment for aircraft equipped with GPS or Flight Management System (FMS) navigational equipment. Questions to ask:

- How are TAA lateral boundaries identified?
- How can the pilot determine which area of the TAA the aircraft will enter?
- When ATC clears you to enter the TAA, what are you expected to do?

Instrument Approach Procedures (AIM 5-4-5)

In addition to reviewing the terms, symbols, and basic steps for flying a conventional instrument approach procedure (e.g., ILS, LOC, VOR, NDB), you will also want to see whether the pilot understands RNAV (GPS) procedures and charting formats, with special emphasis on the minimums section. For example:

- What is LPV?
  - How do you know if you can fly to LPV minimums?
  - Does it include a DA or MDA?
  - At what point does the missed approach begin?
- What is LNAV/VNAV?
  - How do you know if you can fly to LNAV/VNAV minimums?
  - Does it include a DA or MDA?
  - What limitations (e.g., temperature) apply if using a WAAS receiver?
  - Can you use a remote altimeter setting with a WAAS receiver?

- What is LNAV+V?
  - At what point does the vertical glide path intercept the MDA?
- What is LNAV?
  - How do you know if you can fly to LNAV minimums?
  - Does it include a DA or MDA?

Another area to cover is the use of visual descent points (VDPs), which are described in AIM 5-4-5. For example:

- What is a VDP?
  - How is the VDP identified on the chart?
  - What techniques are required to fly a procedure with a VDP?
  - If the approach includes a VDP, when may you descend below MDA?

Missed Approach Procedures

Missed Approach (AIM 5-4-21 and AIM 5-5-5)

The missed approach procedure (MAP) is one of the most challenging maneuvers a pilot can face, especially when operating alone (single pilot) in IMC. Safely executing the MAP requires a precise and disciplined transition that involves not only aeronautical knowledge and skill—the natural areas of focus in most training programs—but also a crucial psychological shift. There is little room for error on instrument missed approach procedures, and a pilot who hesitates due to deficits in procedural knowledge, aircraft control, or mindset can quickly come to grief. Important MAP topics to cover in the IPC ground review include:

- At what point must you execute the MAP:
  - When flying a precision approach?
  - When flying a non-precision approach?
- What is the proper procedure if the decision to miss is made prior to reaching the MAP?
- Do rules and procedures require you to fly to the filed alternate after a missed approach at the intended destination?
- After executing the missed approach, what factors should you consider when deciding whether to make a second attempt, as opposed to proceeding to an alternate?

Step 3: Flight Activities

A proficient instrument pilot must possess knowledge and skill in three distinct, but interrelated, areas:

- *Aircraft control skills* (i.e., basic attitude instrument flying, or (BAI)—crosscheck (including effective scan), interpret, and control. If the pilot flies in "glass cockpit" aircraft, the discussion should include appropriate and effective scanning techniques for these aircraft.
- *Aircraft systems knowledge* (i.e., knowledge and proficiency in instrument procedures and aircraft systems, including GPS/FMS, autopilot, datalink);
- *Aeronautical decision-making (ADM) skills* (i.e., higher-order thinking skills, flight planning and flight management, cockpit organization, weather analysis/anticipation).

There may be a temptation to focus the flight portion of the IPC on the first of these three areas (aircraft control), and to proceed sequentially through the required items chart in the ACS (FAA-S-ACS-8). While these activities can provide a snapshot of the pilot's aircraft control skills, a series of approaches and other maneuvers conducted "out of context" will tell you little about the pilot's knowledge of avionics and other aircraft systems, and even less about the pilot's ability to make safe and appropriate decisions in real-world instrument flying.

Having the pilot fly the cross-country trip you assigned and discussed in the ground review is a good way to make a more thorough and integrated assessment of the pilot's knowledge, skills, and judgment. Since ATC procedures are a critical part of instrument flying, ask the pilot to file and fly one leg "in the system." A leg that involves flying from departure to destination gives you an opportunity to evaluate the pilot's communication skills, systems knowledge and day-to-day decision-making skills, including risk management.

The other leg (which can come first, depending on how you choose to organize the exercise) can focus more on basic attitude instrument (BAI) flying, approaches, and holding patterns. For example, you might fly the return leg of the cross-country under VFR, putting the pilot under the hood for BAI exercises. At some point, give the pilot a scenario that requires a diversion (e.g., mechanical problem, unexpected weather below minimums). Ask the pilot to choose an alternate destination and, using all available and appropriate resources (e.g, chart, basic rules of thumb, "nearest" and "direct to" functions on the GPS) to calculate the approximate course, heading, distance, time, and fuel required to reach the new destination. Proceed to that point and, if feasible, do some of the basic aircraft control work (approaches, including circling approach, missed approach, and holding) at the unexpected alternate.

The diversion exercise has several benefits. First, it generates "teachable moments," which refers to those times when the learner is most aware of the need for certain information or skills, and therefore most receptive to learning what you want to teach. Diverting to an airport surrounded by high terrain, for example, provides a "teachable moment" on the importance of obstacle awareness and terrain avoidance planning. Second, the diversion exercise quickly and efficiently reveals the pilot's level of skill in each of the three areas:

- *Aircraft control skills:* The PTS task chart requires one precision approach and one non-precision approach, plus loss of primary flight instruments. Does the pilot maintain control of the aircraft when faced with a major distraction, and/or when flying the missed approach procedure? Consider as well asking the pilot to remove the hood and land out of a practice approach to DA or MDA. For a satisfactory IPC, the pilot should be able to perform all maneuvers in accordance with the Airman Certification Standards (ACS) for the pilot certificate that he or she holds. If the pilot is flying a multi-engine aircraft for the check, a single-engine approach is essential.

- *Aircraft systems knowledge:* Does the pilot demonstrate knowledge and proficiency in using avionics and aircraft systems, including GPS moving map navigators and the autopilot? The pilot should be thoroughly familiar with both normal and abnormal operation of all systems, and understand how they work together in IFR flying. In technically advanced aircraft, does the pilot understand the significance of indicators for "ENR," "TERM," and "APR?" Does the pilot correctly manage the sequence for selecting navigation source and arming the autopilot's approach mode? Does the pilot effectively access and manage the information available in onboard databases?

- *Aeronautical decision-making (ADM) skills:* Give the pilot multiple opportunities to make decisions. Asking questions about those decisions is an excellent way to get the information you need to evaluate ADM skills, including risk management. For example, ask the pilot to explain why the alternate airport selected for the diversion exercise is a safe and appropriate choice. What are the possible hazards, and what can the pilot do to mitigate them? Be alert to the pilot's information and automation management skills as well. For example, does the pilot perform regular "common sense" cross-checks of what the GPS and/or the autopilot are doing? Does the pilot always keep track of position when being vectored, using cross radials? Does the pilot maintain awareness of weather, personal minimums and alternates at all times?

Step 4: Post Flight Debriefing

Most instructors have experienced the traditional model of training, in which the teacher does all the talking and hands out "grades" with little or no student input. There is a place for this kind of debriefing; however, a collaborative critique is a more effective way to determine that the pilot has not only aircraft control skills and systems knowledge, but also the situational awareness and judgment needed for sound aeronautical decision-making. Here is one way to structure a collaborative post flight critique:

Replay: Rather than starting the IPC post flight briefing with a laundry list of areas for improvement, ask the pilot to verbally *replay* the flight for you. Listen for areas where your perceptions are different, and explore why they don't match. This approach gives the pilot a chance to validate his or her own perceptions, and it gives you critical insight into his or her judgment abilities.

Reconstruct: The reconstruct stage encourages the pilot to learn by identifying the "would'a could'a should'a" elements of the flight—that is, the key things that he or she *would have*, *could have*, or *should have* done differently.

Reflect: Insights come from investing perceptions and experiences with meaning, which in turn requires reflection on these events. For example:

- What was the most important thing you learned today?
- What part of the session was easiest for you? What part was hardest?
- Did anything make you uncomfortable? If so, when did it occur?
- How would you assess your performance and your decisions?
- Did you perform in accordance with the Practical Test Standards?

(continued)

Redirect: The final step is to help the pilot relate lessons learned in this flight to other experiences, and consider how they might help in future flights. Questions:

- How does this experience relate to previous flights?
- What might you do to mitigate a similar risk in a future flight?
- Which aspects of this experience might apply to future flights, and how?
- What personal minimums should you establish, and what additional proficiency flying and training might be useful?

Step 5: Instrument Practice Plan

Offer the pilot an opportunity to develop a personalized IFR skill maintenance and improvement plan. Such a plan should include consideration of the following elements:

Personal Minimums Checklist: As noted earlier, one of the most important concepts to convey in the flight review is that safe pilots understand the difference between what is "legal" in terms of the regulations, and what is "smart" or "safe" in terms of pilot experience and proficiency. For this reason, assistance in completing a personal minimums checklist tailored to the pilot's individual circumstances is perhaps the single most important "takeaway" item you can offer. The Personal Minimums Development Worksheet in Appendix 3 is one tool you can use to help the pilot work through issues that should be considered in establishing "hard" personal minimums, as well as in preflight and inflight decision-making.

Instrument Proficiency Practice Plan: Many pilots would appreciate your help in developing a plan for maintaining and improving basic instrument flying skills.

Training Plan: Discuss and schedule any additional training the pilot may need to achieve individual flying goals. For example, the pilot's goal might be to develop the competence and confidence needed to fly IFR at night, or to lower personal minimums in one or more areas. Use the form in Appendix 7* to document the pilot's aeronautical goals and develop a specific training plan to help him or her achieve them.

The IPC is a vital link in the general aviation safety chain. As a person authorized to conduct this review, you play a critical role in ensuring that it is a meaningful and effective tool for maintaining and enhancing GA safety.

---

*Of the FAA full version—see online source reference given on page 273.

FAA AC 61-98 Appendix G: Sample Pilot's Instrument Experience Summary

Pilot's Name: _____

Flight Instructor: _____

Address: _____

Phone(s): _____

Email: _____

Type of Pilot Certificate(s):

_____ Private
_____ Commercial
_____ Airline Transport Pilot (ATP)
_____ Flight Instructor

Rating(s):

_____ Instrument
_____ Multiengine
_____ Rotorcraft
_____ Glider
_____ Lighter-than-air (LTA)

Experience (pilot):

_____ Total time
_____ Last 6 months
_____ Average hours/month
_____ Time logged since last instrument proficiency check (IPC)

Experience (aircraft):

Aircraft type(s) you fly _____
Aircraft used most often _____
For this aircraft:
Total time _____ Last 6 months _____ Average hours/month _____

Experience (flight environment):

Approximately how many hours logged in:
_____ Day visual flight rules (VFR)
_____ Day instrument flight rules (IFR)
_____ Instrument meteorological conditions (IMC)

_____ Night VFR
_____ Night IFR
_____ Approaches
_____ Approaches to minimums
_____ Approaches in last 6 months

Type of Flying (external factors):

What percentage of your flying is for:
_____ Pleasure
_____ Business
_____ Local
_____ Cross-country

Personal Skills Assessment:

Strengths as a pilot? _____

Areas for improvement? _____

Aviation goals? _____

FAA AC 61-98 Appendix J: Sample Flight Instructor's Instrument Proficiency Checklist

References

Title 14 of the Code of Federal Regulations (14 CFR) Part 61, §61.57(d)—Instrument Proficiency Check.
Except as provided in paragraph (e) of this section, a person who has failed to meet the instrument experience requirements of paragraph (c) for more than six calendar months may reestablish instrument currency only by completing an instrument proficiency check. The instrument proficiency check must consist of the areas of operation and instrument tasks required in the instrument rating practical test standards.
(1) The instrument proficiency check must be–
    (i) In an aircraft that is appropriate to the aircraft category;
    (ii) For other than a glider, in a flight simulator or flight training device that is representative of the aircraft category; or
    (iii) For a glider, in a single-engine airplane or a glider.
(2) The instrument proficiency check must be given by—
    (i) An examiner;
    (ii) A person authorized by the U.S. Armed Forces to conduct instrument flight tests, provided the person being tested is a member of the U.S. Armed Forces;
    (iii) A company check pilot who is authorized to conduct instrument flight tests under part 121, 125, or 135 of this chapter or subpart K of part 91 of this chapter, and provided that both the check pilot and the pilot being tested are employees of that operator or fractional ownership program manager, as applicable;
    (iv) An authorized instructor; or
    (v) A person approved by the Administrator to conduct instrument practical tests.

Advisory Circular (AC) 61-65, Certification: Pilots and Flight and Ground Instructors
Completion of an Instrument Proficiency Check: §61.57(d).
I certify that [First name, MI, Last name], [pilot certificate], [certificate number], has satisfactorily completed the instrument proficiency check of § 61.57(d) in a (list make and model of aircraft) on [date].
/s/ [date] J. J. Jones 987654321CFI Exp. 12-31-19

NOTE: No logbook entry reflecting unsatisfactory performance on an instrument proficiency check is required.

Checklist for IPC

Step 1: Preparation
☐ Set Expectations for Pilot Under Review
☐ Regulatory Review
☐ Cross-Country Flight Plan Assignment

Step 2: Ground Review
☐ FAA Aviation English Language Standard (AELS) Requirement
☐ Preflight
☐ Taxi, Takeoff, Departure
☐ En Route
☐ Arrival and Approach
☐ Missed Approach

Step 3: Flight Activities
☐ Aircraft Control by Reference to Flight Instruments
☐ Systems and Procedures
☐ Aeronautical Decision Making (ADM)
☐ Stabilized Approaches and Landing

Step 4: Postflight Discussion
☐ Replay, Reflect, Reconstruction, Redirect
☐ Questions

Step 5: Aeronautical Health Maintenance and Improvement Plan
☐ Personal Minimums Worksheet
☐ Personal Proficiency Practice Plan
☐ Training Plan (if desired)

For aviation safety information and online resources,
visit www.faasafety.gov.

Ground Review

Pilot
- ☐ Recency of Experience (§61.57)
- ☐ Pilot-in-Command (PIC) Responsibilities and Authority (14 CFR part 91, §91.3)
- ☐ Preflight Actions (§91.103)
- ☐ Medical Facts for Pilots (Aeronautical Information Manual (AIM) chapter 8)

Aircraft
- ☐ Fuel Requirements (§91.167)
- ☐ Equipment Check (Very High Frequency Omni-Directional Range (VOR)) (§91.171)
- ☐ Instrument Flight Rules (IFR) Two-Way Radio Communications Failure (§91.185)
- ☐ Malfunction Reports (§91.187)
- ☐ Required Instruments and Equipment (§91.205)
- ☐ Emergency Locator Transmitter (ELT) (§91.207)
- ☐ Aircraft Lights (§91.209)
- ☐ Inoperative Instruments and Equipment (§91.213)
- ☐ Altimeter and Pitot-Static System Tests (§91.411)
- ☐ Air Traffic Control (ATC) Transponder Tests (§91.413)

Environment
- ☐ ATC Instructions (§91.123)
- ☐ IFR Flight Plan (§91.169)
- ☐ ATC Clearance and Flight Plan (§91.173)
- ☐ Takeoff (TO) and Landing (LDG) in IFR (§91.175)
- ☐ Minimum IFR Altitudes (§91.177)
- ☐ IFR Cruising Altitudes (§91.179)
- ☐ Course to be Flown (§91.181)
- ☐ IFR Two-Way Communications (§91.183)
- ☐ Navigation Aids (AIM chapter 1)
- ☐ ATC (AIM chapter 4)
- ☐ Air Traffic Procedures (AIM chapter 5)

External Pressure
- ☐ IFR Two-Way Radio Communications Failure (§91.185)
- ☐ Emergency Procedures (AIM chapter 6)
- ☐ National Security and Interception Procedures (AIM chapter 5, section 6)

Suggested Flight Activities

Note: Structure the flight portion as an out-and-back IFR cross-country (XC), with one leg focused on XC procedures (including missed approach and diversion procedures) and the other leg focused on airwork (aircraft control). Suggested activities include:

Area of Operation
- ☐ **Preflight Preparation**
    - ☐ Weather Information
    - ☐ Cross-Country Flight Planning
- ☐ **Preflight Procedures**
    - ☐ Aircraft Systems Related to IFR Operations
    - ☐ Aircraft Flight Instruments and Navigation Equipment
    - ☐ Instrument Cockpit Check
- ☐ **ATC Clearances and Procedures**
    - ☐ ATC Clearances
    - ☐ Compliance with Departure, En Route, and Arrival Procedures and Clearances
    - ☐ Holding Procedures
- ☐ **Flight by Reference to Instruments**
    - ☐ Basic Instrument Flight Maneuvers
    - ☐ Recovery from Unusual Flight Attitudes
- ☐ **Navigation Systems**
    - ☐ Intercepting/Tracking Navigational Systems and Distance Measuring Equipment (DME) Arcs
- ☐ **Instrument Approach Procedures**
    - ☐ Nonprecision Approach (NPA)
    - ☐ Precision Approach (PA)
    - ☐ Missed Approach
    - ☐ Circling Approach
    - ☐ Landing from a Straight-in or Circling Approach
- ☐ **Emergency Operations**
    - ☐ Loss of Communications
    - ☐ One Engine Inoperative During Straight and Level Flight and Turns (Multiengine Airplane)
    - ☐ One Engine Inoperative—Instrument Approach (Multiengine Airplane)
    - ☐ Loss of Primary Flight Instrument Indicators
    - ☐ Automation Failure: Failure of Autopilot and Avionics
- ☐ **Postflight Procedures**
    - ☐ Checking Instruments and Equipment

Appendix 4

Instrument Proficiency Check
Flight Record

Instrument Proficiency Check Flight Record

Date: _____ Aircraft Type: _____

Flight Time: _____ Aircraft Tail Number: _____

Simulated Instrument Time: _____ Actual Instrument Time: _____

Pilot Name: _____ Instructor Name: _____

Task	Notes	N/A	Satisfactory	Unsatisfactory
Holding Procedures				
Recovery from Unusual Attitudes				
Intercepting and Tracking Navigational Systems and DME ARCs				
Non-Precision Approach				
Precision Approach				
Approach with loss of Primary Flight Instruments (Non-Precision Approach)				
Missed Approach				
Circling Approach				

Task	Notes	N/A	Satisfactory	Unsatisfactory
Landing from a Straight-In or Circling Approach				
One Engine Inoperative During Straight and Level Flight and Turns (Multi-Engine Airplane)				
One Engine Inoperative Instrument Approach (Multi-Engine Airplane)				
Postflight—Checking Instruments and Equipment				
Comments:				

Pilot Signature: _____ Instructor Signature: _____

Notes

Notes

Notes

Notes

Notes

Notes